THE GAG MAN

THE GAG MAN

CLYDE BRUCKMAN AND THE BIRTH OF FILM COMEDY

MATTHEW DESSEM

THE CRITICAL PRESS
Raleigh, NC

Portions of this book were originally published
in *The Dissolve* (thedissolve.com). Used by permission.

Publisher's Cataloging-in-Publication Data
Dessem, Matthew
The gag man : Clyde Bruckman and the birth of film comedy / Matthew Dessem.
pages cm
LCCN 2015948878
ISBN 978-1-941629-19-2 (hbk.)
ISBN 978-1-941629-18-5 (electronic bk. text)

1. Biography. 2. Film criticism.

10 9 8 7 6 5 4 3 2 1

For Yasmin

"This ascent will be betrayed to Gravity."

—*Thomas Pynchon*

"Any man can change his signs!"

—*Clyde Bruckman*

Contents

NO END OF CREDIT

The September 27, 1924, issue of the film journal *Exhibitors Trade Review* has a small box in the lower right-hand corner of the fourteenth page, headlined "An Acknowledgement":

In reviewing Buster Keaton's latest Metro-Goldwyn picture, "The Navigator," we neglected to give credit to the authors of the story. Buster's famous gag men Jean C. Havez, Clyde Bruckman, and Joe Mitchell were responsible for the story and the highly humorous subtitles. It seems to us that all three, as well as Buster himself, are entitled to no end of credit for "The Navigator," certainly one of the most amusing feature comedies we have ever seen and it is with regret that we failed to mention the three authors.

Almost exactly sixty-five years later, on September 21, 1989, *The New York Times* ran its own correction box at the bottom of page A3:

A listing yesterday of 25 American films to be placed on the National Film Registry omitted Buster Keaton's co-director for "The General."

He was Clyde Bruckman.

And as recently as July 12, 2015, *The New York Times* published a brief history of pie-throwing in movies, under the headline "In Comedy, Some Weapons Are Sweet." The occasion was the rediscovery of the long-lost second reel of *The Battle of the Century*, a 1927 Laurel and Hardy film containing what the *Times* described as "the greatest pie-throwing fight ever recorded." But although there was room on the page for several stills from the film, a detailed account of its inception, production, and historical importance, and no fewer than four stills from *another* pie fight film (1941 Three Stooges short *In the Sweet Pie and Pie*), there wasn't space for the name of the man who directed *The Battle of the Century* and wrote the screenplay for *In the Sweet Pie and Pie*. He, too, was Clyde Bruckman. And so a long tradition headed into its ninth decade.

But for everywhere he's gone missing over the years, Clyde Bruckman shows up in the strangest places. He's in the credits of a 1999 Chris O'Donnell vehicle, a remake of a screenplay he co-wrote seventy-four years earlier. He's the title character in an episode of *The X-Files* that has nothing to do with him. He even has a cameo in the *Weekly World News*, where he appears as the lawyer defending a Scrabble champion after a rampage instigated when the crowd jeered his client's misspelling of "CAT." (The story claimed Bruckman was planning to sue the hapless Scrabble champ's kindergarten for failing to teach him the correct spelling.) And yet in discussions of early film comedy, when he's mentioned at all, Clyde Bruckman is often relegated to a footnote, an aside. A correction.

Judging him only by his résumé, he should be famous. In the course of his thirty-six years in film and television, he wrote, co-wrote, or directed films for nearly every major comedy figure of his time: Buster Keaton, Harold Lloyd, Laurel and Hardy, W. C. Fields, Abbott and Costello, the Three Stooges—everyone except Chaplin and the Marx Brothers. And yet he faded from living memory so quickly that Tom Dardis, in his 1983 biography, *Harold Lloyd: The Man on the Clock*, was able to accurately write:

> Clyde Bruckman appears in American film history as an almost mythical creature, a strangely elusive figure about whom little is known.

Looking past his film credits at his life, it becomes clear that Bruckman had as much to do with his own disappearance as anyone. The popular conception—to the extent a writer from cinema's early days can be said to have a popular conception—is that he was a fraud and a plagiarist, an imposter who drank himself to death when his thievery was publicly exposed. The plagiarism is a complicated question, but the drinking isn't—and there's no amount of talent that can't be drowned in enough liquor, no bridge an addict won't eventually burn. Here's Dardis again, in 1979's *Buster Keaton: The Man Who Wouldn't Lie Down*, on the gap between Bruckman's résumé and his reputation:

> This is an impressive list of credits for a man who has always seemed a little on the dim and shadowy side. People who knew him well, like Harold Goodwin and Ben Pearson, seem agreed on two things about him: he was not very funny, and he drank too much.

But Goodwin and Pearson both worked with Bruckman on *The Buster Keaton Show*, toward the end of his long downward spiral. Goodwin had to patch up work Bruckman was too drunk to finish; Pearson had never even met him before then. A lot of burned bridges there. Later assessments have been harsher still.

Ted Okuda and Edward Watz, in their 1986 guide to the Columbia two-reel short films, paint Bruckman as a hanger-on from the beginning:

> . . . he has been given prestige by association only: having collaborated with so many great comedians, he has basked in the spotlight of reflected glory. Bruckman may have been a competent gagster, but his own writing lacked the qualities that could be considered "great."

Well, maybe.[1] But Clyde Bruckman managed to bask in a remarkable amount of reflected glory for a remarkable length of time, as less talented or lucky coworkers and employers lost their grip and went spinning off from Hollywood's bright center. Harold Lloyd, who would know, named Clyde Bruckman and Sam Taylor as his most valuable employees. W. C. Fields, who would also know, named Bruckman as one of the four directors he'd be willing to work with in a 1938 contract negotiation—long after he was considered too unreliable to hire. And Buster Keaton, who would know more than anybody, said that of all the writers he'd worked with over the years, "the two best I ever had were Jean Havez and Clyde Bruckman." So who to believe?

Part of the problem with Bruckman's reputation is clear in the Okuda and Watz quote—they draw a hard line between "gagster" and "writer." Most of Bruckman's work in film was in positions that are neither well understood nor much valued today. His first job in the motion picture industry was writing intertitles for silent films, a task that would vanish completely in less than a decade. By all accounts, his best work was as a gag man, a position that is perhaps even more forgotten today than intertitle writers. Keaton

---

1. Okuda and Watz go on to criticize Bruckman for reusing material, which is a little rich in a book about the Columbia two-reelers, where jokes, routines, plots, and even footage were reused as a matter of policy.

had as much to do as anybody with spreading the idea that his gag men's work was less important than what *writers* did, as this passage from his autobiography shows:

> One reason I never took extravagant praise seriously was because neither I, my director, nor my gagmen were writers in any literary sense. The writers most often on my staff were Clyde Bruckman, Joe Mitchell, and Jean Havez. They never wrote anything but gags, vaudeville sketches, and songs. I don't think any of them ever had his name on a book, a short story, or even an article in a fan magazine, entitled, "How to Write Gags for the Movies."
>
> They were not word guys, at all.

But Keaton had it wrong: Clyde Bruckman *was* a word guy. Before the movies, he had a successful career as a sportswriter and author of short fiction. His name is on plenty of short stories. It's true that coming up with sight gags and routines that will work on screen, especially for silent films, doesn't have much in common with writing soul-searing monologues or witty repartee or three-act structure or whatever else we think of today as modern screenwriting. But try it sometime; there's more to it than throwing pies.

François Truffaut didn't help Clyde secure a place in film history either. Auteur theory, which Truffaut first articulated, embraced directors who managed to express a personal style and vision, even through the morass of the Hollywood studio system. It's an approach to cinema that brought many overlooked artists their due, but Clyde worked almost exclusively with stars whose personalities dominated their films (which they often co-directed). Clyde made Buster Keaton films, Harold Lloyd films, Laurel and Hardy films, W. C. Fields films. There's no such thing as a Clyde Bruckman film, and no place in the auteurist pantheon for a chameleon—even one who served so many different comedic styles so well. To be fair to the auteurists, Clyde was never going to be anybody's favorite director. He chose projects poorly, working again and again as a cinematic disaster artist, attempting to salvage films other directors had—usually wisely—abandoned. And he himself abandoned many of the films that were his from the beginning, usually by default, usually by drinking; many of his screen credits should have asterisks next to them. Still, the popular idea that a *serious* director imposes his own style and concerns on his films didn't help.

But the greatest blow to Clyde Bruckman's reputation was one he struck himself. The one thing every story about him gets right, no matter what else is botched—the films he made, the women he married, his birthday—is the way he died. On January 4, 1955, destitute and unhireable, he shot himself in the head in the bathroom stall of a restaurant and bar in Santa Monica. It's sad and it's lurid and it's the most famous thing he ever did, the one place no one omits his name. And it happened either years too soon or years too late. If Clyde Bruckman had died in 1927 after *The General*, or in 1932 after *Movie Crazy*, or even as late as 1935, after *Man on the Flying Trapeze*, he'd be remembered today as a man whose promising career was cut tragically short. If he'd died in 1974 at the ripe old age of eighty, he might have been able to rebuild his reputation as critics and audiences rediscovered his work. But he chose the time and manner of his own death, and he chose 1955. Here's what dying in 1955 meant for Clyde Bruckman:

He lived long enough to hear his own lawyers argue in court that his work was worthless, "dated and old fashioned," "a museum piece."

He didn't live long enough to see the movies he'd made find

6

new audiences (and make new money) through revival screenings, television broadcasts, restorations, and home video.

He lived long enough to see Harold Lloyd, the man who delivered the humiliating coup de grâce to his career, receive an Honorary Academy Award for being a "master comedian and good citizen."[2]

He didn't live long enough to see his lifelong friend Buster Keaton receive his own Honorary Academy Award, "for his unique talents which brought immortal comedies to the screen," the greatest of which they'd written and directed together.

He lived long enough to see Chaplin's *City Lights* and *The Gold Rush* tie for second place in the first *Sight and Sound* critics poll of the greatest films of all time, a list that contained nothing he'd worked on.

He didn't live long enough to see *The General* surpass Chaplin and peak at number eight in that same poll, or outrank Chaplin on the American Film Institute's list of the One Hundred Funniest American Movies of All Time—though he probably wouldn't have been surprised that, at least on their websites, both organizations fail to credit him.

Clyde Bruckman lived long enough to see his own obsolescence, but he didn't live long enough to tell his own story. He died at exactly the wrong time, and as with so many of the tragedies and failures that defined his life, he had no one to blame but himself. But what story would he have told, had he lived to tell it?

It's easier to say what stories he wouldn't have told. He wasn't a lost titan of the silent era, abandoned by the march of time.

---

2. The "good citizen" part of the inscription was a dig at Chaplin, who had just had his visa revoked over suspected Communist sympathies, making this one of the few Academy Awards at least partially given out of spite.

That story was already a cliché by the end of 1955, when Buster Keaton stooped to playing forgotten silent film star "Kelsey Dutton" on *Screen Directors Playhouse*. But it's not Clyde Bruckman's story; he managed the transition to sound better than many of his contemporaries, and his long twilight came after a spectacular implosion, not years of neglect. Then there's the myth of the tortured artist whose genius is fueled by the addictions that consume him. But that's not Clyde's story either—it's not really anybody's story. Addiction doesn't feed talent, it undermines it. There was nothing heroic about his drinking. And he was never comfortable painting himself as an artist, much less a genius. That's not how he'd tell it.

Then there are the Clyde Bruckman stories that he could never have told, by definition—the ones suggested by the existence of this book. There's the story about the great artist whose work was too ahead of its time to be recognized, finally getting due credit. That's the story we tell about Buster Keaton. But filmmaking, a collaborative art, only ever supports this narrative uneasily. In the case of Clyde Bruckman, who made as many terrible films as masterpieces, it doesn't support it at all. Or maybe this is a redemption story, where a great historical wrong is exposed at last: Clyde Bruckman Got A Raw Deal. It's true that things didn't go well for him, and it wasn't all fair. But it's never fair, and he wasn't innocent. Worst of all, this could be the story of the great man who shaped an era, or its disguised twin, the one about the forgotten man who secretly embodied the spirit of an age. But these are as damaging in their way as the myth of the addiction-fueled genius. Clyde didn't live in eras or ages; he had hours and days to fill, like all of us.

He filled them haphazardly—sometimes well, sometimes

poorly. If he had a genius, it was as much for navigating the vagaries of Hollywood as it was for filmmaking. As careers flamed out around him, he seemed to arrive and leave at just the right time, moving from employer to employer, project to project, one step ahead of disaster, with the alacrity and grace of Buster Keaton avoiding a pursuing train. Eventually, inevitably, he slipped. The fall took years. But at the height of his powers, he worked on a series of masterpieces that defined film comedy as we know it today. He didn't accomplish this by design: there's no manifesto, no Great Man theory, no smithy-of-my-soul posturing—just this film, then the next one. His days and hours trace a shape that is immediately recognizable not because it is exceptional but because it is secretly familiar: He really had something, for a while.

A HAPPY LIFE

Clyde Adolph Bruckman was born on June 30, 1894, to Rudolph and Bertha Bruckman of San Bernardino, California.[1]

Rudolph—Rudy to his friends—arrived in California from his hometown of Elgin, Illinois, in 1888 at the tail end of the citrus boom, when the combination of new railroad lines, publicity surrounding the 1886 Southern California Citrus Fair in Chicago, and a rate war for train tickets west spurred a wave of migration and a real estate bubble. Bertha Smith's family moved to California from Denmark, Maine, the same year Rudy did. They were married on December 23, 1889. Marriage brought Rudy into an enormous family: Bertha had four brothers and five sisters, most of whom had travelled west at the same time. Despite the boom, San Bernardino was still a tiny town—just over four thousand residents in the 1890 census, with only twenty-five thousand in the entire county—and the Bruckmans almost immediately became an important part of the growing city. Their first son, Earl Ronald

---

1. Bruckman's birthday is sometimes given as September 20, an error that seems to appear for the first time in the California Death Index. Multiple sources, including a newspaper account of his tenth birthday party, confirm that he was born on June 30.

Bruckman, was born a scant seven and a half months after the wedding. Whether he was premature or the reason for the marriage, he seems to have been a prominent local baby, one of four mentioned as guests at a masquerade ball attended by many of the town's luminaries at which Rudy gave a demonstration of club swinging. (Now mostly forgotten, this form of synchronized gymnastics with weighted clubs was popular enough at the time that it was an event in the 1904 Olympics.) Rudy had trained in Illinois as a barber, and in 1891, he bought his way into a partnership with one George Silveria at the Palace Barber Shop on Third Street.

By fall of 1892, when the Bruckmans' second child, Lloyd, was born, Rudy was running the Palace solo, and had become a beloved local figure—one newspaper story refers to him as "our popular young barber and champion club-swinger." And business at the Palace was booming: Just before Thanksgiving, he expanded to add a sixth barber chair. For Christmas that year, his employees pooled their funds to buy a baby carriage for their boss's new arrival. Then disaster struck. On Tuesday, January 10, two-month-old Lloyd Bruckman died. There's no record of what killed him, but it was probably contagious; Earl followed his brother less than a week later. Once again the Bruckmans were childless. It must have felt like a second chance when they discovered Bertha was pregnant again toward the end of the year—they disappear from the society pages entirely for the rest of 1893, until a club-swinging demonstration Rudy gave in early December. By then they would have known. In January, Rudy planned extensive renovations of his barbershop, moving to a temporary location in March, and on June 30 Clyde was born.

As Clyde grew up, so did San Bernardino. Rudy Bruckman was a Republican—not surprisingly for someone from Illinois—and he got involved in politics, serving as one of several vice presidents of the local McKinley Club during the McKinley-Bryan election. In 1897, he ran for office in his own right, seeking the Republican nomination for city marshal. After tying in the convention's first round of voting and denying his opponent a majority in the second, he lost in the third round to local rancher James C. Cole. (Cole promptly lost to the Democrat in the general.) Rudy didn't hold a grudge against the party; only a month after the primary, he played shortstop on a Republican baseball team in an exhibition game, a nineteenth-century-style shellacking in which the Republicans were defeated by a combined team of Democrats, Populists, and Silver Republicans by the astonishing score of 24 to 62. Rudy joined not just the Odd Fellows but also the Royal Arch and the Eagles, served as the founding president of the San Bernardino Athletic Club, and managed a local baseball team. In May of 1895, he and his wife performed as "gondoliers" in a town performance of probably-not-very-accurate dances from around the world—also featured were a "Gypsy Dance," the "Anvil Dance," and a performance by the "Daughters of the Nile."

In other words, the Bruckman family participated in all of the ways the city of San Bernardino asserted that it was part of civilization rather than the frontier: politics, sport, religion, culture. And commerce—Rudy exerted a civilizing influence on the town's least civilized business: alcohol. In March of 1898, he bought his way into a partnership with James Murray at the M. & O., a saloon on Third Street. (The bar's name had come from Murray and his original partner, Al Oakley.) There was more money in drinking than grooming, and by 1900, the year Clyde turned six, the family home had a telephone—putting them in roughly the top 3 percent of American households—and a dachshund. Clyde, simultaneously their third son and only child, led a privileged life. A childhood photo shows a dapper young boy carefully posed in a wool suit, one hand in his jacket pocket. His tenth birthday party made the society pages, complete with guest list.

Against this background of civic virtue and domestic tranquility stood San Bernardino's history as a frontier town. The M. & O. seems to have been a relatively upscale establishment, but Third Street was also home to rougher places—brothers Peter and George Beam ran a number of bars around this time that catered to miners, and ran them violently. In 1895, Peter shot a black customer in the head for being "obstreperous," though to be fair, Beam's definition of obstreperous included waving a knife around. Charges against Beam were dismissed; the customer, "Bronco Charley," survived the bullet and was thrown out of the city for his trouble. Peter Beam's bars were the kinds of places where fights routinely ended in jail time; where patrons didn't just throw punches, but attacked each other with axes. So it wasn't out of character in 1903 when Beam responded to a request for a loan by beating a customer over the head with a shovel handle. The unlucky man, a wealthy miner named Jack Forsythe, collapsed with a blood clot in his brain while walking the police over to the Sunbeam Saloon to identify his assailant. This time, Beam's victim died, and he was arrested. After a great deal of legal maneuvering, he managed to get his charges dropped on a technicality, but he got out of the saloon business, selling the Sunbeam to his brother, who then sold to Rudy in 1906.

To be clear, it's not as though Rudy Bruckman was the sheriff who cleaned up San Bernardino—the town was undergoing an inevitable process of gentrification as it grew. But cleaning up the Sunbeam couldn't have hurt matters. Comparing Rudy's sole scrap with the law to Beam's criminal record is illuminating. In July of 1894, when Clyde was only a month old, Rudy was arrested, hauled before a judge, and charged with violating San Bernardino's Ordinance no. 157. The complaint sworn against him by the town marshal tells a story of reckless lawlessness:

> The said R. Bruckman in the said city of San Bernardino on Sunday the 29th day of July 1894, did keep open a place of business, to wit, a barber shop, for the purpose of transacting the business of such barber shop therein, and did then and there in said place, carry on and conduct the business and occupation of a barber Contrary to the form, force and effect of the Ordinances of said city in such cases made and provided, and against the Peace and Dignity of the People of the State of Califarnia [sic].

His offense, so wounding to the peace and dignity of Califarnians, was operating his barbershop on a Sunday. The law he broke, requiring all but essential businesses to be closed, had only passed that February; in the heat of July, the City Council hastily amended it with Ordinance no. 165, "ALLOWING ICE CREAM, SODA WATER AND CANDY TO BE SOLD AND FURNISHED ON SUNDAYS." So: two San Bernardinos, with the Bruckman family firmly representing the newer, less violent town.

Under Rudy's tenure, the Sunbeam stopped showing up in the newspaper for fights, fires, and attempted ax murders, and started appearing for things like donating prizes for the town's May Day horseraces. By 1907, San Bernardino had calmed down to the point that it made the newspaper when Clyde's bicycle was stolen, and rated a follow-up the next day when it was found a few streets over, "probably the work of boys who just wanted to ride about for a while."

It's not surprising that Clyde, growing up in a household of city boosters, became something of a booster himself. His father had his fraternal organizations; Clyde joined the Boys' Brotherhood, a predecessor of the Boy Scouts of America. He loved fishing and camping, and nearly every summer went on an extended fishing trip at the family cabin in the mountains. In fact, the earliest piece of published writing he may have had a hand in was from summer camp: an indignant open letter to the local paper, reassuring them that they had adequate food supplies, and to disregard any reports to the contrary from boys who "would have been sent home had they stayed much longer."

In high school, Clyde immediately joined the staff of the *Tyro*, San Bernardino High's yearbook and literary quarterly. His first published comedy writing was in the 1909 Thanksgiving issue, in which he and John Conrad wrote the "Joshes" section, full of jokes with all the sophistication you'd expect from high school freshmen. He also contributed fiction, penning a regrettable short story about a friendship between a white explorer and his noble, self-sacrificing Indian companion. (Sample dialogue: "An Indian never forgets, Dick, and I am an Indian.") As with the "joshes," he was young, and this was 1910.

By sophomore year, he was heading the *Tyro*'s athletics section, not only covering San Bernardino High's season but also writing a brief history of sport in San Bernardino. He played basketball that year, a forward on the second league team, and when he wasn't playing, he was cheering, leading the "yell section" at high school games. As the year wound to a close, he was elected class treasurer and chosen as captain of the basketball team for the upcoming school year. Now nearly seventeen, he had access to his family's car, an Overland, and was known to drive himself and his friends "to where the girls abide," according to a bit of doggerel in the yearbook.

Things continued to go wonderfully for everyone in the Bruckman family until the warm summer night of June 11, 1911. Bertha's brother Frank Smith was engaged to a woman named Mabel Smith, who was throwing a party that night for her roommate, Cornelia Knott. Bertha, Rudy, Frank, Bertha's sister Laura, and Laura's husband, Frank Gould, all piled into the Bruckmans' Overland to attend. Rudy drove until they left San Bernardino, then let Frank Smith take the wheel. At the corner of Orange Street and Pioneer Avenue, Frank attempted to pass another car, realized he wouldn't make it, and swerved back into his own lane. The rear axle snapped, and, although everyone else in the car was thrown free, Frank "was caught by the wheel until the machine was upside down in mid-air when he dropped to the ground, and one of the heavy wheels of the automobile settled upon him." He died instantly; his wife-to-be, waiting for her dinner guests, was devastated when news finally reached her. Witnesses to the crash thought it was quite remarkable that the other people in the car weren't seriously injured.

But as it turned out, Rudolph Bruckman *had* been seriously injured; he'd landed on his head when he was thrown from the car. As Clyde kicked off his junior year of high school with a fishing trip to celebrate his seventeenth birthday and a hayrack party with his classmates in Harlem Springs, Rudy began to suffer from blinding headaches. As his father's condition declined, Clyde got his first professional job as a writer, filing a bi-weekly "High School News" column and covering sports for the *San Bernardino*

Daily Sun. His work for the *Sun* shows a flare for the dramatic not present in his first efforts for the *Tyro*—describing an 8–3 win, he wrote, "The murder scene in Shakespeare's Macbeth is like an old maid's social compared with the seventh-inning 'doin's.' " By late fall, Rudy was beginning to become paranoid about his own mental state, worrying that he'd end up institutionalized. He made jokes about his condition, but friends started to worry.

It was a dismal year for sports in San Bernardino, and Clyde's year-end wrap-up shows that he'd started to develop a morbid sense of humor. "When it becomes necessary to set forth our athletic feats, or rather lack of feats," he wrote, "the feeling is the same as when we discuss the character of a friend who has passed away . . . A brief summary will convince the reader that deep grief can be best expressed by silence or at least a little of it."

He also wrote another short story for the *Tyro*: "The Decision," a sentimental bit of teenage wish fulfillment about a young baseball player with an ungrateful fiancée who doesn't properly appreciate the great American pastime. ("It is always baseball first and then I come afterwards," she tells him while breaking off their engagement.) He finally finds true love with a woman who has the kind of selfless passion for her boyfriend's interests that could only be imagined by an eighteen-year-old. ("I haven't seen you for such a long time and wanted to congratulate you on your great success with the Crimson's [sic] and also wish you good luck in the final game. I want you to come and tell me about it soon after it's all over. I will see the game of course.") It's neither extraordinarily good nor extraordinarily bad work for a teenager in 1912. But reading it, it's hard not to wonder what things must have been like in the Bruckman home that spring, as Rudy slowly lost his mind. "The Decision" has a wholly unnecessary subplot Clyde inserted between the protagonist and his father, tacked on in a single paragraph that allows the father to say, "My boy . . . I am proud of you and want you to forgive me for the way I have wronged you."

It was thought that a change of scenery might do Rudy good. The Bruckmans planned to move to Maine to live near Bertha's sister; Clyde was to be enrolled in a boys' school in Fryeburg (presumably Fryeburg Academy). Like anyone entering their senior year, Clyde didn't want to leave his friends behind. On the trip East, he filed a story with the *Daily Sun* about watching the Detroit Tigers play the Washington Senators and the Philadelphia Athletics—by the end of the summer, he'd convinced his parents to let him return to San Bernardino to finish high school. He returned home alone in September, went back to covering sports for the *Sun,* and was elected class president in the few months before his parents returned at the end of October.

But Maine hadn't improved Rudy's condition. He spent his last two weeks in San Bernardino in a daze—his brother-in-law later told the newspapers that he was baffled by business problems that "a child could almost have solved." Rudy was convinced that if his condition didn't improve, he'd "land at Patton," the town's Gothic nightmare of an insane asylum. He bought his business partner, G. F. Hewins, out of the Sunbeam Saloon, and, that first week of November, made vague statements to his family about selling the entire business and moving to the beach to recover.

He didn't move to the beach. Rudy spent the morning of November 7 settling his financial affairs and closing out his bank accounts. After leaving $3,100 in cash in a bureau drawer (the equivalent of nearly $75,000 in 2015), he went into the alley behind his bar, drew a revolver, and shot himself twice in the chest.

His last moments are documented in the transcripts from the coroner's inquest the next day. Here's Paul Maher's account:

I went over to get a glass of beer. I heard a shot. I went through the back fence from the kitchen. Bruckman was sitting up against the wall and said good-morning. I saw blood on him and a gun under his coat. I called Ward the bar-tender and said Bruckman has shot himself. He did not speak any more. I think he must have shot himself. The gun was still smoking.

And this is A. A. Garner:

I am well acquainted with Mr. Bruckman and I saw him yesterday noon. He was talking with Mr. Smith. I went in the Sunbeam Saloon and saw him go out of the saloon. The Jap run in and said Mr. Bruckman has shot himself. He was lying over against the wall. I ran out and asked him what was the matter but he never spoke. I put my hand under his head. Dr. Aldrich came in a few minutes but he said it was all off. The last few days he seemed to be studdying about something. I never heard him make any remarks about being despondent. I asked him to have a drink but he said he did not want any. He told me on Election Day that his head hurt him and every-thing seemed dark to him. He was well fixed financially.

In addition to the cash at home and a check made out to his wife, Rudolph left a note addressed not to his wife or son but to his brother-in-law. The papers published part of it:

I am going to leave this world. It looks dark. Say good-bye to the wife and boy. I hope they will have a happy life.

Nearly two hundred people attended the funeral. Clyde's little brothers Lloyd and Earl were re-buried next to their father at Mountain View Cemetery. Despite his blurry thinking, Bruckman had neatly wrapped up his financial affairs; the Sunbeam Saloon was sold to a local baseball player named Norman Brashear before Christmas. The week the news about the saloon broke, Clyde returned to work at the *Daily Sun*, where he continued to cover sports as his senior year played itself out. He appeared in the minor role of a servant in the senior class play, a production of *The Importance of Being Earnest*, but, except for a ceremonial students-vs.-faculty game after graduation, there are no stories after Rudy's death of Clyde playing baseball or leading pep rallies.

In May of 1913, the *Daily Sun* ran a story on the graduates' plans for the future. Many were staying in San Bernardino; a few were going off to UC Berkeley, USC, or other nearby colleges and universities. Clyde's entry simply reads "Los Angeles."

THE SPORTSWRITER

The surviving Bruckmans arrived in Los Angeles in the fall of 1913, after Clyde took his usual summer fishing and camping trips, including a candy pull at Thousand Pines hosted by the family who was now running his father's bar. The 1914 phone directory lists Bertha as the apartment manager of the Pleasant View Apartments at 516 South Rampart. The building was constructed in 1911 and had been leased in February of 1913 to W. P. Peyton and T. C. Smith (seemingly no relation to Bertha), though a news report from when she left Los Angeles gives the impression she owned it. It's still in use as an apartment complex today. The Bruckmans' new home was just a few blocks away from Westlake Park (now MacArthur Park) on the outskirts of the Wilshire-Westlake district. Though the park itself seems to have been a common location for suicides, the neighborhood was on its way up: Several high-end apartment buildings began construction on its borders the year the Bruckmans arrived. They were in Los Angeles by October—Clyde reported on a football game between San Bernardino and Los Angeles High for the *Daily Sun*—and in February of 1914, not yet twenty years old, he was hired to cover the upcoming baseball season for the *Los Angeles Times*.

The *Times*, still under the control of anti-labor stalwart Harrison Gray Otis, had five major competitors that year: the *Examiner* and *Tribune* in the mornings and the *Evening Record*, *Evening Express*, and *Evening Herald* in the afternoons. Although circulation numbers were difficult to directly compare because the *Times* had a Sunday edition, it was firmly in last place when Clyde was hired. He began with a column, "Foul Tips," covering the exploits of individual players rather than entire games. The first one ran on April 4, 1914.

As a sportswriter, Clyde was inducted into the boozy fraternity of a relatively new profession. The sportswriters at all six papers worked together, traveled together, drank together, and several times a year battled each other in exhibition games of baseball or football, pitting morning papers against afternoon. (Their teams were called the "Morning Glories" and the "Evening Squirts," which gives some idea of the spirit of the thing.) The games were alcohol-soaked ("refreshments will be placed at third base in considerable bulk," reads one account) and open to the public, with a special invitation to professional baseball players "who want to learn a few pointers from the intellectual gentlemen who have been telling them all year how the game should be played."

Los Angeles sportswriters were an odd bunch even for pre–World War I newspapermen. In addition to Clyde, that year the *Times* lineup featured De Witt Van Court, an ex-boxing coach who'd trained heavyweight champions "Gentleman" Jim Corbett and Jim Jeffries in the nineteenth century. The sporting editor at the *Times*'s morning competitor, the *Examiner*, was Harley M. "Beanie" Walker, a chain smoker and cat fanatic whom *Examiner* city desk editor James Richardson recalled had a habit of wearing "a black fedora hat with the brim tipped down over his eyes" and carrying "a cane with a silver knob." (Richardson also tells the story of a night when Jim Jeffries—by then running a bar—cold-cocked Walker in the jaw to cure an ulcerated tooth, before the assembled newspapermen returned to their drinking.) The *Examiner* would eventually add "Gentleman" Jim Corbett himself to their lineup, running a syndicated column called "In Corbett's Corner," which ran next to a large portrait of the ex-boxer in white tie. But the president emeritus of this band of eccentrics—and the man who got Clyde his job—was Charles Emmett Van Loan.

Van Loan, like Clyde, was a graduate of San Bernardino High. He'd started as a freelancer with the *Los Angeles Examiner* before being hired full-time at the *Morning Herald* in 1904; from there he'd moved east to Denver to write for the *Post*, and then further east to the *New York American* in 1909. In New York, Van Loan successfully transitioned into writing short fiction, churning out a whopping nine short story collections in a single decade. At the end of 1913, around the time the Bruckmans moved to Los Angeles, he returned to California, wealthy and nationally famous, so he could golf year-round. Van Loan had an eye for young talent—in Los Angeles, he promoted Beanie Walker, who succeeded him at the *Examiner*; in Denver, he found Damon Runyon, whom he'd brought with him to the *New York American*, and in late 1913 or early 1914, he brought Ring Lardner's short stories to the attention of his editor at *The Saturday Evening Post*. Clyde was his latest discovery.

That summer, as World War I began, Clyde chronicled the fortunes of long-forgotten teams of the Pacific Coast League, whose six teams had names ranging from the unimaginative (the Los

Angeles Angels, the Oakland Oaks) to the apt (the Sacramento Wolves) to the positively baffling (the Venice Tigers, whose name had been less of a mismatch when they were in Vernon). At the *Times* Bruckman either had better editors, his writing had improved, or both. Though his prose is occasionally purple—a game played "with slaughter-house rules covering the affair"—or unintentionally funny—"Ty Lober spread wreck and ruin all over the local ball yard yesterday afternoon"—compared to Grantland Rice, he was Ernest Hemingway.

Clyde was much younger than his coworkers, but his access to the family cabin in the San Bernardino Mountains seems to have made him popular. In June he took Beanie Walker and De Witt Van Court there on a fishing trip. In July he returned with Charles Van Loan, who wrote about their trip in a story for the *Times*. Van Loan painted a wonderfully deranged portrait of Clyde, who he referred to as "Ay-dolf," after his middle name. Clyde, according to Van Loan, was "extensively German in his thought processes, slow, sure, and methodical to an alarming degree and cloudy weather depresses him." Here's his account of the Bruckman cabin:

> Ay-dolf owns a cabin, that is to say, the property stands in his name, but the real owners are the mice and the ants. When we moved in, the mice disputed possession and the ants marched to their support, seven hundred million strong. The first time we went away on a hike Ay-dolf carelessly left a ham exposed and when we returned, all the red ants in the world were using it for a race track.
>
> "Well, wouldn't that scald you!" say Ay-dolf. "It could have been worse, though. Think of the trouble it would have been to kill these ants a hundred thousand at a time! Now we've got 'em all in a bunch."

Thereupon he immersed the ham in kerosene and set fire to it. A few of the ants escaped flood and holocaust and these Ay-dolf murdered methodically with a hammer.

"Gen. Custer had a chance," said he, between thumps, "but these ants are up against a cinch."

But the trip ended badly when the two men drove to the Skyland Heights Inn to mail Van Loan's story of ant massacre to the *Times*. Van Loan was behind the wheel of his prized 1914 Cadillac when the front left wheel slid onto the soft shoulder. The car skidded along for about twenty feet as he attempted to regain the road—"I wanted to jump, but I just couldn't move," Clyde recalled at the scene—before lurching over the cliff. The car flipped sideways twice in its thirty-foot descent, throwing both Clyde and Van Loan free on the first revolution—but it landed on Van Loan in the process, injuring his hip, shattering his arm, and fracturing his skull. He had to be taken down the bumpy mountain roads in a hastily-converted truck.

Despite his injuries, Van Loan returned to Los Angeles within a week; by the first week of August he felt well enough to trade barbs in the pages of the *Los Angeles Times* about the fishing bait he'd used on the trip. Even the Cadillac was fine, although Clyde told reporters "I don't want to see an automobile again." On his return to Los Angeles, he published an article about the roads in the San Bernardino Mountains, warning that the Skyline Heights road was "unsafe for the average driver" without mentioning the crash. And the summer and the baseball season rolled on.

At the end of the season, Clyde left the *Times* for the *Examiner* to work for Beanie Walker; his last *Times* byline was in August. Leaving one paper for another didn't really affect his place in the brotherhood of sportswriters—he was still at a morning paper, so he still played with the Morning Glories rather than the After-noon Squirts. That fall, he hit an eighth-inning home run in their baseball matchup—not that a single run made any difference in a game his team won 14–2. The fraternal tomfoolery reached its apex in 1916, when Clyde represented the *Examiner* at spring training camp for the Los Angeles Angels. The Angels trained that year at Lake Elsinore, where Clyde joined his fellow sportswriters in a late-night drinking society they christened the Owls Club, presided over by team manager Frank Chance. One morning, the players all received professionally printed invitations at breakfast mail call:

> You are cordially invited to attend an al fresco dinner and dance given by the Girls' Glee Club of Elsinore at the Hotel Lucerne at 9 p.m. on Saturday night. Come, trip the light fantastic and let joy be unconfined.

This caused a great deal of excitement, particularly among the married players, a couple of whom bought new shirts for the occasion. That Saturday, the team rented a truck for the voyage to the party, some distance away. As *Los Angeles Times* sportswriter Bob Ray recounted years later:

> It would have been a perfect evening except for the fact that the Hotel Lucerne was an old wreck which had not been occupied by anything except rodents for twenty years, that there was no such thing as a Girls' Glee Club in Elsinore, and that the invitations, paid for by one of the baseball writers, were based on pure figments of fancy.

It was his last hurrah as a bachelor. Before the summer was out, he'd married Lola Margaret Hamblin, his first wife. The Hamblins came from Missouri, but migrated west in the 1910s, starting with Lola's brother Simeon Albert ("Al") Hamblin, who arrived in Los Angeles in 1911. Lola and the rest of her family followed him in 1913. Al was in the film industry, working at Biograph as an actor before transitioning to production roles, and Raymond, another Hamblin brother, also had a variety of film-related jobs, from cameraman to prop man. But Lola left the movie business to her brothers; she had been a telephone operator in Kansas City and took the same job in Los Angeles. By the time Clyde started at the *Examiner*, she was working in the mechanical department, which is probably how they met. They were married the summer after his Lake Elsinore idyll, on Saturday, July 29, 1916. He had just turned twenty-two; his bride, described by the newspapers as "a charming blonde," was twenty-one.

Clyde and Lola delayed their honeymoon until September (perhaps waiting for the end of the baseball season), then spent it in the San Bernardino Mountains, first at the Bruckman cabin and then on a tour of the area's resorts. Although Clyde, gun-shy after his trip with Van Loan, attempted to take a horse and buggy rather than a car ("Safety first," the newspaper quoted him as saying), the horse balked at the steep grades, and Clyde and Lola ended up abandoning both animal and vehicle at a Pacific Electric station before continuing by automobile.

The newlyweds moved to a home on Santa Barbara Avenue, near Exposition Park and USC, and Clyde began the next stage of his career as a writer. He'd been writing baseball stories since high school, but shortly before marrying Lola he sold one to *The Saturday Evening Post*. The story, "Reverse English," ran on October 21, 1916. It's years ahead of his high school work, and whether or not it benefited from Charles E. Van Loan's association with the *Post*, it's clearly in imitation of his style. As with "The Decision," there may have been some wish fulfillment in his story: it's about a young baseball player going on the wagon after discovering he'd bet against himself in the throes of a bender. Observers doubt he can reform: "If he's done anything with his habits it's a cinch they're worse. It's born in him an' you can't change them kind." But as the narrator puts it, "There was one bet they overlooked—any man can change his signs!"

There was no reason for Clyde to doubt this at twenty-two. His second story, "Joe Gum," ran in *The Saturday Evening Post* in May, two days before his third, "O Upright Judge," in *The Popular Magazine*. That summer, as more stories ran in *The Blue Book Magazine* and *The Red Book Magazine*, he wrote an autobiographical letter for a series on contemporary writers running in *The Editor*, describing the eternal limbo of professional writing. After listing his published works, he made sure to note, "I have still more under way or out for consideration." And there's this: "I am twenty-two and hopeful."

Bertha left Los Angeles for Denver that November, selling off the apartment complex on Rampart. Clyde continued along the same path Van Loan had taken before him: sportswriting at the *Examiner*, writing fiction in his spare time. Between September of 1917 and September of 1918, he published six stories in *The Popular Magazine* and *The Blue Book Magazine*. He was ineligible for the draft in the summer of 1917 because of his wife, but World War I affected him in other ways—he was jailed in June of 1918 under the Sedition Act, presumably because of his German heritage. He was released in a few days, "it having developed that he is harmless and has shown patriotic moves toward this country." On his release, he seems to have gone immediately to a baseball game.

In November the war ended, just as the flu epidemic started killing people off at a faster rate than the Browning machine gun. One contemporary report estimated the worldwide death toll at six million, but the CDC currently suggests at least fifty and perhaps as many as one hundred million people died. The bodies began piling up in Los Angeles, and businesses, theaters, schools, and churches were closed in October. As Christmas approached, city authorities believed the flu was under control; at noon on December 2 the theaters reopened, many with gala shows. Grauman's (the Million Dollar Theater—the Chinese was nearly a decade away) welcomed back audiences with Paramount's *Out of a Clear Sky*, a full orchestra, and a new "four-system lighting effect." Less visibly, but perhaps more importantly, they'd installed a $7,000 ventilation system to help prevent the spread of infection. But the Bruckmans weren't going to the movies—they had both caught the flu in early December, and were sick enough that Clyde's mother travelled from Denver to care for them. (Later that winter, she decided to move back to Los Angeles permanently.) Reopening the theaters caused a brief resurgence in cases, and in late December, the city began enforcing a house-to-house quarantine, with warning cards posted on the doors of infected houses, blue for flu and white for pneumonia. The Bruckmans presumably ended up with a blue card on their door.

But by mid-January, the worst was past. Clyde and Lola had survived the flu, theaters were reopening across the country, and Universal Pictures, which had closed for a month at the height of the pandemic, began to staff up again. There's no record of how Clyde got his first break in the motion picture industry—he could have been introduced to people through his brothers-in-law at Famous Players-Lasky, or through his boss at the *Examiner*,

Beanie Walker, who had been moonlighting for Hal Roach since 1917. However it happened, in February of 1919, he got the opportunity to do a new kind of writing: intertitles for the one-reel films of comedy duo Lyons and Moran at Universal.

He'd only been at the job for a few weeks when terrible news arrived from Philadelphia. Charles E. Van Loan had moved there in November to work for *The Saturday Evening Post* full-time; on March 2, he died of nephritis in a Pennsylvania hospital. Doctors blamed injuries he'd incurred when he and Clyde careened off the mountain that summer five years ago. When Van Loan's father got the news, he immediately died of a heart attack.

Charles E. Van Loan was dead. Clyde was writing movies now.

MISSING REELS

Clyde entered the film industry at the end of a tumultuous decade that saw one monopoly broken up and new ones spring into being. The industry's early days had been dominated by the Motion Picture Patents Company, a cartel of producers and distributors that controlled access to Thomas Edison's film patents. Their strategy had been to sue non-members out of existence, and at their peak they'd controlled 60 percent of the U.S. film market through General Film, their distribution arm. The MPPC's near-monopoly was a major factor behind a westward migration of film production from New York to Los Angeles, as producers tried to escape Edison's legal reach—though the sunshine didn't hurt. But by the middle of the decade, the MPPC began losing anti-trust actions, and as their legal position weakened, new distributors and producers lined up to stick the knife in. The most successful of these was Paramount, formed in a three-way merger of the original Paramount Pictures, a Utah-based film distribution company, and Adolph Zukor's Famous Players and the Jesse Lasky Feature Play Company, two independent production companies that had been using Paramount to handle distribution. The new firm began buying movie theaters in 1919, moving toward a system of complete integration that was nearly as monopolistic as the Motion Picture Patents Company.

This process of rapid vertical integration led to a three-tier class system in Hollywood. At the top were companies like Paramount and their rival First National, where production, distribution, and exhibition were managed under a single corporate roof—their films had guaranteed audiences nationwide. Mid-tier companies like Universal had distribution arms, but didn't own their own theaters. Still, they were able to negotiate with theater chains from a position of strength, since they controlled all of their films; the process of "block-booking," requiring exhibitors to purchase less-popular short films to gain access to hit features, meant that a studio like Universal could leverage their more expensive films to sell filler. At the bottom of the barrel were independent producers like Hal Roach's Rolin Film Company. Roach had to submit each individual film his studio made to their distributor, Pathé (a survivor from the Motion Picture Patents Company cartel), which was under no obligation to accept any of them.

Genres, too, had their own caste system. Films were planned and sold to exhibitors on a system that had more in common with industrial goods than art, based on the number of reels (General Film had literally priced films on a per-foot rate). A reel ran between ten and fifteen minutes depending on projection speed; a typical program might include one feature running between three and five reels (sometimes more for prestige pictures), fronted by several single-reel shorts. The bulk of the box-office receipts went to the feature, and comedies were almost never feature-length. Accordingly, most of the earliest comedies were cheaply made slapstick affairs, with little time for star-making performances. A few actors had built enough of an audience to move into two-reel shorts: Charlie Chaplin, Roscoe "Fatty" Arbuckle (whose shorts featured Buster Keaton in supporting roles), and, eventually, Harold Lloyd. One-reel comedies were already something smart actors tried to escape from. When Mabel Normand made a move into "light comedy dramas" in 1916, newspapers reported that she was seeking "More Plots and Fewer Pies."

So when Clyde began working on one-reel comedies at Universal, he was at the very bottom of one hierarchy and the middle of another, working on films that exhibitors and audiences saw as filler material, but for a studio that could strong-arm theaters into booking them anyway. And by writing for Eddie Lyons and Lee Moran, he was joining an experienced team. Lyons had been at Carl Laemmle's Independent Motion Pictures in 1912; Moran started working for Al Christie at Nestor the same year, before both companies were swallowed at the end of the summer in the merger that formed Universal. They first appeared together in Al Christie's *Hearts and Skirts* in secondary roles as cowboys that October before moving on to starring roles together. In 1914, they were well enough known as a duo to be referred to in a news story as "the unheavenly twins"; by 1916, when their longtime director Al Christie left Universal, they were described as "the mainstay of the Nestor-Universal Comedy Company," and stayed on to co-direct their own features under the Nestor label. They were on a grueling schedule: a new one-reel comedy every week. Around the time Clyde got married, they celebrated making their fiftieth film together. By the time he was hired they'd made nearly 250, and the studio had given them their own release label, Lyons and Moran Star Comedies. The schedule burned writers out quickly—before Clyde, the roster was headed at various times by Fred Palmer, C. B. "Pops" Hoadley, and the delightfully named "Captain Leslie T. Peacock."

Although they were a crucial part of Universal in its early years, few of their movies survive today. James Roots described their screen personas in *The 100 Greatest Silent Comedians*:

> . . . they seemed to be doing nothing so much as playing the buddy team of ex-college pals in a 1950s television sitcom, always getting into romantic scrapes in a very clean-cut way, in a well-scrubbed society that bore only the most superficial connection with the real life around them offscreen. They're indistinguishable from each other in their white-bread WASP appearance: watching Lyons and Moran is like watching a couple of mirrors have a stare down.

Their clean-cut reputation may help explain why a spot was available for Clyde: in December, it was announced that J. Grubb Alexander—another comedy writer with an amazing name—had decided that the next Lyons and Moran film he wrote would be *You've Got It*. According to *Moving Picture World*, the script would

> . . . [take] its fun as a burlesque of the recent 'flu' epidemic. Mr. Alexander, the author, was a sufferer from the dread disease himself, and obtained from his experience some very lucid facts to work with.

So perhaps by February, Lyons and Moran wanted to work with a writer like Clyde, who drew inspiration from stories and experiences he'd had at the ballpark, rather than from a pandemic that had killed a significant percentage of humanity. (J. Grubb Alexander, for his part, switched to projects more suited to his sensibility, including adapting Victor Hugo for Paul Leni's horror/swashbuckler/Joker-inspiration masterpiece, *The Man Who Laughs*.)

Clyde didn't leave the ballpark or the *Examiner* right away, however, and his job for Lyons and Moran was not very much like modern screenwriting. Lyons and Moran came up with many of the scenarios for their films themselves, though some were contributed by freelancers or Clyde himself. The comedy came from the situation more than gags or quips, a style Al Christie had insisted on at Nestor. Clyde's primary job was writing the intertitles once the films had been shot—inserting jokes and witticisms to suit already finished footage. He did this at night and in the early mornings, attending baseball games during the afternoon for the *Examiner*; some of his lines were sanitized versions of taunts from the crowds at the games. During the spring of 1919, he alternated films with Melville Brown, a former vaudevillian who'd written for Chaplin; by June, World War I correspondent Frederick Bennett had come on board as well.

Since the Lyons and Moran films are mostly lost, it's difficult to attribute any in particular to Clyde. But during the time period he was writing nights and mornings, they released fifty-five one-reel shorts; the Internet Movie Database only credits Clyde for one of these, *Three in a Closet*. The titles give some idea of the subject matter: mostly domestic farces like *The Expert Eloper*, *Wise Wives*, or *A Model Husband*, with occasional pseudo-political comedies like *The Bullshiviks* (in which Eddie and Lee get addicted to Russian cigarettes) or *Ten Nights in a Tea Room* (in which Eddie and Lee, in a post-prohibition 1950, become addicted to "tea, cubeb cigarettes, malted milk, etc."). The titles couldn't always be trusted, however, especially when it came to what seemed like expensive locations—a review of *The Smell of the Yukon* notes that it takes place in a dance hall. As far as the plots go (not far), *The Moving Picture World*'s review of *Three in a Closet* gives the general idea:

Eddie Lyons and Lee Moran appear in this pleasing comedy, assisted by Mildred Moore and Fred Gamble. Lee, who appears as "Swat" Dugan, is employed by the girl's father to keep her away from Eddie. Instead Swat makes a series of errors and assists Eddie to get the girl. The number is typical and amusing.

In December of 1919, Lyons and Moran were finally fed up with the breakneck pace and limited possibilities of one-reel films. But rather than making the move to two-reelers that had served Chaplin, Arbuckle, and Lloyd so well, they jumped all the way to a series of five-reel films—"comedy-drama" rather than situation comedy. Fewer pies, but much, much more plot. Clyde contributed intertitles for at least two of these, *Everything but the Truth* and *Once a Plumber*, both adaptations of stories by Edgar Franklin, but they weren't as successful as the one-reelers. In particular, *Once a Plumber* was singled out even among the features—*Wid's Daily*'s review noted that it "doesn't compare with the first two feature comedies produced by the team" and warned exhibitors that "those who will perhaps appreciate it do not make up the high class audiences." Faced with audience walkouts from *La La Lucile*, another of the Lyons and Moran features, a theater owner from Davis, California, wrote, "Seems as though patrons are loathe to accept Lyons and Moran in five reel stuff." Carl Laemmle got the message, bouncing them down to two-reelers in January of 1921 before the team split permanently that summer.

But by then, Clyde was long gone. He'd kept other irons in the fire all along. Though the Morning Glories seem to have been disbanded, he pitched for a new team of sportswriters, the Scribes, against a team of ringers led by Vernon nightclub impresario Baron Long. (Clyde pitched nineteen strikeouts, albeit in a game that ran for nineteen scoreless innings before being called on account of darkness.) He began 1920 by covering the Rose Bowl for the *Examiner*, filing a story that hit the national wires with the unlikely news that Harvard had won. That spring, while writing titles for *Everything but the Truth*, the first of Lyons and Moran's doomed features, he was named sporting editor at the *Examiner*. (Beanie Walker was finally making enough writing for the movies to retire from the newspaper business.)

Though assignments at Universal would have been spotty as Lyons and Moran downshifted production, Clyde found work that summer writing for Italian-American comedian Mario Bianchi, who billed himself as "Monty Banks." Banks, at least by his own account, was an all-American success story. He'd arrived in Hollywood barely speaking English, and managed to land work as an extra. His break came when directors started complaining about him to Mack Sennett: Unable to understand what they'd asked him to do, he'd do anything that seemed funny to him, usually succeeding in stealing the scene. Sennett saw talent where his directors only saw an annoyance, and Banks was off to the races.

It's unclear how Clyde and Monty Banks started working together, but they may have met at Universal. Banks had made one of the occasional Lyons and Moran Star Comedies that didn't star Lyons and Moran, a film called *A Hero 'n Everything*, shot in May 1920 and released on June 7. However he met Clyde, when he shot *A Hero 'n Everything*, Banks had just signed a deal with Warner Bros. to produce eighteen two-reel comedies to be distributed by Federated Film Exchanges. These films are even more obscure than the Lyons and Moran comedies—according to film historian David Levy, reused titles and tangled copyright registrations mean it's hard to be sure which ones have even survived. That summer, Banks made his first four of these films: *A Rare*

Bird, His Naughty Night, Nearly Married, and *A Bedroom Scandal.* Robert Farr and Joe Moore, drawing from David Turconi's 1987 biofilmography, *Monty Banks: Biofilmografia,* credit Bruckman with writing all four of these two-reelers. It must have been a summer filled with late nights and early mornings, because Clyde was also covering the baseball season for the *Examiner.* What's more, in early August, Lola fell seriously ill and lingered near death after an operation at Los Angeles's Clara Barton Hospital.

She recovered, but things didn't slow down. In the fall, in addition to his normal duties as sportswriter and editor at the *Examiner,* Clyde was dragged into a grand jury investigation into the 1919 Pacific Coast League season. According to W. Baker "Babe" Borton, first baseman for the Tigers—by now back in Vernon—the players had put together a $2,000 pool to bribe their opponents into throwing games. Clyde testified on November 15, and Babe Borton and three other men were indicted. Eventually, a judge ruled that deliberately losing baseball games was not a crime—at worst, it was a civil matter, if the players' contracts contained a clause averring they would play their best—and threw out the charges. (The National Association of Minor Leagues promptly expelled them from baseball, an important precedent for the Black Sox scandal that went to trial that summer.)

At the same time, Clyde wrote the titles for Lyons and Moran's *Once a Plumber,* as well as both scenarios and titles for Monty Banks's *A Flivver Wedding, Kidnapper's Revenge, His Dizzy Day, Where Is My Wife,* and *Peaceful Alley.* The pace must have been even more hectic than it sounds, because at the end of October, Banks, "ahead of his production schedule," went home to Italy for a vacation.

Something had to give, and in spring of 1921, it did. Lisle Foote, in her excellent guide to Keaton's collaborators, *Buster Keaton's Crew*, identifies Clyde's last byline at the *Examiner* as April 5, 1921. He wrote that day about the Pacific Coast League's upcoming season opener, ending his career as a sportswriter the same place he'd begun it seven years earlier. A few weeks later, *Variety* reported that Clyde had left the *Examiner* to write both scenarios and intertitles for the Special Pictures Corporation. The company had been founded by bankers rather than filmmakers, and advertised itself in a way that seemed to take direct aim at the star system in general (and the Lyons and Moran comedies in particular), as in this ad in *Exhibitors Herald*:

> ARE *you* looking for comedies carrying *every week* the same little cast of "so-called" stars—whose names mean nothing at your box office—whose peculiar type fits them for only a certain type or kind of comedy story, so that the same situations and comedies must be rehashed, week after week, to fit that little cast? If so—we have nothing for *You*.

Special Pictures ran into financial trouble after losing their distribution deal with Federated that February, and in March, the Warner brothers took over the distressed company. Monty Banks was moved to their label and Clyde was hired full-time. He described his first full-time job in the motion picture industry to Keaton biographer Rudi Blesh in the 1950s:

> Warners at that time consisted of Jack, Sam, and Harry Warner, Monte Banks, and a few extras and props, in an old barn of a studio at Bronson and Sunset, where the big bowling alley now is.

Clyde probably only wrote one film here while employed full-time; Farr, Moore, and Turconi credit him with *A Peaceful Alley*, released in September. Though the story that announced Clyde's hiring described Special Pictures as having been "rescued from the financial scrap-heap," it wasn't rescued for long—by June, both director Lloyd Brierly and Keaton gag man Jean Havez were suing for unpaid wages. By fall, the entire thing had dissolved into lawsuits—*Variety* called it "the fiasco of the Special Pictures Corporation." But once again, Clyde was gone before the hammer fell.

Sometime in early June he'd run into Harry Brand, another ex-sportswriter who'd made his way into the movie business (he'd played first base for the Scribes in their game against Baron Long a year and a half earlier). By 1921, Brand was running publicity for Buster Keaton, as Bruckman later explained to Rudi Blesh.

" 'Why don't you come over with Keaton?' he asked.

" 'How do I know Keaton wants me?'

"Next day Brand phoned, said, 'Come over for lunch with us.'

"I did and was hired, to start the next Monday. I went back and saw Jack Warner. 'Jack, I have a chance to go with Keaton—better job, better opportunity. I'd like to close Saturday.'

" 'Can you keep a little secret?' said Jack. 'We're all closing Saturday.' "

And so Clyde Bruckman's golden age of comedy began the next Monday, in the early summer of 1921.

THE PLAYHOUSE

In retrospect, Clyde was such a natural fit for Keaton's production company that it seems odd he didn't land there sooner. Working on intertitles and gags hadn't given him much experience with structure, but that wasn't what Keaton was looking for, as he explained to Harry Brand that fall for an article in *The Photodramatist* addressed to freelancers submitting work to his studio:

> "If I were to start out to write a comedy, I wouldn't know how myself. Because, after all, we 'write' more with the camera than the typewriter. In other words, we have one idea before starting, or perhaps two, say, a start and a finish, and the rest is ad lib. . . .
>
> "The beginner, that is, the one who writes his first comedy," the agile star said with emphasis, "tries to write a continuity so that every move of the comedian is known. That is all right for drama, but for comedy most of the humor is spontaneous, and the best laugh provokers come while the picture is under way. The script is a mere skeleton and a comedian must improvise as he goes along.
>
> "I would suggest, to those who are writing for the comedy-end of motion pictures, that they concentrate on 'gags.' Novelty and origi-

nality are essential. We usually get an idea as to what our picture will be, then erect a set and start 'shooting,' improvising as we go along.

"So, I recommend to those who are inclined along comedy-writing lines that they do away with story and just mail in 'funny pieces of business,' and I am sure they will succeed," Buster said. "We want 'gags,' not story."

Gags, not story. That was something Clyde—whose work for Lyons and Moran had involved inserting jokes in already-finished films—excelled at. And there was another reason Clyde was ideal for Keaton's company: Buster was a baseball nut and always had been, as he explained in his autobiography:

As far back as I can remember baseball has been my favorite sport. I started playing the game as soon as I was old enough to handle a glove. A sand lot where baseball was being played was the first thing I looked for whenever The Three Keatons [his family's vaudeville act] played a new town. We always had a team in Muskegon, and later I organized baseball teams at my own studio and at M-G-M. I also played in the annual Comedians-Leading Men games that amused Hollywood for years. Each September I did my best to finish my fall picture in time to go to New York for the World Series.

The team he put together, the Keaton Nine, was well known enough that the *Los Angeles Times* covered their games, and according to Rudi Blesh, one sportswriter joked that Keaton's employment application looked like this:

Please Check One of the Following Questions:
  Are you a good actor? ☐ Yes ☐ No
  Are you a good baseball player? ☐ Yes ☐ No
Passing Grade: 50%

So Clyde, high school athlete, sportswriter, amateur baseball player, *and* gag man, was right at home. Though he'd played infield and sometimes pitched for the Morning Glories and Scribes, Keaton hired him in a dual role as "outfielder and writer"; he'd stepped up a league. (One of Keaton's stunt doubles, Ernie Orsatti, even made the leap into professional baseball, playing in the Pacific Coast League and then for the St. Louis Cardinals.) There was no firm line between playing and working, as Clyde told it years later:

"Oh, we'd get hung up on sequences. Throw down your pencils, pick up the bats. The second, maybe third inning—with a runner on base—Bus would throw his glove in the air, holler, 'I got it!' and back to work. 'Nothing like baseball,' he always said, 'to take your mind off your troubles.' "

Clyde's new boss had been performing in vaudeville from the age of three, as part of a family act with his parents in which he was pushed around on the floor as "The Human Mop" (one early billing succinctly described their act as "grotesque comedy.") Keaton's first film appearance came in 1917 with a minor role in Fatty Arbuckle's *The Butcher Boy*; he followed Arbuckle to Los Angeles in October. Arbuckle had started at Keystone, but in January of 1917 created his own production company, Comique Films, with Joseph Schenck. Comique specialized in two-reelers; as *Motography* reported at its formation, Arbuckle believed that "you cannot make people laugh for five reels so he is going to make them 'simply scream' for two." Comique was a straight production company, which had to sell films to distributors—but then, so was Keystone, and Comique had Arbuckle's fame to leverage when negotiating distribution deals. Famous Players-

Lasky ended up distributing the Comique shorts, but early in 1919 Adolph Zukor, who by this time could buy whatever he liked, decided to bring Arbuckle into the corporate fold. The deal was worth the exorbitant sum of three million dollars. This left Comique in need of a star, and so Keaton was moved into leading roles in 1920, landing his own distribution arrangement with Metro. Comique had filmed in rented space, but to sweeten the deal for his new star, Schenck bought a studio at Lillian Way and Cahuenga from Charlie Chaplin, rechristening it the Keaton Studio.

Nineteen twenty-one hadn't started well for Keaton. He broke his ankle in February when an escalator malfunctioned during his first attempt to make *The Electric House* and was in a cast for months. In May, still unable to work, his distribution contract with Metro expired, and he signed with First National. When Clyde started, Keaton had just returned from marrying Norma Talmadge in New York; although his leg was healing rapidly, he wasn't ready for the kind of athletic slapstick he'd made his name with.

So Clyde was faced with the problem of creating gags for an actor who couldn't rely on the acrobatics that had propelled much of his work to date. But it wasn't a problem he faced alone. The scenario department was headed by ex-vaudevillian Joe Mitchell, Fred Gabouri had been recently hired as the technical director, and Elgin Lessley, a one-time still photographer who'd started with Keaton back in the Arbuckle days, was in charge of the camerawork. At the time, Keaton had planned on alternating directors for his First National shorts between longtime collaborator Eddie Cline and cartoonist and ex-Keystone Kop Malcolm St. Clair; Cline was assigned to Clyde's first project.[1] Clyde's workday started at the civilized hour of ten in the morning and ran until six, six days a week.

Keaton was always open to ideas from anyone on his staff, but Blesh credits him with the central idea for *The Playhouse*: a vaudeville show in which Buster played all the roles. Since duplicating Buster would depend on visual gags more than acrobatics, Keaton could make the film while his ankle continued to heal.

The film's showstopper is a shot of nine Buster Keatons on stage at once, an effect Keaton, Cline, and Elgin Lessley achieved through extraordinary camera trickery. (Its technical virtuosity is perhaps overshadowed for modern audiences by the fact that all nine Keatons are performing in a blackface minstrel show.) Clyde explained the shot to Rudi Blesh, emphasizing that it was a multiple exposure, not double exposure—instead of shooting the entire frame of film twice or using an optical effect to superimpose images in post-production, the camera itself was rigged to only expose a small portion of the film at any one time, then rolled back, modified to expose a different section of the film, and reshot. The resulting effect was completely finished on the original negative—entirely in-camera.

This wasn't a new technique, but it had only been done at that point with two exposures—and even then, it was hard to do well. It required extraordinary precision rigging the camera, then equally precise timing on the part of the actor, who had to respond to his or her performance from the first exposure. In the days of hand-cranked cameras, the cameraman had to be as skilled as the actor, as a failure to match the camera speed would throw

1. Although many writers, including Rudi Blesh, put Jean Havez on staff at this point, he'd actually jumped ship after Keaton was injured, landing at Special Pictures while Clyde was there before joining Harold Lloyd's team when the company collapsed. He doesn't seem to have returned to Keaton until he switched to features in 1923.

the whole thing off. It was an excruciatingly difficult effect to pull off with two exposures. Buster did it with nine.

Part of the solution was technical. The exposure was handled through a contraption Clyde credited to Keaton himself:

"He built a lightproof black box, about a foot square, that fitted over the camera. The crank came out the side through an insulated slot. It was in the front that the business was: nine shutters from right to left, fitted so tight you could have worked underwater. You opened one at a time, shot that section, closed that shutter, rolled the film back, opened the next shutter and shot, and so on.

The secret to getting the timing right, as Keaton explained years later, was banjo.

". . . it was hardest for Elgin Lessley at the camera. He had to roll the film back eight times, then run it through again. He had to *hand-crank* at *exactly* the same speed *both* ways, *each* time. Try it sometime. If he were off the slightest fraction, no matter how carefully I timed my movements, the composite action could not have synchronized. But Elgin was outstanding among all the studios. He was a human metronome.

"My synchronizing was gotten by doing the routines to banjo music. Again, I got a human metronome. I memorized the routines very much as they lay out dance steps—each certain action at a certain beat in a certain measure of 'Darktown Strutters' Ball.' Metronome Lessley set the beat, metronome banjo man started tapping his foot, and Lessley started each time with ten feet of blank film as a leader, counting down, 'Ten, nine, eight,' and so on. At 'zero'—we hadn't thought up 'blast off' in those days—banjo went into the chorus and I into routine. Simple."

So simple, in fact, that Keaton managed to execute it perfectly in eleven separate setups:

- A double-exposure of Keaton playing a young couple in an opera box.

- A double-exposure of Keaton playing an old woman and her lollipop-wielding child in another opera box.

- A double-exposure of Keaton playing an elderly couple in yet another opera box.

- A double-exposure of Keaton playing both halves of a dancing act, from a distance.

- A closer double-exposure shot of the dancing act.

- A triple-exposure of Keaton playing all three musicians on the left side of the stage.

- A triple-exposure of Keaton playing all three musicians on the right side of the stage.

- A triple-exposure of the left three Keatons in the minstrel show.

- A triple-exposure of the three center Keatons in the minstrel show.

- A triple-exposure of the three Keatons on the right in the minstrel show.

- The ludicrous *nonuple-exposure* long shot of the entire minstrel act.

Besides the wide shot of the minstrel show, the close shot of the dancing act was probably the most challenging for Lessley and the banjo player, given that it's a single twenty-second take and the two Keatons perform a complicated routine in perfect synchronization. As Patricia Eliot Tobias notes in her visual essay about the film, "Only someone as athletic as Buster Keaton would think that dancing was a good way to recuperate from a broken ankle."

The result is dreamlike—director Albert Lewin called it "a phantasmagoria of masks"—as Keaton after Keaton interact and perform with each other. The trick shots are, in fact, part of a dream sequence, and the second half picks up on the theme of doubling, putting Buster through his paces with mirrors, symmetrical sets, and even twins, only one of whom is Buster's love interest. And it's hilarious. So even from his first day, Clyde was working with the very best in the business, stretching the boundaries of what was possible in film comedy both technically and thematically. Moving to the outfield was a small price to pay.

Between the summer of 1921 and fall of 1922, Clyde worked with Keaton on eleven short films, one masterpiece after another. These include *Cops*, with its manic chase scene in which hundreds of uniformed policemen pursue Keaton; *The Paleface*, which has one of Buster's best bits of slapstick, an odd little soft-shoe that turns into a fall as Keaton tries to dance along with the Indians who mean to kill him; and *The Boat*, with its iconic image of Buster going down with his ship. (Members of the International Buster Keaton Society call themselves the Damfinos after the boat.) All of these shorts are extraordinarily funny, but they have their dark places. *Cops* ends with a shot of Buster's tombstone after the police either execute him or beat him to death.

Some of the sharp edges may have come from Clyde; just as many came from Keaton. This period of professional accomplishment for both men was not a happy time for Clyde's boss, as it coincided with the public vilification of his old collaborator and lifelong friend, Fatty Arbuckle. In September of 1921, shortly before the release of *The Playhouse*, actress Virginia Rappe died under questionable circumstances at a party thrown for Arbuckle in San Francisco. He was tried three times for his alleged involvement in Rappe's death before finally being acquitted in April of 1922. The costs were ruinous; he had to sell his remaining interest in Comique to raise funds for his legal defense. Even with an acquittal, the publicity destroyed his career, and Keaton took it hard. During Arbuckle's third trial, Keaton made *The Frozen North*, perhaps his darkest film, an angry parody of the works of popular Western star W. S. Hart in which Keaton attempts to rob a saloon, murders an innocent couple (he mistakes them for his wife and another man), and chases violently after an entirely unwilling love interest. It's the only Keaton film where Buster is a complete jerk, replacing his stone-faced stoicism with snarls and glares. According to biographer Marion Meade, the idea came from Arbuckle himself, who was angry at Hart's public statements about the case. Hart didn't speak to Keaton for two years afterward.

But whatever personal misery and bitterness were swirling around the edges of Keaton's First National shorts, they're almost all masterpieces. The time he spent with Buster Keaton was Clyde's greatest period of happiness and accomplishment, both personal and professional, and he never found anything quite like it for the rest of his life. As he put it years later:

> "We were one big happy family. And that's something you don't know until—and if—you've been in one. In such a situation, gags are never a problem. You feel good. Your mind's at ease, and working. . . .
>
> "Buster was a guy you worked *with*—not *for*. Oh, sure, it's a cliché, like the 'happy family.' But try it sometime. I even hate to mention the playing. It sounds like a buildup. But late afternoons we chose

sides and had our ball game—fights, arguments. Rainy days it was bridge in a dressing room—fights, arguments. And we made pictures." Bruckman sighed. "Harold Lloyd was wonderful to me," he said. "So was Bill Fields. But with Bus you belonged."

Keaton had finished eleven of the twelve films he'd agreed to make for First National by late October of 1922, and got out of making the last one when First National sent a regrettable telegram during what they thought were opening contract negotiations:

WE DO NOT WISH TO RENEW KEATON CONTRACT STOP WE CANNOT BE BOTHERED WITH HIS SHORT SUBJECTS

Buster called their bluff, stopped production of his final short, since they couldn't be bothered with it anyway, and travelled to New York to see if he could get a better deal elsewhere. His new contract with Metro was officially announced in January. Clyde was already at Metro—he'd left Keaton almost immediately after *The Balloonatic* was finished to work for Hunt Stromberg, writing titles for the Bull Montana shorts *Glad Rags* and *Rob 'Em Good*. It's unclear if he simply remained under contract with Metro now that Buster had returned or if Keaton hired him back, but whatever the contractual details, he was back on Keaton's team, where he joined a murderer's row of comedy talent: Eddie Cline, Joe Mitchell, Thomas Gray, and even Jean Havez, back at last from working for Harold Lloyd.

There was one problem, as Keaton and his team would soon discover. Feature films needed story, not gags.

NAVIGATORS

Clyde didn't have to reckon with the challenges of longer narratives immediately. Keaton had already starred in one feature, 1920's *The Saphead*, but that had been a loanout arrangement for an adaptation of a play, and he'd had little creative control. Now he was running the show, betting his career on the idea that audiences would like him as much in features as they had in shorts. With Clyde on staff, he surely would have been aware of the fate of Lyons and Moran, who never recovered from their disastrous attempt to reinvent themselves in five-reelers. So Keaton and his writers found an ingenious way to hedge their bet. His new contract called for longer films; for his feature debut, he and his writers tackled one of the longest: D. W. Griffith's 210-minute epic *Intolerance*.

Griffith's 1916 film had been a boondoggle for the director, and its (undeserved) public reputation at the time—too long, too expensive, too self-serious—made it a great target for a spoof. More importantly for Keaton, its innovative structure—crosscutting between four parallel stories at different moments in history—provided a fallback position. *Three Ages*, the first feature Keaton controlled, would similarly intercut three stories of love: one set in the Stone Age, one in ancient Rome, and one in the present day. If it flopped, he could repackage and resell it without much trouble. As he told Rudi Blesh, "Cut the film apart, and then splice up the three periods, each one separately, and you will have three complete two-reel films." Complete, maybe, but not as good. Not much would be lost by losing Keaton's straight-faced sendup of Griffith's introduction; the rocking cradle is replaced by a bearded Father Time, the same device of flipping pages of a book is used. But in Griffith's version, serious as could be, one of the opening titles quotes Whitman—"Out of the cradle endlessly rocking"—before grandiloquently elaborating: "Today as yesterday, endlessly rocking, ever bringing the same human passions, the same joys and sorrows." Keaton's version of this is delightful, using the same high-flown language before deflating it with the names of his cast:

> In every age Beauty
> is sought by the
> Adventurer
> . . . Mr. *Wallace Beery*

Cut to Wallace Beery on an elephant, wearing an obviously fake beard and mustache, gesturing grandly. And although *Three Ages* is nowhere near as structurally complex a film as *Intolerance*, its best joke depends on interplay between the three stories. It's in the epilogue, which gives a glimpse of Keaton and leading lady Margaret Leahy's domestic bliss to come in each of the ages. Stone Age Buster leaves his cave with his wife and nine children, then

Roman Buster with his wife and *five* children. Modern day Buster is accompanied only by his wife and their pet dog.

The production seems like it was a nightmare for Keaton—Margaret Leahy had literally won a contest to star in a movie, and could neither act nor be recast—but the film turned out fine. It's not Keaton's best work by any means, but it was more than good enough to proceed with production of his next feature before it opened. In fact, Clyde and the rest of the gag men started work on the next film, *Our Hospitality*, as *Three Ages* was shooting in the late spring and early summer of 1923. The crew met with Keaton each night and had finished the script by the time Buster wrapped.

Jean Havez's story idea—framing the film around a Hatfield–McCoy-style feud—was barely enough to justify six reels. Tackling a longer story for the first time, especially with limited feedback from their boss, may have made things tenser than usual: one newspaper noted that Keaton had installed a radio in the writers' room while they were working out the story for the dual purpose of stress relief and breaking up arguments. "The making of a comedy is a severe nerve strain," the paper explained. Keaton was probably as much to blame as anyone else—according to Rudi Blesh, the writers deliberately chose a story that would require location shooting in the country, in an effort to check Buster's "ceaseless parties," which were beginning to wear on everyone. Still, despite the tensions, they managed to write a better film than *Three Ages*—while abandoning the parallel structure they'd cribbed from *Intolerance*, they lifted something better: the steadily increasing pace that made Griffith's film work. *Our Hospitality* starts off like a melodrama, then slowly starts dropping in gags until the furious final chase. It was a matter of learning to handle pace on a larger canvas, as Keaton described in his autobiography:

> In one or two of my later two-reelers I had tried putting in a story line. But this had not always proved feasible, and the faster the gags came in the short comedies, the better. In the features I soon found out that one had to present believable characters in situations that the audience accepted. The best format I found was to start out with a normal situation, maybe injecting a little trouble but not enough to prevent us from getting laughs. That permitted us to introduce the characters getting in and out of situations that were not too difficult. It was when we approached the final third of the picture that we had the characters in serious trouble which permitted bigger laughs, the biggest of all coming when catastrophe threatens.

Buster cast his wife, his one-year-old son, and his father in the film, and by all accounts had a wonderful summer in the mountains, at least until his longtime heavy Joe Roberts suffered a stroke. (He insisted on finishing the film but died before it was released.)

Clyde probably didn't travel with the company, however; that summer he made one of his occasional attempts to branch out from comedy, writing intertitles for Harold Shaw's *Rouged Lips*, a backstage melodrama adapted from a Rita Weiman short story that had run in *Cosmopolitan*. The film shot in May and production was finished by early June, so Clyde's work would have begun roughly when Keaton was heading for the mountains. *Rouged Lips* beat both *Three Ages* and *Our Hospitality* to the screen; *Variety*'s reviewer singled out Clyde's subtitles for special praise, quoting his description of a character "whose main ambition is to yawn without stretching." The film as a whole had a pacing problem, however: the reviewer complained, "Were it forty-five minutes it would be an ideal program attraction, but that extra quarter of an hour causes it to drag unmercifully toward the finish." Although Clyde would attempt genres other than comedy later in his career, *Rouged Lips* was the only time his efforts made it to the screen.

That fall the Keaton features opened two months apart, *Three Ages* on September 24, and *Our Hospitality* on November 20. Both films made money, and money for Keaton meant money for Clyde. By January (and probably sooner; he's not listed in the 1923 phone directory) he and Lola had moved to 1660 North Orange Drive, on the east side of the street just south of Hollywood Boulevard. (Though the Egyptian Theatre was already down the block, Sid Grauman wouldn't announce construction of the Chinese Theatre on the north side of Hollywood Boulevard until September of 1924; the Roosevelt Hotel on the western corner of Hollywood and Orange came later still, in October 1925.)[1]

While Keaton's first features were having their theatrical runs, Clyde and the other writers had moved on to the next one. The idea this time came from a film Keaton didn't get to make—*Merton of the Movies*. The stage adaptation of Harry Leon Wilson's 1919 serial novel had had a phenomenally successful Broadway run, landing its star, Glenn Hunter, a five-year movie contract in the spring of 1923. On its face, the premise seems ill-suited for Keaton: the hero is a wannabe actor whose overacting is unintentionally hilarious, so he is cast in a comedy but told he's performing in a drama. It's hard to imagine Keaton overacting, but both he and Chaplin circled the role. They were outbid by the deepest pockets

---

1. Maybe Clyde got a real estate tip; both projects must have increased the value of the land immensely, and the consortium that built the Roosevelt was headed by Keaton's business manager Joseph M. Schenck. There is an H. Bruckman listed at 1664 Orange Dr. in the 1923 directory and nowhere else, and Clyde is unlisted, so perhaps he bought several lots.

in town—in January 1924, Famous Players-Lasky, having already bought Glenn Hunter, bought their new star the role he'd originated on Broadway.

Edged out of one story about a Hollywood outsider, Keaton and his writers came up with another: *Sherlock Jr.*, the story of a projectionist who wants to be a detective. It's a return to the kind of hallucinatory gags that marked the best of the shorts, especially *The Playhouse*, and although it breaks every rule Keaton set for himself concerning features—no impossible gags, no distractions from the main plotline—the gags are so extraordinary that it's one of his very best films. In this case, it seems that Fred Gabourie came up with the structure. The gag men and cameraman Elgin Lessley had a collection of gags they wanted to use and, according to Buster, "the technical man" came up with the idea of using a film-within-a-film to string them together:

> "You can't do it and tell a legitimate story, because there are illusions, and some of them are clown gags, some Houdini, some Ching Ling Foo. It's got to come in a dream . . ."

Sherlock Jr. opened in the spring of 1924, and although it is rightly seen as a triumph today, neither contemporary audiences nor critics were impressed. *Variety*'s reviewer was particularly unhappy with its gag-anthology structure, complaining that "the picture has about all the old hoke that there is in the world in it." The reviewer at least noted the genius of the meta-gag where Keaton jumps into the motion picture screen and finds himself at the mercy of jump cuts, noting, "That is clever. The rest is bunk."

Perhaps this is what Keaton had in mind when he set out to make his next feature, *The Navigator*, which has the cleanest plotline of anything up until *The General*. The original idea once again came from Fred Gabourie, but it wasn't a plot so much as a prop. Gabourie had been hired by Metro between Keaton projects to look for antique ships for use in *The Sea Hawk*. While travelling along the Northwest coast on Metro's dime, Gabourie discovered that the *Buford*, an ocean liner scheduled for demolition, could be purchased outright for $25,000. Gabourie immediately saw the possibilities and contacted Keaton: "You can do anything you damn please with her—sail her, burn her, blow her up, sink her." Keaton chose to rent rather than buy—a gag in *The Blacksmith* where a Rolls Royce had been gratuitously smashed up had fallen flat, so he was wary of destroying luxury property—but short of sinking the boat, anything was fair game.

It fell to Keaton's writers to decide exactly what that "anything" would be. According to the *Los Angeles Times*, Keaton took Clyde, Jean Havez, and Joe Mitchell to the *Buford*, off the coast of Catalina Island, and told them, "There's the boat, now write me a comedy." But by Keaton's own account, they already had the basic plot before the boat arrived: Jean Havez had the idea of setting two spoiled rich kids adrift, alone, on the open sea. Shooting involved ten weeks at sea in the spring of 1924, during which time Clyde, Jean Havez, and Joe Mitchell shared the *Buford*'s Imperial Japanese Suite.

Despite conflicts with director Donald Crisp—Keaton had hired him for his experience with drama, only to find he had lots of terrible ideas about comedy—and technical challenges shooting underwater, the resulting film is funny, evocative, and, particularly in the sequences in which Keaton and leading lady Katherine McGuire are alone on the deserted boat, haunting. It's one of Keaton's absolute best, and was his favorite after *The General*. It was also the impetus for Keaton and his team to finally give up on gags that weren't related to the matter at hand. At preview screenings, an intricately constructed gag that showed Buster directing a school of fish as though it were traffic fell flat:

> It took us a while to figure out why that wonderful gag laid an egg. One of my gagmen, Clyde Bruckman, was so stunned he almost took the pledge. It is always an interesting problem to me when an audience rejects any such sure-fire laugh getter.

After realizing the gag worked in the film's trailer but flopped in the context of the film, when Keaton's character should have been repairing the boat, he formulated a theory that would inform *The General*:

> . . . once you got the audience interested in what the hero was doing, they deeply resented anything that interrupted him. It didn't matter what terrific gag you gave them.

The finished version of *The Navigator* has only a few moments of outright absurdity, and those—Buster dueling a swordfish with another swordfish, for example—are directly related to his goals. *The General* may be the masterpiece, but *The Navigator* was the breakthrough, in which Keaton and his writers figured out how to build a comedy around a story, rather than trying to find a story to fit already-conceived comedy bits.

The Navigator opened in October of 1924, and quickly became Keaton's greatest financial success. But rather than giving Keaton more freedom to choose his next project, producer Joseph Schenck locked him into *Seven Chances*, a Broadway adaptation he'd purchased without discussing it with anyone, even hiring a director in advance. Though *Seven Chances* has a better reputation today, at the time no one but Schenck was thrilled about it.

Keaton owed Schenck favors, but Clyde had no such obligation. The success of *The Navigator* and its widespread press—which, even in the ads, mentioned he and the other gag men by name—meant Clyde now had a reputation of his own. He spent the fall working on adapting the play for Keaton, but by the time filming began in January, he was ready to take what he'd learned from the transition to features and strike out on his own.

BUILT-TO-ORDER COMEDIES

Clyde's first job in 1925 was with Mack Sennett, the prolific producer whose career in film dated back to bit parts for D. W. Griffith at Biograph in 1908. He'd bought out Thomas Ince's studio in Edendale in 1912 and built an empire from Keystone Kops and Bathing Beauties shorts. Keaton had never worked for Sennett, but virtually everyone else had: Chaplin, Lloyd, Arbuckle, Harry Langdon, W. C. Fields, Gloria Swanson, Carole Lombard, even Bing Crosby. According to Buster Keaton, the only problem was that Sennett underpaid his stars—they got poached away by other studios after building their reputation at his studio.

Clyde started work at Sennett in January, where he reunited with Eddie Cline, who'd left Keaton after *Three Ages*. He joined a scenario department that was, in its own way, as illustrious as Keaton's team: headed by Arthur Ripley, his coworkers were Jefferson Moffatt, Brian Foy, Hal Yates, and, of all people, Frank Capra. Intertitles were handled by a separate department consisting of A. H. Giebler and Felix Adler; Adler would become one of Clyde's most frequent collaborators in his later years.

Clyde's work for Sennett was a step backward in one sense: he was back to shorts, moving away from the larger canvas that he'd only just mastered with Keaton. But it also gave him the opportunity to see an industrialized process of short film production that would serve him well when he began to direct shorts himself. Sennett's studio was nicknamed the "Fun Factory," and as the surviving documents show—Sennett kept virtually everything—the "factory" part was well earned. Clyde's first project was a Ralph Graves vehicle called *Bashful Jim*, and virtually all of the documents created during the film's production are at the Academy of Motion Picture Arts and Sciences' Margaret Herrick Library.

The scenario department was responsible for the initial story, and for *Bashful Jim*, it is found in a document whose title speaks to the industrialized nature of the work: "Graves Story no. 171." (Arthur Ripley wrote "Bashful Jim" on the title page in pencil at some point during the production.) It bears no author's name, but Clyde and Brian Foy were credited for the film's scenario. A Sennett scenario was the ancestor of a modern film treatment, not a modern screenplay—it has the plot laid out in prose without any special formatting. In this case, Bruckman and Foy used the actors' names instead of character names throughout; these were written for a particular cast. Some of the gags, especially the ones that would require work from the prop department, are laid out in great detail:

> Pick up on [Marvin] Loback driving his Ford. His dog is on the seat beside him . . . Loback takes out a package of Bull Durham and papers to roll a cigarette. He takes a rod from the floor of the car and inserts it in a special slot in the steering-wheel, so that the rod extends over in front of the dog, who takes the rod in his teeth and thus controls the car which allows Loback to roll the cigarette.

Other parts are very sketchy; one scene ends with, "This is a spot where gags are to be added." Eddie Cline went straight to filming with nothing more detailed than this scenario. Here's a complete scene, which obviously draws from *Sherlock Jr.*, and gives a good sense of what he and his cast were working with. Ralph Graves is working at a movie theater and Alice Day, the love interest, arrives with his rival, played by Marvin Loback:

Loback and the girl arrive and are seated by Ralph, who then finishes his work and sits next to Alice, with Loback on the other side of her.

The picture, of the "HIS HOUR" type, begins. The lover on the screen is a handsome male vamp with caveman methods.

Ralph is greatly impressed with the way the screen-sheik makes love, and gets over that he has a great idea.

Possibly show a strong love-scene on the screen, and then come to a reverse angle shot showing all the women in the audience raise their shoulders and all sigh at once.

Possibly, an old maid next to Ralph becomes excited and unconsciously takes Ralph by the hand and otherwise embarrasses him. He can see Alice watching this, and becomes terribly confused.

It's more of a brainstorming session than a screenplay—the entire thing is filled with "possibly" suggestions for Cline to use or discard as he liked. Once filming was complete, the finished picture was handed off to Geibler and Adler in the intertitle department, who went through it looking for places to put titles. Some of these were clearly necessary for the plot to make sense, while others were opportunities they saw for gags. Here's the same section of the film as it appears in the Title Spots list:

15. Title for picture within a picture—Film Ralph sees on screen.
16. Possible title for Sunshine Hart in audience at picture show.

17. Spoken title for Alice to Ralph in picture show. "Oh, Ralph, ain't he great?" marvelous.

Intertitle 16 shows that Cline had taken the treatment's suggestion of having an old maid in the audience watching the film, and cast Sunshine Hart in the role. Note that the Title Spots list is still tentative—"marvelous" is proposed as an additional option for "great," and Giebler and Adler are not certain Sunshine Hart should have a line of dialogue. Once title locations had been identified, presumably by Cline, the intertitle writers brainstormed about thirty options for each one. Here are just some of the pitches for Sunshine Hart's line: multiple approaches for each joke, many of which cast her character in different lights:

"If he don't kiss her pretty soon I'll scream!"
"Don't love get grander and grander all the time?"
"I'll bet she marries him at the end. They always do!"
"That girl sure puts up a fine struggle!"
"They always struggle that way in the first reel!"
"Just think, she gets paid for doin' that!"
"Ain't he just adorably cruel?"
"I wouldn't struggle that way if I was her—He might quit!"
"He played the hero in 'Life's Red Lemonade!' "
"He was the dissapointed [sic] lover in 'Life's Cracked Record!' "
"I saw her in 'Passion's Purple Romance,' "
"Did you see him in 'Passion's Purple Tint'?"
"He was grand in 'Life's Broken Suspenders'!"
"I got his picture in a box of prunes!"

These were presented to Eddie Cline, one sheet of paper for each intertitle, and the final choices were made. In this case he crossed out "picture" and wrote in "photo" before writing "OK" next to the line about the box of prunes. The final continuity sheet, used to print the intertitles and cut the whole thing together, shows the final intertitle, including a note to format it as dialogue. It's now number 25 because the opening titles and credits have been added:

25. (Spoken) "I got his photo in a box of prunes!"

Clyde wrote at least one more short before leaving Sennett: *Remember When?*, starring Harry Langdon, a comedy star who briefly rivaled Keaton, Chaplin, and Lloyd but—like Clyde, Felix Adler, and Arthur Ripley—would eventually crash land at Columbia. In February, Clyde was hired away to work for Harold Lloyd—his first encounter with the man who would ultimately bring about his downfall.

Harold Lloyd was temperamentally very different from Keaton, the inveterate prankster, card player, and partier. For one thing, he neither smoked nor drank. In his 1928 autobiography, he tells a horrifying story of being taken on a childhood trip to Colorado Springs by a family friend who fell definitively off the wagon before their train had even arrived. Thirteen-year-old Lloyd had to lock his chaperone in his hotel room, threaten a whiskey-selling pharmacist with the police, and practically carry the man home from a bar—earning jeers from the locals—before giving up and wiring home to Denver for help. "As a moral lesson it was worth ten thousand temperance tracts to a boy," he wrote. Lloyd had come up from theater, not vaudeville, and started appearing in films in 1913 only because he had hit a slump in his theatrical career in San Diego. He began as something less than an extra, sneaking onto the Universal lot by wearing makeup and joining extras returning from lunch; there he met Hal Roach, working in similarly modest circumstances. When Roach unexpectedly raised the money to become a producer, Lloyd joined him, left briefly for Sennett, returned to Roach and in 1917 put on the horn-rimmed glasses that would make him famous. In 1918 he'd blown off most of his own hand when a prop bomb turned out not to be a prop; he'd fought his way back to health from an injury that would have ended most careers. Keaton played cards and base-ball—for Lloyd it was handball, fast and furious. While Keaton was the calm center around which chaos whirled, Lloyd's char-acters were strivers, with a touch of Dale Carnegie about them. Critic Walter Kerr zeroed in on his comedic persona, writing that Lloyd's glasses "masked and justified the nakedness of the aggres-sion."

By the time Clyde went to work for him, Harold Lloyd was more successful than anyone except Chaplin. *The Navigator*, Keaton's biggest success at that time, had grossed $680,406 domestically; Harold Lloyd's 1924 features *Girl Shy* and *Hot Water* had grossed more than $1.7 million. Each. And Lloyd got to keep much more of that money than Keaton did. Because Keaton had risen at Comique after Arbuckle left, it wasn't really his company, despite bearing his name; Lloyd's production company was his own, formed in 1923 when he severed relations with Hal Roach, long after he was a star. His distribution deal with Pathé was a rich one: his share totaled more than $2 million in 1924 alone. And Lloyd, much more than Keaton, had a head for business—his autobiography is filled with the details of contract negotiations. So the chance to work for Lloyd was a step up for Clyde.

Which didn't mean he wasn't a smart hire for Harold Lloyd. Clyde came on board on February 23, 1925, during the last weeks of shooting on *The Freshman*. It had been a troubled production: with nothing more than the idea to make a "football film," Lloyd had started shooting football footage in October of 1924, for what he imagined would be the ending of his film. Shooting the ending first turned out to be a bad idea. As he later recounted, he told his writers:

> It isn't going to work, boys. I haven't got the spirit into it. I've got to know what's going to happen before this, in order to catch the quality and the spirit of wanting to win this game.

The footage was thrown out and the crew started over. Since moving to features, Lloyd had been alternating between character-driven and gag-driven stunt comedies; this was meant to be one of Lloyd's character-driven comedies, but it wasn't holding together. As it happened, Clyde had just spent several years working out how to build coherent character-driven comedy features with Keaton. It's likely his contributions were more in the nature of punch-ups and gags, since the production wrapped at the end of March, but Lloyd biographer Tom Dardis says his contributions were crucial.

As soon as his work on *The Freshman* was finished, Clyde was off to rescue another production, this time for Monty Banks, his old friend from his Warner Bros. days. Banks had made a mildly successful feature comedy for Associated Exhibitors called *Racing Luck*, and, with a contract for three more features in hand, formed his own production company in New York in November of 1924. Leveraging star power to deal directly with distributors had been working well for Chaplin, Lloyd, and Keaton; Banks thought he could make it work for him. Back in Los Angeles in the spring of 1925, he began shooting his new film, *Keep Smiling*, in March, but could only have brought Clyde in during mid-April when he finished his work for Harold Lloyd. So as with *The Freshman*, it's likely that Clyde's work was more in the nature of triage than creation—but unlike Lloyd, Banks gave him a credit. This may have been a mixed blessing when the film opened in September. Although *Exhibitors Trade Review* called *Keep Smiling* "a corking motor boat thriller," *Variety* was less kind:

> One of those built-to-order comedies for a former two-reel come-dian . . . so palpably an elaboration of what might have originally been a two-reeler that it creaks at the joints as far as the story is con-cerned and the last twenty minutes of it are given over entirely to a motor boat race filled with gag stuff . . . it will get by if the audiences are not too particular.

Photoplay was the most succinct, and harshest; their review simply reads, "In which Monty Banks again tries to prove that he is a comedian."

In brighter news, when *The Freshman* opened a few weeks after *Keep Smiling*, it was met with near-universal acclaim. It made $2.6 million, dwarfing all of Lloyd's previous efforts, and is today seen as one of Lloyd's greatest silent films. As with *The Navigator*, Clyde had worked on his employer's biggest success.

But Clyde probably wasn't paying too much attention to the reviews that fall, as he'd been drawn into a family scandal involving his mother. Bertha had remarried in 1922, to a real-estate broker named Clark Horsford. Horsford had a somewhat shady reputation, though Bertha might not have known about it—in 1916 he had been sued for tricking an Austrian pensioner who spoke no English into assigning him power of attorney, then selling her house out from under her. It wasn't even his first offense—he was already on probation.

He wasn't any more scrupulous in marriage than he had been in real estate. Clark had met Bertha's family; they'd all celebrated Christmas together in San Bernardino in 1923. But after Bertha's brother Chauncey W. Smith died in 1924, Clark began an affair with his widow, Mary. Bertha, suspecting this, hired the W. B. Luckenback Detective Agency to investigate in November of 1924, shortly after *The Navigator* opened. They filed their report in February of 1925, informing her that Clark and Mrs. Smith "have ridden in an automobile together in San Bernardino and elsewhere," and, more damningly, had checked into a number of hotels together under false names. Bertha separated from her husband.

In November, she sued for divorce—it was a knotted enough case that it made the papers in Los Angeles and San Bernardino, with the *Los Angeles Times* running photos of both Clark and Mrs. Smith, though not Bertha, captioned "Two Sides of Unusual Triangle." ("Unusual" because everyone involved was older than forty.) Reached by the San Bernardino papers, Mary was indignant:

> "Mrs. Hersford [sic] was my husband's favorite sister, so I wouldn't say a word against her," said Mrs. Smith. "After nursing my husband for five years until his death in February last year, I cannot lower myself to drag his family name into an affair of this nature—I hold those memories too sacred for that."

Clyde may have still had some pull with the *Examiner*, because they buried the story on the last page before the classifieds, below the daily sermon ("1925—A Year of Prayer") and above a fast-breaking story from Sacramento headlined: "Vertical Rising Plane Company Incorporates."

Bertha returned to San Bernardino, newly single, where she remained until her death. Clark and Mary continued to see each other, though Clark does not seem to have become any more reputable after his divorce. It was Clark who found Mary's body in 1927, when she mysteriously fell to her death from her front porch. He claimed not to have seen her fall, which coincidentally happened just as he was pulling up in front of her house, but told the police she'd been suffering from "nervous attacks" and had perhaps slipped.

While his mother's sad drama played itself out in the Los Angeles papers, Clyde was writing comedies for Harold Lloyd again, this time for one of his gag-driven films, *For Heaven's Sake*. When *The Freshman* hit, Adolph Zukor had once again seen something he wanted, and signed Lloyd to an insanely lucrative contract—77.5 percent of domestic gross, 90 percent of foreign. *For Heaven's Sake* was the first feature produced under the new terms. As a film, it didn't turn out well at all; Lloyd hated it, and today it's nearly forgotten. But it made nearly as much as *The Freshman*, and Lloyd got far more of it.

Maybe Buster Keaton noticed that Clyde was making his rival rich. Maybe he missed his input on *Go West*, the not-very-successful film he'd made in 1925. Or maybe he just needed an outfielder. Whatever the reason, he hired Clyde back again in March of 1926. By summer, they'd begun work on one of the greatest comedies of all time.

AN IMPORTANT PLACE IN
MOTION PICTURES

———————

Most screenwriters who move into directing do it because of something they've written. Clyde managed to do it because of something he'd read: William Pittenger's *The Great Locomotive Chase*. The book is an account of the Andrews Raid, a Civil War incident in which a group of Union spies, including Pittenger, stole a Confederate locomotive and headed north, sabotaging tracks in their wake. They were pursued by a dogged conductor from the General, the train they'd hijacked—he followed them on foot, by handcar, and finally by commandeered locomotive.

On its face, *The Great Locomotive Chase* seems as unlikely a sub-ject for a comedy as the 1918 flu epidemic. It was originally written while Pittenger recovered from injuries incurred during his cap-ture, and the first edition was published in 1863 while the war was still raging. The bulk of the edition Clyde read takes place in Con-federate prison camps, and the tone is anything but comic, as the opening paragraph attests:

———

It is painful for me to recall the adventures of the year beginning April 7, 1862. As I compose my mind to the task there rises before me the memory of days of suffering and nights of sleepless apprehension—days and nights that in their black monotony seemed well nigh eternal. And time has not yet dulled the sorrow of that terrible day, when comrades made dear as brothers by common danger and suffering were suddenly dragged to a fearful death that I expected soon to share. A man who has walked for months in the shadow of the scaffold and escaped at last almost by miracle will never find the experience a pleasant one to dwell upon, even in thought.

Perhaps only Clyde Bruckman would read that paragraph and start dreaming of a comedy. But despite its unpromising beginning, Clyde realized that the locomotive chase would provide as great a structure for gag construction as the empty ocean liner in *The Navigator*: two trains careening across the Confederacy, with the fate of the war in the balance. Sometime around the release of *Battling Butler*, Clyde loaned his copy of the book to Keaton and suggested he think about adapting it for his next film. Buster later described Clyde's pitch:

> Clyde Bruckman run into this book called *The Great Locomotive Chase*, a situation that happened in the Civil War, and it was a pip. Says, "Well, it's awfully heavy for us to attempt, because when we got that much plot and story to tell, it means we're goin' to have a lot of film with no laughs in it. But we won't worry too much about it if we can get the plot all told [laid out] in that first reel, and our characters—believable characters—all planted, and then go ahead and let it roll. And every other situation is more dramatic than it is funny."

Even with this extreme soft-sell, Buster saw the potential, at least after one crucial adjustment. Pittenger and the Union spies were the heroes of the book (and the 1956 Disney film adaptation), but since the real story ended with eight of the spies being simultaneously hung by the Confederacy for espionage, he thought perhaps a different angle would make for a funnier comedy. And in 1926, making the Confederates the villains wasn't something Buster thought would work. "The audience resents it. They lost the war anyhow, so the audience resents it," he later told Kevin Brownlow.

So instead of Pittenger and the Union, they decided that *The General* would focus on the Confederate conductor (promoted, for the film, to engineer) in pursuit. Clyde and Buster worked closely on the script together that winter. Though Keaton always claimed that he never worked with a screenplay, including on *The General*, this wasn't true. Clyde's copy of the script resurfaced and sold at auction in 2014, and the catalog includes a photograph of one page. It doesn't look like a modern screenplay, but the detailed descriptions of each shot make it immediately apparent that *The General* required careful planning and coordination that wouldn't have been possible on the fly:

> Scene 310. Profile long shot of switch and loading trestle. The "General" backs in and stops clear of the switch, letting the Texas [the other locomotive] pass onto the siding up the trestle. The "General" pulls forward as soldiers on the tender of the Texas raise their guns and take aim at Buster and Virginia. They are stopped by the bump of the supply train which fails to stop in time and hits the rear of the Texas, nearly sending it off the trestle.

When trying to choreograph hundreds of extras as well as three wood-burning locomotives, it pays to have a written plan. It's clear that this was written before the film was shot (as opposed to some sort of cutting continuity created after the fact), because in the finished film, the business with the trestle takes four shots: the long shot described in the screenplay, another long shot from a different angle as the Texas passes, a close-up of the train collision, and a medium shot of the front of the Texas hanging off the trestle.

It was obvious that a period piece with locomotives like *The General* would be incredibly expensive, but Buster was running with a richer crowd now. His longtime business manager, Joseph Schenck, had joined United Artists once D. W. Griffith left in 1924; in 1926, he was elected president. The other UA artists—Charlie Chaplin, Douglas Fairbanks, and Mary Pickford—didn't waste time making small bets; *The General*, Buster's first UA film, would be no different. They had originally planned to shoot in Tennessee, but by Keaton's account, on visiting, he found the railroads in disrepair and was unimpressed with the locations:

> . . . the scenery didn't look very good. In fact, it looked terrible . . . They didn't have so much gravel rock to put between the ties, and then you saw grass growing between the ties every place you saw the railroad, darn near.

Marion Meade gives a different explanation: Keaton had planned to use the actual General, the locomotive from the chase, but descendants of the men who'd participated in the raid protested, not wanting their story to be told in a comedy. Instead of the South, they decided to use the tiny town of Cottage Grove, Oregon. Keaton and a party including Clyde and Lola toured the area in early May and on Friday, May 28, Keaton, Clyde, and the rest of the crew returned to begin shooting.

Keaton later described Clyde's directorial credit on *The General* as though it were a favor he'd done after the film was completed.

"Oh, I'd put one of my writers' names—or something like that—on there. Says directed by . . . Give 'em a promotion. I did that with Clyde Bruckman."

Clyde definitely got his promotion as a favor for coming up with the idea, but it wasn't as simple as having his name put on a completed movie. *Variety* reported that he would be co-directing a few days after the crew arrived in Cottage Grove, and the position came with responsibilities, even if they weren't exactly directing. In a 1965 interview with John Gillet and James Blue, Buster was forthright about the division of labor.

JG: *What exactly would the co-director do?*

BK: Co-direct with me, that's all. He would be out there looking through the camera and I'd ask him what he thought. He would maybe say, "That scene looks a little slow," and then I'd do it again and speed it up. As a rule, when I'm working alone, the cameraman, the prop man, the electrician, these are my eyes out there. I'd ask, "Did that work the way I wanted it to?" and they'd say yes or no. They knew what they were talking about.

JG: *You would choose the actual camera setups yourself?*

BK: Always, when it was important for the scene I was going to do. If I had an incidental scene—someone runs in, say, and says, "Here, you've got to go and do this"—the background wasn't important. Then I generally just told the cameraman that I had these two characters in the scene, two full-length figures, and asked him to pick a good-looking background.

So Clyde's duties as co-director on *The General* probably fell somewhere between yes-man and crew member—but the important thing is that he had some. No one was more aware of the gap between the credits and what he'd actually done than Clyde himself. In fact, as he told Rudi Blesh, he'd never been entirely comfortable even back in the days of the two-reelers.

> "You seldom saw his name in the story credits. But I can tell you—and so could Jean Havez if he were alive—that those wonderful stories were ninety percent Buster's. I was often ashamed to take the money, much less the credit. I would say so.
>
> "Bus would say, 'Stick, I need a left fielder,' and laugh. But he never left you in left field. We were *all* overpaid from the strict creative point of view. Most of the direction was his, as Eddie Cline will tell you."

Overpaid or not, being Buster's eyes at the camera for *The General* would have been more of a challenge than usual, since the cameras were often on a different moving locomotive than the action, running on a parallel track. And the shoot was a logistical nightmare beyond the inherent difficulties of wrangling locomotives, requiring eighteen freight cars of cannons, props, and costumes. Nearly the entire town of Cottage Grove was commandeered all summer long: the Bartell Hotel was headquarters, a prop house was set up in a local garage, and Oregon National Guardsmen were drafted as extras for the battle scenes. Housing was so scarce that extras lived in train cars rented from Union Pacific.

For the film's grand finale, Buster built a railroad bridge across a creek, strategically sawed through some of the supports, set it on fire, and blew the whole thing up with dynamite while a locomotive piloted by a dummy chugged across it. The result is spectacular, but that single stunt cost $42,000—more than half a million dollars today. And it wasn't just the budget that spiraled out of control: The wood-burning locomotives threw sparks that kept setting the surrounding wilderness on fire. The day after the bridge collapse, a train caused a forest fire the crew couldn't put out, the smoke made filming impossible, and the production shut down for most of August.

Despite all the chaos, Cottage Grove was thrilled to be part of the film business, however briefly. Buster spent a lot of time that summer on public relations, giving lengthy interviews to the *Cottage Grove Sentinel*, paying to have the local baseball field leveled, and playing third base on a local team in an exhibition game. But although the *Sentinel* ran features and interviews with everyone from the cameramen to the explosives expert, Clyde barely appears. He seems to have promised them an autobiography he couldn't get around to writing—in mid-August, while the crew was waiting out the forest fire back in California, the paper wrote that their Movie Edition was delayed because "important copy has failed to arrive from Hollywood, but word from there is to the effect that it will be there at once."

Finally, the rains came, the smoke cleared, and Buster and a diminished company returned to Cottage Grove to get the last remaining shots. On September 18, when filming was finally complete, everyone got roaring drunk and shot fireworks down the town's main street.

The final film had Clyde's name on it, and had been Clyde's idea to begin with, but the cinematic vision is Buster Keaton's. In *The General* he finally achieved the unity between plot and comedy he'd been reaching for since he moved to features. No gag is unmotivated; everything proceeds from character and situation. And the camera is in on the joke in ways that go beyond the visual punning in earlier films, as in the sequence where Keaton stages a massive advance of the Union troops on the Confederates—the kind of thing that makes an epic—and then relegates it to the background of the frame as he passes by obliviously in the foreground. But neither critics nor audiences were ready for Keaton as an action-comedy star.

Rumors of the out-of-control budget reached Hollywood during production, and the film's release was delayed because it wasn't testing well. When Keaton traveled to New York to attend the premiere, after arranging for the original General locomotive to be displayed in the lobby, he discovered that the theater decided to hold over *Flesh and the Devil* instead. Locomotive or no, he had to leave town before the film finally screened.

Variety's reviewer called it a flop, and for once Clyde may have been glad to have his name left out as Buster Keaton took all the blame: "The action is placed entirely in the hands of the star. It was his story, he directed, and he acted." Regardless of the acclaim *The General* has received in decades since, in its day it was a financial disaster—missing profitability in its initial release by $400,000; about five million dollars today. This debacle was the first step toward Keaton losing his creative and financial independence.

But Clyde had once again moved on. As far as anyone in Hollywood knew, he was a full-fledged director, and whatever private qualms he might have had about his qualifications, they didn't stop him from moving up in the world. That meant leaving Buster Keaton and *The General* behind for the time being. By the time the film finally opened in New York in February, he'd already directed his first solo feature and begun work on his second.

In the meantime, the town of Cottage Grove—so proud to have

been "the Hollywood of Oregon" during production—was getting its own lesson in how quickly Hollywood abandoned people once they'd served their purpose. When the film was complete in November, the local paper openly wondered whether its Oregon premiere would be in Cottage Grove, noting that "it was understood that Buster intended to favor this city." By the middle of the month, they confidently predicted that "the Arcade theater here will have the first booking in Oregon for the picture." In December, the town was shocked to discover that *The General* was booked for its Oregon premiere at the Majestic in Portland; tiny Cottage Grove was invited to send a delegation in lieu of screening the film themselves. The manager of the Arcade, furious, assured the public that, outside of Portland, Cottage Grove would surely come first, going so far as to travel to Seattle to square things away with the film exchange, "to make certain that there shall be no slip-up in these arrangements." "There Is Slip Up Somewhere in Contract with Film Exchange," the *Sentinel* reported on January 6: *The General* had already been shown in several other cities across the state. The filmmakers had been happy to set the surrounding wilderness on fire all summer, but they didn't manage to get a print to Cottage Grove until January 25.

Later that month, *The Cottage Grove Sentinel* finally ran their long-delayed biographical sketch of Clyde:

One of the important men in the Keaton organization but one who says little is Clyde Bruckman, assistant director and also of the scenario staff. The Sentinel failed to receive data from which to prepare a biography but "Bruck" has worked his way up to an important place in motion pictures.

LICENSE TO DRIVE

Years later, Buster remembered Clyde's directorial career as a prank he'd played on Harold Lloyd.

> . . . Lloyd didn't know any better and hired him and kept him for about four pictures—four or five pictures. He was there for about three years, or something like that. But he turned out good for Lloyd, so there was no harm done. Made him a good director. But up to then he had no experience of directing at all.

In fact, Clyde's career was a prank Buster played on Monty Banks, although Harold Lloyd had a hand in it. When Lloyd left Pathé for Adolph Zukor's impossibly rich deal at Paramount in the fall of 1924, the company found themselves without a comedy star. Banks must have had a great public relations rep as he began angling for the job; the *Los Angeles Times* alone ran four profiles of Banks in the space of five months, under headlines like "Merit Won His Start in Films: Monty Banks Achieves High Place in Cinema World by Own Efforts," and "Comedian Winner by Hard Work: Monty Banks Attains High Rank by Tugging at His Own Boot Straps."

His PR campaign worked. In April of 1926, Pathé signed Monty Banks to a twelve-picture deal and announced he was being groomed to take Harold Lloyd's place. That summer, while Clyde was in Oregon, Banks was shooting *Atta Boy*, his first feature under the new contract, directed by Edward H. Griffith. For his second outing, *Horse Shoes*, he hired Clyde to direct, at least partially on the strength of his experience "directing" *The General*.

Banks, acting as his own producer, had shot *Atta Boy* in space rented on the Hal Roach lot; the crew returned for *Horse Shoes*. In the years since Hal Roach and Harold Lloyd were extras at Universal, Roach had been incredibly successful. Even losing Lloyd hadn't slowed him down, and by the time he'd built a studio in Culver City that rivaled Mack Sennett's in Edendale. Hal Roach's studio was known as "The Lot of Fun," and just like Sennett's "Fun Factory," the nickname was apt. Employees of Roach's studio uniformly reported an informal, collaborative working environment, without the hierarchies or castes that characterized other studios. Actor Henry Brandon put it succinctly: "It was the friendliest lot in Hollywood." It would have been particularly friendly for Clyde, because Beanie Walker, his old boss from the *Examiner*, was running the title department. In early November, Clyde began his first job as a genuine director.

Screenwriter Charles Horan's plot for *Horse Shoes* was simple: Monty Banks plays a new law school graduate with a superstitious belief in a lucky horseshoe. On his return from school, he and a stranger (Jean Arthur, in one of her first starring roles) are mistaken for a married couple on the train; on reaching their destination, Arthur turns out to be the daughter of the head of the law firm where Banks is starting his career. Compared to shooting *The General*, this must have been a dream—filming was finished by

December, when Banks was suddenly called back to Italy for the death of his mother. Despite Clyde's lack of experience behind the camera, Banks was pleased with his work; he hired Clyde for his next feature before leaving town.

On Monday, January 17, after stopovers in Paris and New York, Banks returned to Hollywood, and he and Clyde went to work on their next film, another Charles Horan screenplay, at the time titled *Clear 'n' Cloudy*. This time Ruth Dwyer took Jean Arthur's place as the female lead and an etiquette guide took the horseshoe's place as Banks's lucky talisman. Banks plays a lowly teller who blows his wedding to the bank president's daughter by showing up drunk, then attempts to reform his manners. (There's also an elaborate subplot involving Banks foiling the plans of South-American revolutionaries; Clyde seems to have forgotten whatever he learned with Keaton about keeping things simple.)

Filming began in late February under a new title, *A Perfect Gentleman*, and continued through March, including a sequence shot aboard the SS *Ruth Alexander*, a steamship en route from Los Angeles to San Diego, where further location shooting was to be done. Clyde may have become a director through a fake credit and a misunderstanding, but he was settling in to the job and handling a complicated shoot well.

Nineteen twenty-seven was also the year Clyde began to live up to the style of his new position. An apartment in Hollywood was all right for a gag man, but he was a director now. Everyone around him was moving up just as fast: in 1925, Buster Keaton bought an enormous Italian villa in Beverly Hills, with a trout stream, a playhouse for his children, and a large swimming pool at the base of a grand outdoor staircase; Clyde helped him move in. Harold Lloyd did things on an even grander scale. Greenacres, his

Beverly Hills estate, had been under construction since 1925 (and wouldn't be ready for Lloyd to move in until 1929), but the plans included a nine-hole golf course, an Olympic-size swimming pool, a reflecting pool, a lake, and a 110-foot waterfall.

Clyde and Lola couldn't afford Greenacres or the Italian Villa, but they could at least buy their way into the same neighborhood. In 1927 the couple moved into a newly constructed home at 717 North Elm Drive—just south of Sunset Boulevard, right in the center of Beverly Hills. The house is still standing; it underwent extensive renovations in 1950 and was last assessed in 2006 at more than $5 million. Donald P. Swisher, Clyde's nephew from his second marriage, visited often as a child and remembers a sunken living room, an extensive library, a huge dining room, a fishpond, and servants' quarters. Into the living room went a baby grand piano, though neither Clyde nor Lola played; into the library went stacks of books, many of which Swisher later noticed were clearly unread; onto the walls went portraits by Hollywood artist John Decker of "stage personages," though Clyde had had nothing to do with theater since his high school production of *The Importance of Being Earnest*. The house became a social center for everyone around, from film personages to family: Lola's nephew Richard Hamblin recalls that her extended family was a little starstruck when they were invited over: "The house became *the house*." According to Hamblin family stories, Lola presided over parties and dinners, while Clyde reaped the benefits. "Lola attracted people, and in many ways bolstered Clyde's career, in that she was beloved by people."

Horse Shoes was released in April to modest commercial success and critical acclaim. The *Los Angeles Times*, which had done so much to build Banks up as a leading man, was kindest, calling it "a very funny, exceptionally human comedy without unnecessary slapstick or unreal situations." *Motion Picture News* was also positive, though the reviewer noted that "the production has its slow moments which could have undoubtedly been improved by the dint of more application on the part of the editors in its cutting." History has been less kind—none of Banks's features are readily available. He rated only a single paragraph in Walter Kerr's *The Silent Clowns*, and not a good one:

> It is almost impossible now to describe a once-popular comedian like Monte Banks by speaking of his mannerisms; he doesn't seem to have any. He is short, on the plump side, possessed of a miniature mustache that would seem suave on a head waiter but is somehow a badge of apprehension on him. He is likable . . . The stunting is impeccable, worth keeping in film anthologies; but we cannot quite remember the man.

In May, as *A Perfect Gentleman* neared completion, Banks readied his next feature, once again by Charles Horan, to be titled *An Ace in the Hole.* (Presumably, Banks would have had a lucky playing card this time around.) Clyde was tapped to direct.

But before that could happen, Monty Banks's career descended into farce and tragedy. On June 15, a few days after Banks unaccountably decided to retitle his new film *The Flying Fool*, Banks received his third speeding conviction and had his driver's license revoked. "Walking is good for one's health, I've heard," he told reporters. "And then, too, it's such a cheap means of transportation. Perhaps I'll try it." Later that summer, he fired his longtime manager, Arthur MacArthur, and the two ended up dueling in the courts; MacArthur was eventually barred from going to the lot where Banks was working. In September, MacArthur had his revenge when someone swore a warrant claiming that he'd seen Banks drive by at Santa Monica and Las Palmas; Banks was arrested and charged with driving on a suspended license. Banks suspected MacArthur, telling reporters, "I believe the man who swore to the warrant is related to a certain person who recently brought suit against me over business matters." MacArthur followed his wrongful termination suit with by suing for slander, reporting that Banks had ruined him professionally by telling anyone in the film industry who would listen that "he does more harm than good."

By the end of October, Pathé was displeased enough with Banks's bad press and lack of progress on his next film that they canceled his contract. Banks had to ask for a continuation in his suspended license case to rush back to New York, as his lawyer told the court, "in a desperate effort to avoid financial ruin." He'd been able to use the press to his advantage when angling for the Pathé contract in the first place, so naturally Banks did his best to turn his legal troubles into a publicity stunt, arriving at the courthouse in a horse and buggy. "I am taking no chances," he told the papers. It didn't make any difference. He ended up with a suspended sentence of thirty days in jail, two years' probation, and no film career. Pathé held *A Perfect Gentleman* from release until January of 1928, when it was met with lukewarm reviews ("Funny Now and Then," raved *Motion Picture News*). It was Monty Banks's last starring role in America. In 1929, he was forced to file for bankruptcy; by then, he was down to $150 in assets against $90,701.86 in debt. Ill-equipped for sound film because of his strong accent, he spent the rest of his career working mostly as a director.

But just as he had with *The General*, Clyde leapt from the deck of the burning ship before it really started blazing. In May, he signed a long-term contract to direct films for Hal Roach. Clyde's escape route probably came from Beanie Walker, whom Roach had just promoted to vice president. Also under contract to Roach at the time were two little-known actors named Stan Laurel and Oliver Hardy.

THE BOYS

When Clyde started work at Roach Studios in the spring of 1927, the biggest stars on the lot were Charley Chase and Max Davidson. (The studio had just made its final film starring Rex the Wonder Horse, so this represented progress of a sort.) When he left early in 1928, Laurel and Hardy were unquestionably the studio's biggest draw, and well on their way to becoming the most successful comedy duo in history. This was not Clyde's doing: the idea of pairing them was Leo McCarey's, the promotional muscle was MGM's, and the comedy chops were Stan Laurel and Oliver Hardy's. But between August and December of 1927, Clyde directed Roach's new comedy team in four landmark films in a row, each one crucial to the development of their act. In the first of these, *Putting Pants on Philip*, Laurel and Hardy's comedic personas were rudimentary at best; as film historian Randy Skretvedt put it, "What's typical about an L&H movie where Stan plays a Scottish sex maniac?" But by *The Finishing Touch* four months later, they had recognizably become Stan and Ollie, the roles they'd play for more than twenty years to come. Along the way, they staged history's greatest pie fight.

Clyde's first job for Hal Roach presaged none of this: His assignment was cleaning up another director's mess. A week before he was hired, Roach tested a Louis Gasnier film called *Cowboys Cry for It*, starring Eugene Pallette. The results were so disastrous that Roach threw Gasnier off the project and brought in Clyde, with instructions to somehow salvage things. The solution they arrived at was removing Pallette entirely and replacing him with one of Roach's stock actors, Stan Laurel.

Laurel, four years older than Clyde, had begun his career at the age of sixteen on the British vaudeville circuit. He first came to the U.S. on a 1910 vaudeville tour with Fred Karno's company in which he was Charlie Chaplin's understudy, and had been sporadically appearing in films since 1917. Monty Banks's problem was that he never found a distinctive comic persona; Stan Laurel's was that he'd settled on one audiences hated. Director George Stevens called Laurel in those days "one of the unfunniest comedians around," for, among other things, laughing at his own jokes. By 1927, Hal Roach had hired him three times and fired him twice: in 1918 for a job pitched as a "permanent engagement" that lasted less than a month, in 1923 for a five-year contract that lasted two years, and in 1925 as a writer and director only. (Laurel was initially barred from appearing in Roach films as an actor during his last go-round because of an existing acting deal with producer Joe Rock.)

In 1926, while battling Rock in the courts, he returned to the screen in *Love 'Em and Weep* as a last-minute replacement for future co-star Oliver Hardy, who'd been injured.[1] By the time of *Cowboys Cry for It*, Laurel had been in several films for Roach—a few with Oliver Hardy—but had met with no great success. So it wasn't as if Roach was throwing his best talent at the problem; he gave it to his new hire and an underperforming actor.

Nobody exactly exceeded expectations. As Ted Okuda and James L. Neibaur point out, the main problem with the film is that neither Laurel nor co-star James Finleyson have much to do with the plot, a Western love triangle in which Stuart Holmes and Theodore von Eltz battle for the hand of Martha Sleeper. Instead, the comedy exists on the sidelines, and although there are a couple of good gags, the film is mostly an experiment in testing the audience's patience with watching Finleyson get chased around by a mule.

But it didn't really matter if *Cowboys Cry for It* was any good; it only mattered that it was finished. Roach was in a transitional period when Clyde came aboard: For years, Pathé had distributed his films, but by 1926 the partnership was fraying. For one thing, Pathé was also distributing Mack Sennett's films, so Roach had to compete for distribution within his own company, never mind the larger market. In January of 1927 he jumped ship for Metro-Goldwyn-Mayer. The deal was arranged by Fred Quimby, who had worked for Pathé while Roach was building his studio; he was able to parlay his experience with Roach into a position at MGM as head of the short subjects department. A side effect of all this shuffling was that Roach was required to deliver a few more films to Pathé in exchange for being released from his contract early. *Cowboys Cry for It*, which might as well have been titled *Contractual Obligation*, was one of these final films.

---

1. Hardy's injury was the painful result of real-life slapstick: his wife had fallen down a hill while running from a rattlesnake; while she was recuperating, he attempted to cook a leg of lamb himself, managed to spill hot grease all over his hand, then fell and twisted his leg while racing out of the kitchen to try to treat his burn without disturbing her.

Regardless of what Pathé may have thought of the quality of their last films from Roach, they managed to squeeze some money out of them by holding the ones with Laurel or Hardy until they could ride on the coattails of MGM's promotion of their new comedy team. *Cowboys Cry for It*, which Pathé registered for copyright in September, didn't make it to theaters until January of 1928, when it was inexplicably retitled *Should Tall Men Marry?* Stan Laurel, despite his minor role in the film itself, was given top billing. By then, his name meant something.

In fact, although audiences wouldn't know it for months, inside Roach Studios, Laurel's name meant something by June, when Clyde directed his next film. Between *Cowboys Cry for It* in May and *Call of the Cuckoo*, Roach had wrapped up his contract with Pathé. Wanting something new for MGM, at Leo McCarey's urging, Roach decided to test Laurel as part of a comedy team with another of his not-too-successful stock actors: Oliver Hardy.

Hardy had entered the film industry in an unusual fashion in those days of ex-vaudevillians: Rather than appearing in theaters, he'd run one, the first movie theater in Milledgeville, Georgia. The films he booked there were terrible enough that he decided he could do no worse, and left Georgia in 1913 not for Los Angeles or New York but Jacksonville, Florida. At the time—the days of the Motion Picture Patents Company—Jacksonville was a larger center of film production than Los Angeles: it was easily reached by train from anywhere on the East Coast, so New York studios spent winters there and used it for location shooting. Agile despite his great size, Hardy found steady work as a comic villain, the kind of role Joe Roberts played in Buster Keaton's early shorts. He was turned down because of his weight when he attempted to enlist during World War I, and headed west in late 1918, eventually landing with Hal Roach. Like Laurel, he'd made many films, but no one quite knew what to do with him.

No one, that is, except for Leo McCarey. McCarey, who would go on to a legendary career as a director in the 1930s and '40s, had been at Roach Studios for several years, working his way up to directing. That spring, he'd begun pitching the idea that Laurel and Hardy might work well as a team. Hal Roach was amenable; Oliver Hardy was positively overeager, according to Venice Lloyd, whose husband, Art, was a cameraman:

> "He was anxious to be part of a team . . . They were grooming him for it. So he came over one night, and he was asking Art, 'Have you heard anything? Do you think I'll really get on steady, do you think I can really be part of a team?' He was so anxious to work with Laurel."

Stan Laurel, on the other hand, wanted nothing to do with any of it; he was convinced his future lay in writing and directing. Nevertheless, in late June he and Oliver Hardy went in front of the cameras for a film called *The Second Hundred Years*. This was the first time Roach would sell Laurel and Hardy together, although the publicity department couldn't settle on whether or not they were selling "Stan Laurel and Oliver Hardy," "Hardy and Laurel," or the "famous comedy trio" of Hardy, Laurel, and Finlayson. Clyde wasn't involved, but Roach and McCarey liked the results, and asked Clyde to shoehorn the new comedy team into his next assignment, a Max Davidson film called *Call of the Cuckoo*.

Max Davidson specialized in Jewish humor, often to the point of offensiveness. By the fall of 1928, he would be sidelined at the request of MGM executives Louis B. Mayer and Nicholas Schenck, both of whom were concerned that his work was helping stoke anti-Semitism. But he's not particularly offensive in *Call of the Cuckoo*, in which Davidson sells his house to avoid his obnoxious neighbors, only to end up with a catastrophic, poorly constructed new house and the same neighbors. Davidson's house is more than a little reminiscent of the one in Keaton's *One Week*, though the gags are nowhere near as impressive.

Laurel and Hardy, put into the film because "the boys were just too good to be kept inactive," according to George Stevens, give no indication of being too good for anything. At least this time Clyde wasn't reediting an existing film, but their appearance is as peripheral as Stan Laurel's in *Cowboys Cry for It*. What's more, their performance has no relation to the act they were supposedly promoting. Instead, along with James Finlayson and Charley Chase, they play the lunatic neighbors, doing manic, not-very-funny bits viewed through a window, impersonating radio announcers and singers and generally behaving ridiculously. Anyone could have been cut into these shots, and perhaps someone else should have been. The film's funniest performance comes from none of the stars but from Spec O'Donnell as Davidson's dimwitted son, introduced via intertitle as "Love's Greatest Mistake." Still, compared to *Cowboys Cry for It*, it's a masterpiece.

Clyde followed this mediocre performance by snagging a directorial credit on *Love 'Em and Feed 'Em*, another Max Davidson film, although he was barely involved. The Davidson series was beginning to falter—MGM's sales force hadn't liked the first film they'd delivered, *What Every Iceman Knows*—and so Hal Roach himself directed most of his next outing in an effort to get things back on track. The film is now mostly lost, but it featured Oliver Hardy, without Stan Laurel, in a supporting role, and may have been originally planned as a Laurel and Hardy film. Clyde took the reins from Roach only for the last few days of the production, although he received sole screen credit. There's no indication from the surviving footage that the film was particularly good.

Clyde's rocky start makes his next four excellent pictures in a row all the more remarkable. The first, *Putting Pants on Philip*, made enough of an impression on Stan Laurel that he misremembered it as being the first official Laurel and Hardy film years later. (It *was* the first film made after Roach Studios announced via press release that they'd work as a team from then on, which may have been the source of his confusion.) Despite its billing, this is not quite a Laurel and Hardy film: Hardy is a pompously respectable American; Stan is his fresh-off-the-boat Scottish cousin Philip, with a fondness for women and kilts. But the two men have a rapport that is starting to resemble their later work.

Cinematically, *Putting Pants on Philip* is both impressive and innovative. Biographer John McCabe gives Stan Laurel credit for working with his directors to develop a technique of holding on a gag to allow time for audience laughter, to the point of reediting films after timing the laughs at test screenings. The timing isn't that precise yet, but there's an inkling of this technique in *Putting Pants on Philip*, which has several beautiful slow builds. The most impressive is a long tracking shot of Laurel and Hardy walking down Culver Boulevard. In the foreground, Hardy is increasingly embarrassed and exasperated as Laurel keeps taking his arm. As they move down the street, bystanders see the commotion and follow, laughing and pointing. Clyde lets this run for a full minute and eighteen seconds without cutting, as the camera tracks backward down the entire block, slowly bringing more and more people into frame. Critics tend to describe the Laurel and Hardy long takes as an attempt to recreate the theatrical experience, but this is a uniquely cinematic shot. The film's final gag—too good to spoil—works by shock rather than a slow build, but it depends on an optical illusion, which Clyde stages almost as gracefully as anything Keaton and Fred Gabourie ever dreamed up. Both Hal Roach and MGM were thrilled with the results, with one MGM executive calling it "one of the funniest things I have ever looked at" in an internal memo. The next film would be even better.

The inspiration for Clyde's second outing with Laurel and Hardy, like *The General*, came from American history. But this time, instead of looking back decades before he was born, he only had to recreate the events of a few weeks before filming began. On September 22, 1927, Gene Tunney successfully defended his heavyweight title from Jack Dempsey in one of the most-hyped sporting events of the century. The fight broke all the records; the next day, the crowd at Soldier Field in Chicago was estimated at 150,000; the gate was $2,800,000. It also descended into controversy in the seventh round, when Dempsey knocked Tunney off his feet and the referee gave him several extra seconds to get back up. At issue was a new rule that required Dempsey to retreat to a neutral corner before the referee began counting. Dempsey, whether dazed or forgetful, didn't do this right away, which gave Tunney enough time to come to his senses. Depending on who was asked, Tunney's "long count" lasted between twelve and fourteen seconds, during which, according to the AP's reporter, "Pandemonium was loose in the vast arena," as spectators screamed at the boxers and referee. Many sources assume the idea to shoot a version of the fight with Laurel and Hardy came from Leo McCarey, who received a "Supervised by" credit on the film; his father was a boxing promoter and he loved sports. And a decade later, in a profile written during the production of *Make*

Way for Tomorrow, the sports section of the *Los Angeles Times* said McCarey had "seized on the commotion" surrounding the fight.[2] On the other hand, no one loved sports as much as Clyde, and among those screaming ringside was one Lola Bruckman, who had traveled to Chicago alone to attend the fight as the guest of some of her husband's former sportswriter colleagues.

Whoever's idea it was, it was decided that Laurel and Hardy's next film would be a version of the "Long Count" fight. *Putting Pants on Philip* had gotten great mileage from reaction shots of Oliver Hardy; by casting him as the manager to Stan's incompetent boxer, they created a situation that would naturally be fueled by Hardy's impotent rage as Stan blows it in the ring. Noah Young, Harold Lloyd's frequent comic foil, was cast as the other boxer, and the scenario basically wrote itself, down to Stan getting in a fight with the referee.

But the boxing match of the century only took care of the first reel. For the second, they planned something *really* spectacular. Buster Keaton had instituted a strict rule against pie-throwing when he started making features, feeling the gag was played out; and pies had the same reputation around the Roach Lot—"early Sennett, mid-Chaplin, and late everybody," according to John McCabe. But a classic thrown-pie gag involved one pie and one face; Stan Laurel had something more ambitious in mind. Philip K. Scheuer summarized it a couple of years later:

His method would consist, simply and directly, of throwing more

2. Also in that profile is the fact that McCarey, like Clyde, owed his career to Charles Van Loan. McCarey worked briefly as a sportswriter; sent to cover a boxing match for the Los Angeles Times, he was seeking a post-fight interview with the young winner. Van Loan correctly told him the real story would be found in the dressing room of the man who'd just become an ex-champion after more than a decade.

pies. Not one, not two, not ten or twenty, but hundreds, even thousands.

Leo McCarey didn't want to do it, but Laurel went over his head and sold Hal Roach on the idea. So the studio bought the entire day's output of the Los Angeles Pie Company and Clyde came to direct a battle scene as challenging, in its way, as Keaton's Civil War recreations: 3,000 pies soaring gloriously through the air. And yet the result is not chaos, until the very end; the pie fight is even more meticulously staged than the boxing match. The secret, as with *Putting Pants on Philip* and the first reel of *The Battle of the Century*, turned out to be not action, but reaction:

> "It wasn't just that we threw hundreds of pies," Laurel explained, "that wouldn't have been very funny; it really had passed out with Keystone. We went at it, strange as it may sound, psychologically. We made every one of the pies count.
>
> "A well-dressed man strolling casually down the avenue, struck squarely in the face by a large pastry, would not proceed at once to gnash his teeth, wave his arms in the air and leap up and down. His first reaction, it is reasonable to suppose, would be one of numb disbelief. Then embarrassment, and a quick survey of the damage done to his person. Then indignation and a desire for revenge would possess him; if he saw another pie at hand, still unspoiled, he would grab it up and let it fly."

The usual take on Clyde as a director is that he dutifully duplicated the house style of whatever comic he was currently working with. So it's worth noting that *The Battle of the Century* is nothing like *Putting Pants on Philip* in terms of direction, editing, or cinematography. Of course, it's possible that Clyde received the credit without doing the work; McCarey's "supervisor" credit sometimes extended to ghost-directing. But in the same letter where Laurel misremembered McCarey as the director of *Putting Pants on Philip*, he credits Clyde with *The Battle of the Century*; and McCarey, whose duties at the time also included the Charley Chase and Max Davidson films, was reportedly rarely on sets during filming in the early days.

George Stevens, the cinematographer on the film, went on to become a great director, and Stan Laurel eventually took more control of the Laurel and Hardy films, particularly once McCarey and Stevens left Roach. So there was no shortage of brilliant cinematic minds working on the film, and it's probably impossible to know who did what. Success has many fathers, particularly years later, particularly when one of the fathers is dead—but in 1927, when it counted, Clyde got the credit.

And what a success. Although, then as now, the pie fight gets most of the praise, the boxing match is also remarkable. It wasn't the first time Clyde had filmed a fight: *Call of the Cuckoo* ends with several brawls. But they're almost all long shots; Clyde set the camera back far enough to capture everything, yelled "Action," and that was that. *The Battle of the Century* uses the camera brilliantly, in ways that have little in common with the Laurel and Hardy long-take house style. Here's how the knockout punch that floors Stan is staged:

- A medium shot of Noah Young from the waist-up, in a boxing stance, glowering at the camera, taking up most of the frame. The ropes form straight horizontal lines behind him, giving no impression of depth. He crowds the frame.

- A nearly full length shot of Stan, fists way too low, looking terrified. Stan's entire head takes up only a little more of the frame than Noah Young's ear in the preceding shot. Stan is shot at a slightly high-angle, so we see the floor of the ring behind him, and at an angle to the ropes, so that the corner behind him makes the ring dwarf him. Ollie is visible in the lower left of the frame, gesturing futilely.

- A long shot of the ring, showing Noah Young and Stan. They're pushed over in the left half of the frame, much closer to each other than the impression given by the earlier shots.

- A terrifying medium shot of Noah Young, with a sadistic grin on his face, throwing a right cross directly at the camera. As his fist takes up more and more of the frame, he steps forward, out of focus.

- And at the moment we expect a shot of the punch landing, Clyde cuts away to a medium shot of Ollie in the corner, wincing in sympathy, then fainting dead away.

The whole thing takes less than seventeen seconds. It couldn't be any more different than *Putting Pants on Philip*, and yet it's perfectly suited to the material. It's difficult to speak with much confidence about the way the pie fight sequence was directed. For years, the only version of the second reel known to have survived was an edit made by director Robert Youngson for use in a 1958 compilation film. It wasn't until 2015 that film collector and historian Jon Mirsalis realized that the film canister labeled "BATTLE OF THE CENTURY R2" in his collection was the long-lost second reel—most likely Youngson's personal copy. The second reel hasn't been seen by audiences yet; Paris-based Lobster Films is restoring it—but the Youngson edit resembles the first reel in that it uses rapid cuts rather than long takes as things slowly descend into chaos. The basic formula for the early stages of the fight is a long shot of someone throwing a pie and missing their target, followed by a shot of an innocent bystander, who is seen for precisely the amount of time necessary to take in their prelapsarian state before the rogue pie flies into frame. Besides *The General*, this is undoubtedly the most influential film Clyde directed: Among the people who considered it a favorite were Blake Edwards, James Agee, John Ford, and, weirdly, Henry Miller, who called it "the greatest comic film ever made." (Ford and Agee both seemed to believe Leo McCarey had directed it; Miller couldn't remember the title.)

Anything would be a step down after *The Battle of the Century*, but *Leave 'Em Laughing*, filmed that October, is great in its own right, at least in the second reel. Once again, the timing and direction are completely unlike anything Laurel and Hardy had done before. The premise, which came from Hal Roach, couldn't be simpler: the boys get dosed with laughing gas. The first reel sets up that Stan has a toothache and can't manage to extract the tooth himself; eventually Hardy drags him to the dentist. The most interesting thing about this section is that it's the first film where Laurel and Hardy share a bed, wearing long nightgowns and projecting the infantile asexuality of their later films: a long way from Stan's rabid heterosexuality (and, in the tailor scene, gay panic) in *Putting Pants on Philip*.

It's the second reel where the film starts to shine. Stan and Ollie wake up in a room full of laughing gas just over halfway through the film. For the next eight minutes, there is exactly one joke: neither man can stop laughing. Where *The Battle of the Century* depends on carefully orchestrated escalation, *Leave 'Em Laughing* works through repetition, like Sideshow Bob on *The Simpsons* stepping on the same rake over and over again. Despite their impaired state, the boys attempt to drive home. Ollie backs up to leave the parking space, smashing into the parked car behind him. They crack up laughing. Ollie pulls forward, right into the car in front of him. More laughter. Then he backs up into the other car, exactly as before. When he finally remembers to steer, he pulls into a passing car. The angry driver jumps out and takes down his information—neither Stan nor Ollie can stop laughing long enough to say anything—and gets back in his car. Ollie merrily smashes into him again. Cinematically, the second reel is built on long shots of the car crashes intercut with medium shots of Stan and Ollie in their car, dying of laughter. Eventually reaction shots of Edgar Kennedy, playing a cop whose attention they've attracted, are added to the mix. That's all there is to it. The crashes get funnier each time they're repeated; Laurel and Hardy's laughter is contagious. And the final shot is positively sublime: the battered car, now driven by the cop who is taking them in, pulls into a street where sewer construction is being done and slowly, inexorably, sinks into a puddle of—best-case scenario—mud. It's an image lifted from Keaton's *The Boat*, but while Keaton's version painted him as a noble figure beset by the world's indignities, the boys are absolutely *delighted* by this turn of events. Ollie stands in the rear seat and doffs his cap victoriously. They're the platonic ideal of boneheads.

Clyde's final film with the duo, filmed in late November and early December, was *The Finishing Touch*. It has an even simpler premise than *Leave 'Em Laughing*: Laurel and Hardy try to help build a house; the house falls down. By this point, Stan and Ollie are entirely themselves, down to Ollie's exasperated eye-rolls at the camera. The great innovation here is that the straight repetition in *Leave 'Em Laughing* has been replaced with a sort of theme and variation, as with Ollie's three attempts to carry a door up a ramp and across a plank to the porch. The first time, Stan moves the plank: Ollie falls forward and crashes face-first through the door. The second time, a few minutes later, Stan tries to reinforce the broken plank with a board that's nowhere near strong enough. Ollie carries the door over his head so he can see where he's going, which means when the plank snaps, he drops the door on his own head and ends up wearing it like a collar. For the final attempt, near the end of the film, he takes no chances, pushing Stan aside to test the plank, sitting on it and bouncing up and down. All seems secure. He makes his way up the ramp with the door, tests his footing on the plank, then dashes across. Success—until he sets foot on the porch, which immediately topples to the ground, sending columns rolling in all directions. It's a perfectly executed misdirection, and it's hilarious. The same cannot be said for the film's topper, the inevitable collapse of the house: due to a construction screw-up, a truck designed to roll through the house got snagged, leaving things only half-destroyed. *The Finishing Touch* is only a run-of-the-mill Laurel and Hardy film—but Clyde had just helped build the mill.

Although Clyde made four great movies with Laurel and Hardy during his brief time at Roach, he didn't stick around long enough to reap many of the benefits. It wasn't until December, as he was wrapping *The Finishing Touch*, that *Putting Pants on Philip* opened; *The Battle of the Century*, which really made Laurel and Hardy stars, would open New Year's Eve. He got along fine with both Laurel and Hardy—they were both frequent visitors at Clyde and Lola's house—and it's possible they would have continued to fruitfully collaborate. But his best professional experience had still been making movies and playing baseball with Buster Keaton. So when Buster, in the midst of professional turmoil, told Clyde he was trying to rebuild his old team, he left Roach Studios to rejoin him. And that's how Clyde, who'd always been so good at jumping ship before catastrophe struck, happened to be on board with his old pal Buster Keaton as he made the worst mistake of his life.

TONG WARS

Nineteen twenty-seven had been a terrible year for Buster Keaton. After the commercial disaster that was *The General*, his next film was the unambitious *College*, his version of Harold Lloyd's *The Freshman*. It was meant to be a safe bet, but the only reason it came close to being profitable was because it had been made so cheaply. He followed it with *Steamboat Bill Jr.*, a great movie, but one which would become as much of a box-office fiasco as *The General* when it was finally released in May of 1928.

Part of the problem was that Keaton no longer had the staff he'd worked with in his heyday. None of the original gag men were still around—Clyde was with Laurel and Hardy, Jean Havez had died, Joe Mitchell was working freelance, and Eddie Cline was trying, unsuccessfully, to move from comedy to drama. With the sole exception of Charles Reisner, who directed *Steamboat Bill Jr.* ("He was a good one," Keaton told Kevin Brownlow), he hated his new collaborators. James W. Horne, director of *College*, was, he recalled, "absolutely useless to me." Carl Harbaugh, credited along with Brian Foy for writing *College*, and the sole credited writer on *Steamboat Bill Jr.*, was even worse:

> He didn't write nothing. He was one of the most useless men I had on the scenario department. He wasn't a good gag man; he wasn't a good title writer; he wasn't a good constructionist.

Keaton wasn't much fonder of his business partners. Joseph Schenck had hired away Keaton's longtime business manager Lou Anger into a position at United Artists and, at Buster's suggestion, promoted Harry Brand to replace him. Brand had worked with Keaton for years in publicity, but now that his job was keeping expenses in check, their relationship started to fray, as Keaton explained:

> . . . once he was on the job he suddenly turned serious. He was grim. He was watching the dailies—how much is spent on this, how much is spent on that? He worries, he frets, he begins losing sleep. He felt he had to do something, like a guy that has to tear down a car that's running perfectly.

Things got tenser when Brand went over his head and talked Schenck into giving him a supervisory credit on *College*. Keaton was generous with credits as long as he was the one assigning them, but Brand's was an unpleasant surprise: he found out about it when he saw it on screen, and their relationship soured. But Keaton still preferred Brand to Schenck's other man tasked with restoring fiscal order, John Considine—Keaton openly loathed him, giving him the nickname "Schenck's fink."

On top of everything else, Keaton's drinking was getting out of hand. He'd been on the downslope since at least 1925, but had managed to hold things together during the period of creative challenges surrounding *The General*. *College* didn't engage him as much, and so he'd spent 1927 bored in his work, bored in his marriage, and constantly hungover.

But none of that was even the bad news. The bad news, as Schenck told him over Labor Day weekend, was that Buster Keaton Studios was shuttering for good. Schenck wanted out of the production business; Keaton, who'd started as an employee, didn't get a vote. Still, everything was arranged—he'd make movies from now on at MGM, working for Joseph's brother, Nicholas Schenck, president of the young studio. The money would be better than ever and he'd have access to the resources of an entire studio; no more worrying about budgets. What's more, he'd never have to negotiate another distribution or exhibition agreement, since MGM, with its roots in the Loews theater chain, was as vertically integrated as Paramount. Keaton fought it the best he could, first trying and failing to make a better deal with Adolph Zukor—but with Harold Lloyd in his pocket, Zukor finally found a deal he didn't want to buy his way into. Keaton then met with Nicholas Schenck to negotiate better terms, but showed up three drinks in, "all softened up." Not surprisingly, Schenck's first offer remained his best and only.

But Keaton didn't see MGM as a disaster right away. His new salary of $3,000 a week was more money than he'd ever made at the Keaton Studios, and he was able to use MGM's money to reassemble some of his old crew for his first film there. Technical director Fred Gabourie came along with him; Al Boasberg, who'd left after *The General*, returned; and Elgin Lessley, the cameraman whose perfect timing had made *The Playhouse* possible, worked with him again for the first time since 1925's *Go West*. And Clyde, too, came home.

Financially, he would have been crazy not to. It's unclear what Clyde made at Roach Studios, but for his work on Buster Keaton's first MGM film, he was paid $34,866—nearly half a million dollars today, and almost twice what Stan Laurel and Oliver Hardy had made combined during their last four films with Clyde. The money wasn't free, however: Clyde had to step down from directing and return to the gag room.

The film was called *Snap Shots*, and the story was as simple as any of the two-reelers: Keaton would play a freelance newsreel photographer, seeking footage to impress the front office and, more importantly, the *girl* in the front office, played by Marceline Day. Keaton thought this would have the added benefit of synergy for his new corporate masters: The film would naturally promote MGM's newsreel division, a joint operation with William Randolph Hearst, and with any luck, that would yield further promotional opportunities in Hearst's papers. Buster fumbling around with a camera would have been enough of a premise to hang a movie on in the days of the Keaton Studio. But those days had just ended.

Schenck had assured Keaton he would have full access to MGM's stable of talent, and he kept his word. What Buster didn't realize was that this access wasn't optional. As he recalled in his autobiography, before he could get in front of cameras and begin dreaming up the gags:

> . . . the *crème de la crème* of the M-G-M writing staff began descending on us in droves. Most of these men were very good writers and resourceful plotters. That was one of the troubles. They were too resourceful, and each naturally wanted to contribute something. In all there were twenty-two staff writers helping us.

Irving Thalberg, the young tyro who was meant to be Keaton's ally in the front office while Nicholas Schenck handled the money from New York, turned out to be no help at all. It was a philosophical conflict—the hard-won lessons Keaton and his staff had learned making *The Navigator* and *The General* were alien to MGM's corporate culture, as Keaton later described:

Well, now here is rule number one with us when we were making our pictures: simplicity in story. And as few characters as possible, too. Well, that was the reverse English when I went to MGM. Irving Thalberg was in charge of production and he wanted—oh—I wasn't in trouble enough trying to manipulate a camera as a cameraman, trying to photograph current events as a news weekly cameraman. In *The Cameraman*, Thalberg wanted me to get involved with gangsters, and then get in trouble with this one and that one, and that was my fight—to eliminate those extra things.

Clyde helped win that fight, although he didn't exactly cover himself with glory in the way he did it. Thalberg wanted gangsters, Keaton wanted fewer characters; Clyde gave them both what they wanted with an elegant, if racist, solution: a central setpiece where Buster, sent to film a Chinese New Year parade, finds himself in the middle of a shootout between Tong factions. The Tong War sequence treats Asian-Americans with exactly as much subtlety and insight as you'd expect from white filmmakers in 1928—lots of minions running around in robes brandishing daggers—and so Thalberg got his crime story without Keaton having to add any characters.

Nothing else about the film was resolved so simply. Thalberg assigned Lawrence Weingarten as producer, and Keaton found himself involved in internecine struggles over budget, schedule, and shooting locations. MGM's front office couldn't stand Keaton's improvisational style—if he didn't stick to a script, they couldn't plan his budgets. And Keaton didn't help his own case: After insisting on shooting in New York, at least partly so that he could see *Show Boat* on Broadway with its original cast, Keaton discovered he was too famous to shoot on public streets without attracting a crowd. Knowing Weingarten wouldn't want to change course mid-stream, Keaton went over his head to Thalberg to have the production called back to California. It was an instance of winning the battle but losing the war; he began to get a reputation, and by the time *Snap Shots* was released under the title *The Cameraman*, the well was poisoned.

The Cameraman, although not on the level of *The Navigator* or *The General*, isn't a bad movie. There's a lovely sequence of Keaton pantomiming a baseball game at Yankee Stadium, and the Tong War is well-orchestrated chaos. One of the finished film's best sequences was made using the old Keaton Studio methods. Shooting Venice Beach in lieu of Coney Island, Keaton, director Edward Sedgwick, Lew Lipton, and Clyde made up the gags on the spot, and the resulting scene of Keaton attempting to change clothes in a tiny changing room shared with a larger man—played by unit manager Ed Brophy to avoid delays from MGM's casting department—is one of the film's highlights. Just Buster clowning for the camera, like the old days.

But the problems Keaton was facing were systemic, and a day's victory couldn't change that. His new crew were MGM's employees, not his, and the incentives were all wrong, as he later recalled:

> Not being on a team they rarely forgot that their next assignment depended on their work standing out, instead of being subordinated

into the picture as a whole. Under M-G-M's system each craftsman was more beholden to the head of his department than to me.

And those department heads acted in the studio's interest, not Keaton's. Fred Gabourie, whose mechanical ingenuity had brought so many of Keaton's wildest imaginings to life, was quickly promoted to head MGM's technical department; other staffers were reassigned or drifted away. *The Cameraman* was the last film where Keaton felt he had creative control. Not coincidentally, it was the last one to touch on the greatness that had been a matter of course in the days of the Keaton Studio. By summer, Keaton was frustrated enough that, according to Louise Brooks, he left a dinner party at his own house for a late night trip to his bungalow at MGM, where he slowly, methodically, shattered every pane of glass with a baseball bat. He then sat down amidst the wreckage as if nothing had happened and offered his guests a drink.

It was no way to work, but then Clyde didn't have to work that way. That summer, he left Keaton once more for Paramount to work as a gag man for Marshall Neilan on a Bebe Daniels film called *Take Me Home*. But before the month was out, he'd been poached once again, this time by Harold Lloyd.

Lloyd had had a better time of it than Keaton; though he hadn't topped *The Freshman*, his last two films had both grossed more than two million dollars worldwide. (Keaton, always a distant third to Chaplin and Lloyd, had never topped one million.) But he was in the midst of his own crisis, along with the rest of the film industry: talking pictures.

Experiments in cinematic sound stretched back over most of the decade, but as late as summer of 1927 the general consensus was that it was only a novelty. So secure was this conventional wisdom that *Motion Picture Magazine* was able to get most of the studio heads of the day on record: Jesse Lasky, Hal Roach, Al Christie, and Samuel Goldwyn all lined up to offer hilariously misguided prognostications. Cecil B. DeMille went out of his way to announce, in the manner of someone who doesn't even own a television, that he had never seen a talking picture. And Irving Thalberg was doubly wrong:

> I do not believe the talking motion picture will ever replace the silent drama any more than I believe colored photography will ever replace entirely the present black and whites.

Only the Warner brothers, who'd sponsored the Vitaphone, declined comment. Director Clarence Brown got the future wrong, but correctly diagnosed the reason for the studios' skepticism:

> There is so much money invested in present-day equipment that there is no danger of the companies throwing out everything and beginning anew on a talking picture basis. If there were inventions that would positively combine color, voice and movement, I do not believe that the big companies would permit an immediate change. To take a concern that has millions of dollars invested in it and turn it bottom side up would result in a tremendous loss of money.

But by the summer of 1928, the industry was clearly "bottom side up." The realization seems to have hit Harold Lloyd abruptly. In June, he announced that he was considering using sound in his next film, scheduled to begin in two weeks for a late fall release. That July, he described sound as "doomed," and joined Douglas Fairbanks and Mary Pickford in announcing that his next film might feature sound effects and music, but would have no dialogue. By September, he'd changed his tune entirely. "I am thoroughly convinced that talking pictures are here to stay," he told a reporter, in an article headlined "Harold Lloyd Plans to Use Both Sound, Dialogue in His Next." But despite grand statements to the press, Lloyd approached sound tentatively. He wanted a silent version of the film for theaters that weren't equipped for sound, so his plan was to create the silent version first, following his normal procedure of constantly previewing and revising, then add sound wherever he thought it might help.

The film was to be set in San Francisco's Chinatown, and it seems likely that Clyde's work on the Tong War sequence for Keaton was part of the reason Lloyd wanted him. He joined Lex Neal, Felix Adler, and Jay A. Howe on staff, and in early September they began work on the silent version of the film that would ultimately be titled *Welcome Danger*. Ted Wilde, who'd just directed Lloyd in *Speedy*, would direct again.

When it was first announced, Lloyd anticipated a quick turnaround; *Welcome Danger* was to start in June and be released in late fall. Cameras finally started rolling in early September, but the production was almost immediately troubled. The fall of 1928 brought a flu outbreak on the West Coast, which spread throughout the film industry and derailed production at every studio. Among those struck ill in late November was Ted Wilde, who left the project for bed rest. By December, Clyde, Lex Neal, and Felix Adler were out sick as well; Lloyd shut down everything for four days. The gag staff came back, but Wilde didn't; his case was complicated by a long-standing injury he'd sustained at the Battle of Saint-Mihiel, and on his doctor's orders, he left Los Angeles for a health resort after the holidays. He wouldn't be well enough to work again until summer, when he reemerged at Columbia.

By this time, press accounts of Lloyd's new production started to betray a certain amount of wavering confidence. None of his gag men had ever written dialogue, so he let it be known that he had began negotiations with unnamed "Top Playwrights." And although he'd started his career on stage, he wasn't sure of his own abilities in the new medium, and conducted several voice tests. Unhappy with the results—he'd been speaking with a falsetto—he met with one of the voice coaches who were springing up around Hollywood. (Whatever Lloyd paid for this service was probably too much: After only five days, he was told he'd mastered voice acting and sent on his way.) The voice tests also made clear that adding dialogue would be more of a technical challenge than he'd anticipated. In early December, his manager announced that he'd signed an open-ended lease on the newly constructed sound stages at Metropolitan Studio. With no director and a rapidly creeping mission, Lloyd ominously abandoned all deadlines:

> Under the deal just negotiated he will have all the time necessary to experiment with sound.
>
> Lloyd has no release schedule to meet and will not be pressed in his efforts to make his first synchronized picture [an] outstanding success.

As the New Year approached, Lloyd found a replacement for his ailing director: Malcolm St. Clair, who'd briefly worked with Clyde on Keaton's First National shorts. St. Clair had been under long-term contract with Paramount, but became available because Paramount was letting contracts expire for their silent film directors and replacing them with theatrical directors as they moved toward talkies. (The thought was that directors with theatrical experience would be better at directing dialogue—but just as importantly, they were cheaper.) Lloyd's production was still described as primarily silent: dialogue was to be inserted once the film was complete, "provided there is a place and a need for it, otherwise it will be released as an 'old-fashioned movie' with a musical synchronization and sound effects."

So that spring, Malcolm St. Clair and Lloyd produced a massive silent film that almost no one would ever see. The first cut was an epic: sixteen reels—two hours and forty-five minutes. After the first preview, Lloyd vowed to remove nearly half of it. But as St. Clair and Lloyd trimmed it down to a releasable length before deciding how or whether to add sound, the preview scores started dropping. Lloyd thought this was as much a function of audiences getting bored with silent films as anything he was doing to the film itself, an impression confirmed when the film was screened with a talkie one-reel comedy on the same program.

> . . . they were laughing at the pouring of the water, the frying of eggs—it didn't matter what—the clinking of ice in a glass. We said, "My God, we worked our hearts out to get laughs with thought-out gags and look here: just because they've got some sound, they're roaring at these things."

Never let it be said that Harold Lloyd didn't try to please his audiences. After months of work, two directors, hours of footage, and a finished silent film, he told his staff, "Maybe we've kind of missed the boat, maybe we should make this film over." That was enough for Malcolm St. Clair, who quit. Fortunately, Lloyd had in his employ a man who had experience salvaging other directors' abandoned projects. Clyde had never directed a sound film, but then neither had anyone else. And so, with Wilde and St. Clair out of the way, he landed a directorial gig that was increasingly looking like an albatross.

Converting the film to sound was a nightmare for everyone involved. Half the footage was immediately discarded; the rest had to be dubbed. "Nobody knew what they were doing, a large studio like that—we had everybody doing something different—it was like an insane asylum," Lloyd recalled. On another occasion, he described their method:

> . . . the dubbing was horrible. We just didn't know what we were doing. We had a screen up there and we'd run the picture with X marks on it and try to hit those things. Cutters didn't know too much about cutting them in. I look at the film today and groan . . .

No one knew what they were doing that year: the new technology had swept all the pieces off the board. But in late summer of 1929, when Paramount executives finally saw the sound version of the film they were distributing, they quickly developed the opinion that perhaps Clyde Bruckman and Harold Lloyd knew less about what they were doing than most people.

Even considering the circumstances under which it was made, it's difficult to find much to love about *Welcome Danger*. The jokes in the spoken dialogue are uniformly terrible, "top playwrights" or no. Tom Dardis singles out the moment when Harold, seeing a sign for the town of Newberry, announces to no one in particular, "Well, I've heard of strawberry and raspberry, but this is a new berry on me," as the dialogue's low point, but there aren't any high points. Keaton's faceless Tong War is here replaced with a complicated plot that somehow manages to be even more racist: in *Wel-*

come *Danger*, Lloyd battles a prominent white citizen who secretly controls Chinatown's opium trade in disguise as "The Dragon." (The less said about the scene where Lloyd fights a shirtless, whip-wielding African-American butler, the better.) But worst of all, Lloyd, whose entire shtick was being a likable up-and-comer, is insufferable here. His voice training doesn't seem to have made any difference, his performance is simpering, and he finally triumphs by putting the villain's head in a book press and tightening it until he confesses, like Joe Pesci in *Casino*.

Paramount knew the film wasn't much good, and attempted to get Lloyd to test it against the silent version—even without seeing the silent film, one executive was "certain that it will please the public much better than the dialogue version." But Lloyd was having none of it. In September, according to a story headlined "Lloyd's First Talkie Beset with Tribulation," he "ordered the negative sent forthwith to Paramount in New York for immediate release." *Welcome Danger* was released in both sound and silent versions in October of 1929. Despite several months of work, Malcolm St. Clair's name was entirely dropped from the film. Ted Wilde and Clyde shared credit on the silent version, but the sound version was all Clyde.

In the end, Paramount had underestimated audiences' curiosity about what Harold Lloyd's voice sounded like. Whether they enjoyed it once they heard it didn't much matter as long as they bought a ticket. And they bought plenty: *Welcome Danger* grossed $23,000 in its first two days alone at the Rivoli in New York. The only film that had done more business there was *The Iron Mask*, which had nine daily showings against Lloyd's seven. That's despite the fact that the Rivoli screenings seem to have had technical difficulties beyond the poor dubbing, unless Martin Dick-stein, the reviewer for *The Brooklyn Daily Eagle*, was exaggerating:

> One saw Mr. Lloyd move his lips as if in speech, but it was not always possible to hear the words until several seconds later. One also observed the audacious Harold belaboring an unfriendly Chinaman or two with a sturdy barrel stave, but the sound of the impact had a way of not reaching the ears until the frightened Oriental had already assumed a horizontal posture. It was not a very convincing demonstration for this day and age of the sound tracks.

Dickstein was one of the only contemporary critics who didn't like the film; reviews were otherwise uniformly positive. Audiences responded as well—an advertising campaign in *Variety* consisted entirely of telegrams from theater owners ecstatic with the grosses. The one place the film was not a success was Shanghai, where student protesters, unhappy with the film's portrayal of the Chinese, rioted at a screening at the International Settlement Foreign Theater. Lloyd's business manager William Fraser took to the papers to make frankly incredible claims in an attempt at damage control:

> When we made "Welcome Danger," we engaged Chinese experts purposely to avoid any embarrassment to the country or its nationals. In fact, we leaned over backward in trying to avoid questionable situations, and felt that we had accomplished that aim in view of the fact that we had not had one single complaint from Chinese in this country.

Chinese experts or no, Chiang Kai-shek's Nationalist government banned the film across China in April. But despite the roiling catastrophes that marked its production, its chilly reputation in Asia, and its questionable merit as a film, *Welcome Danger* grossed more than anything else Lloyd had made since *The Freshman*. There's no artistic disagreement in Hollywood that can't be papered over with enough ticket stubs, and both Clyde and Harold Lloyd quickly reentered Paramount's good graces.

Once again, Clyde Bruckman had talked his way into a job he was wholly unqualified for and somehow triumphed. At this point, his nearly flawless run of luck had lasted just over ten years. But dice get cold, probability is immutable, systems reassert themselves. Just a few weeks after *Welcome Danger* was released, Wall Street—not for the first or last time—cratered the global economy. A matter of luck running out, perhaps. Clyde's lasted only a little longer.

QUEEN OF ANGELS

After *Welcome Danger*'s financial success, Clyde's continued employment with Harold Lloyd was a foregone conclusion. In December of 1929, Lloyd announced that Clyde would direct his next film, whatever it might be. Lloyd and his staff proceeded cautiously; in January they were still torn between a thrill picture set at sea or another college movie. By April, they'd decided: Harold would go to sea. Lloyd's quote in the wire story announcing the film that would ultimately become *Feet First* suggests he felt his recent work hadn't been as good as it should have been:

> I am more enthused over this story than I have been over any of my pictures for a long time. And I believe that enthusiasm will count for a lot. The story is one of the best I have ever had. It is full of thrills, laughs, and a much better romance than I usually have.

It was also, the story noted, the first time he'd used a script since his "Lonesome Luke" days; sound didn't allow for as much improvisation. The script at least had the virtue of not involving a Tong War, but calling it a sea story is a bit of a stretch. Lloyd plays a Honolulu shoe salesman with a crush on Barbara Kent. He mistakenly believes she's the boss's daughter, she mistakenly believes he's a wealthy leather magnate, and misunderstandings lead to complications lead to laffs. Eventually, Lloyd accidentally stows away on an ocean liner bound for Los Angeles; on arrival he ends up on the side of a skyscraper, like in his 1923 hit *Safety Last*. Uncertain of his future, Lloyd returned to something that had worked in the past.

Much of the filming was to be done on board an ocean liner, a technical challenge in the age of sound. Just as Clyde had put his crew on a working steamship travelling from Los Angeles to San Diego for Monty Banks in *A Perfect Gentleman*, Lloyd arranged berths for the cast and crew aboard the S. S. *Malolo*, sailing from San Francisco to Honolulu. Departure was scheduled for May 24, 1930, but was delayed when Lloyd had an attack of appendicitis. He recovered without surgery; appendectomies were not as routine then as now, and Lloyd managed to avoid one until the next year. Filming began with the *Malolo*'s next voyage from San Francisco on June 7. The trip would serve as a proof-of-concept for making sound films at sea: The *Malolo*'s electrical system would have to power sixty-odd sun arcs, spotlights, and side lights, as well as the sound wagon, which was lashed to the front deck and equipped with enough cable to allow a 500-foot microphone range.

Filming went smoothly on the way to Honolulu, where the party spent three days ashore. Lloyd attended a Luau put on by the local Shriners and gave a radio address to the Kalaupapa leper colony, then set sail for home. Despite running into a gale which nearly washed the sound equipment overboard, on June 21 cast and crew returned to Hollywood, bringing back 15,000 feet of sound film, about two hours and forty-five minutes of footage. Clyde and Harold shot the rest of the film that summer, including challenging location shooting on the roofs of several buildings in downtown Los Angeles as they staged a new daredevil climb. *Feet First* was released that October: Clyde's first sound film that had begun production as a sound film.

Not surprisingly, having some experience with sound equipment, a single director, and most of all, a screenplay, resulted in a more coherent film. But *Feet First* is still a long way from perfect, particularly in the first two acts. The highlight of the first act is a sequence at a posh social club Harold has bluffed his way into, in which a drunk played by Arthur Housman keeps insisting on introducing him to everyone, but the great thing about it is Arthur Housman, not Harold Lloyd.[1] The second act takes Harold's bluff further: stowed away aboard the *Malolo*, he must keep up the pretense that he is a millionaire while avoiding detection by the crew. It's not a "sea story" the way *The Navigator* is; the ship is just another environment for Lloyd to mingle with the wealthy. There is one lovely moment when Lloyd is nearly caught in the act trying to remove a magazine page stuck to a female passenger's posterior—it's complicated—and turns his awkward pose into a strange little pantomimed dance, ending with a pratfall. But for the most part, the main benefit to the logistically challenging shoot aboard the *Malolo* seems to have been a free trip to Hawaii for the cast and crew. It's only once Harold arrives back on solid ground that the audience finally gets what they'd paid for

---

1. This seems to have been one of those moments where an actor found his true calling: Housman had been in films since 1912, but none of his credits specify that he was drunk; in the ten years after *Feet First*, he has no fewer than fifty-four roles like "The Drunk," "Al—The Drunk," "Drunk Who Keeps Turning Off Lamp (uncredited)," and, cast against type, "Pickpocket—Posing as a Singing Drunk."

before and, with any luck, would pay for again: Lloyd dangling from the side of a building hundreds of feet above downtown Los Angeles.

It's revealing to compare the way the climb is executed in *Feet First* to the same sequence in *Safety Last*, which Fred Newmeyer directed, to see what Lloyd and his crew had learned in the seven years prior—and what they'd forgotten. As a piece of pure action filmmaking, *Feet First* is in every way superior, filled with near-falls, perilous stunts, and convincing special effects. It's nerve-racking to watch. But as a sequence that serves the larger film, it's a dud. For one thing, it's not very funny, something that Lloyd realized when testing a longer version of the sequence; as he later recalled, the audience was in a "state of horror all the way through."

But the problems are structural as well as tonal. In *Safety Last*, Harold has hired a human fly to climb the side of his employer's building as a promotional stunt. When the human fly gets into trouble with a cop, Harold takes his place at the last minute to save his own job. As he climbs, he keeps hoping he will be able to trade places with the stuntman, who is climbing the stairs inside the building, pursued by cop. Clear stakes, a good reason for everyone to be there, and action that naturally escalates as Harold gets higher and higher. In *Feet First*, on the other hand, Lloyd is hiding inside a mailbag that is mistakenly set on a window washer's scaffolding; he's hoisted by accident. So he can go up, safely return to the ground, or somehow enter the building; his only real goal is not to die. Which is fine, as goals go—universal, even—but it's unconnected to the rest of the film, which is about Lloyd pretending to be rich to impress a girl. As Lloyd put it in the 1970s, "In *Safety Last* we had what we call an idea working for us . . . a gimmick that worked for us all the way through. Well now in *Feet First* we didn't have that."

Feet First does borrow one structural device from *Safety Last*, but in a way that makes things worse instead of better. Harold's increasingly desperate interactions with the human fly in *Safety Last* punctuate the thrills and are funny in their own right. In *Feet First*, Clyde and Lloyd duplicate that rhythm by having Harold attempt to get help from a dimwitted janitor played by African-American character actor Willie Best. Best was trying at the time to launch a career as a sort of cut-rate Stepin Fetchit (he's credited under the stage name "Sleep 'n' Eat"), so his performance is painful to watch to begin with. But structurally, he's literally just a bystander, so having Harold yell at him in frustration is less amusing than in *Safety Last*, where Harold has a good reason to be angry. It doesn't help that Harold immediately nicknames him "Charcoal."

Although *Feet First* met with generally favorable reviews—the *Los Angeles Times* reviewer claimed that the audience at a preview screening "literally rolled in the aisles"—Lloyd's audience had started to dwindle, and everyone who wondered what Harold Lloyd sounded like had already satisfied their curiosity with *Welcome Danger*. As Tom Dardis points out, the first year of the Great Depression was a uniquely terrible historical moment to ask audiences to sympathize with an up-and-comer who bluffs his way into business success thanks to a can-do spirit. *Feet First* ultimately grossed just over half as much as *Welcome Danger*—a precipitous fall, and drastic enough to shake Lloyd's confidence. Before the film had opened, Lloyd had announced his intention to make another college film next—presumably the idea he'd passed over to make *Feet First*—but a month after the premiere, as he realized audiences were no longer responding to his usual formula, he abruptly changed course: the next Harold Lloyd film would be a parody of Westerns. Lloyd's schedule called for Clyde to direct, beginning filming in January of 1931—but filming never began. Even if Lloyd didn't realize what was happening, the public was starting to see flop sweat. That May, *Screenland* ran a fan letter with a succinct diagnosis:

> The old Harold Lloyd is no more. In his place is a cautious business-man who weighs the laughter-chances of every gag before he dares to put it in his million-dollar production.

As he'd done so many times before, Clyde made a move that might have enabled him to stay just ahead of catastrophe. But this time, his foot slipped. While Lloyd figured out his next move, Clyde spent the spring at RKO. He was there to help them with a gamble on one of their fledgling stars, Robert Woolsey.

Though today he is barely remembered, RKO owed its very existence to Robert Woolsey and his partner, Bert Wheeler. The studio's first big hit, the one that had made them, was 1929's *Rio Rita*, an all-talkie Technicolor adaptation of a Ziegfeld Broadway show. Wheeler and Woolsey had starred in the stage version, come to Hollywood for the film, and stayed on at RKO afterward. The studio bet big on them in 1930, putting them in four films, all of which hit. In 1931, facing a weak acting bench, they decided to see if Wheeler and Woolsey could sell tickets on their own. Wheeler, the younger of the two, was cast in *Too Many Cooks*, a play from 1916 that had already been adapted into a failed film in 1920, and Woolsey was given a script by Al Boasberg called *Going, Going, Gone!* Clyde had worked with Boasberg on *The General*, and RKO brought him over to direct the new project. Rather than leave Lloyd outright, he was hired at RKO on a loanout agreement, including a pay raise from $750 to $1,250 a week. (*Variety* reported that RKO had hired Clyde to direct Richard Dix in *Young Donovan's Kid*, but this is likely an error, as the *Los Angeles Times* had him working with Robert Woolsey two days earlier.) In this fashion, Lloyd got him off the payroll while keeping him under contract for his next film, whenever that might be. From Clyde's perspective, too, the move made sense. Lloyd was clearly starting to falter; if Woolsey worked as a solo act, Clyde would have a tie with a new star who'd come up in the age of talkies. It quickly became apparent to all concerned, however, that the move to RKO was a disastrous mistake.

RKO's approach to filmmaking was more factory-like than MGM's, to say nothing of Harold Lloyd. Clyde was only there for two months, with just eighteen days scheduled for filming. Even that was more time than he ended up spending on the film, which he shot in two weeks—less time than he'd spent on his Laurel and Hardy shorts—rushing through the first four days of his schedule on the first day. Given the painstaking work he'd done with Lloyd and Keaton, and especially considering the fact that RKO gave him more time than he used, it seems likely he decided to cut his losses and get out of the project as quickly as possible. The film's one innovation was another step forward in location sound recording, a ground noise eliminator invented by recordist Hugh McDowell Jr. that allowed the crew to capture the sounds of birds, wind, and leaves while location shooting in the Santa Monica Mountains.

But there are hardly any birds, wind, or leaves to be heard in the finished film. There's just Woolsey, Woolsey, Woolsey, prattling his way through jokes that were old when vaudeville was young.

George Burns would later borrow Woolsey's waggling cigar and round eyeglasses, but nothing else from the film is remotely salvageable. The whole thing reaches a sort of negative perfection at a dinner party where Woolsey is pretending to be royalty; he literally just walks around the party doing crowd work with the guests.

SOCIETY MATRON: Years ago, I visited the ruins of Athens.

WOOLSEY (Collapsing in laughter): Visited? You married him!

It's impossible to say enough terrible things about Woolsey's habit of punctuating his jokes with peals of laughter and lines like: "I've gotta have my little quippy!"—"Gosh, you can't stop me now!"—and "Oh, how I suffer!" It's a fascinating film to watch today, but only as a record of how terrible vaudeville could be.

What's worse, Boasberg's plot, about a snake oil salesman with an adopted daughter, was clearly lifted from *Poppy*, a Broadway play W. C. Fields had starred in in 1923 (Fields would make it into a film in 1936). Though Clyde would run into problems later for reusing gags, an RKO memo suggests Woolsey was responsible this time around; he'd had a small role in the Broadway version and was eager to take on Fields's part. So although Clyde's direction couldn't be more perfunctory—especially after the intricate clockwork of the finale of *Feet First*—it's hard to imagine anyone spending more time on the project than contractually required. As Bert Wheeler reportedly said about his own equally doomed solo venture that spring, "It stinks, but they gotta pay us for doing *something*."

The film, ultimately titled *Everything's Rosie*, was shown to unhappy critics in late May, barely three months after Clyde had been hired. Andre Sennwald got the assignment for the *New York Times* and filed a masterpiece of vitriol:

> One of cinema's minor indiscretions, an item entitled "Everything's Rosie," was inflicted last evening on a small audience at the Globe which found it as lacking in wit as in intelligence and ordinary good taste. Its intention possibly was to while away sixty minutes or so in a mild and harmless spirit of fun, so that one should not hold too strongly against it the unfortunate fact that its net achievement reached new depths of low vaudeville humor and backstairs conduct.

Clyde had made great movies that were terribly received, like *The General*; he'd made terrible movies that were well received, like *Welcome Danger*. Now he'd hit the perfecta: a terrible movie with terrible reviews. *Variety* was no kinder, but at least noted that there was very little he could have done:

> Exculpation should be granted to Clyde Bruckman, the director. Direction is all right for what there is to direct. Bruckman had to direct what he had, which he did. At least he cannot be charged with the story or the rest.

Everything's Rosie had a brief theatrical run that summer, and Clyde hurried back to Harold Lloyd. Bert Wheeler's solo film did no better than Woolsey's, and so RKO reunited the duo. The entire episode seemed best forgotten by everyone involved, except Wheeler and Woolsey, who, according to Woolsey, hung onto each other's bad solo reviews to read when they needed cheering up.

Back with Harold Lloyd, Clyde found him no closer to making a film than when he'd left. He'd been busy with other things:

a son, Harold Jr., born prematurely in January, another bout of appendicitis in March, then his long-overdue appendectomy in April. He recovered by early summer, but wouldn't commit to a story idea. Or rather, he kept committing, telling the press, then changing his mind. First the Western parody was out; he'd make a baseball movie from a story by Al Boasberg. By midsummer, he'd thrown out the baseball idea for lacking international appeal—instead, he'd make a movie about the foreign legion. Finally, as August ended, he made a decision he stuck to: the next Harold Lloyd film would be a Hollywood satire. Once again, Clyde would direct.

But long before cameras rolled, Clyde's world came crashing down. His drinking had been getting worse, and it was starting to put a strain on his marriage. His nights got later and his hours got odder. Years later, Lola's brother Albert would say she'd confided to him that she suspected he was having an affair. Then the records get blurry. On Sunday, October 4, 1931, Lola Bruckman was admitted to Queen of Angels hospital for what papers later called an "emergency operation." Whatever it was, it required surgery, which caused horrible complications: adhesions, intestinal obstruction, and gangrene. There's no good way to die, but that's a bad way. She hung on until early in the morning of October 8, and then she was gone.

Her funeral was held on Saturday, October 10, at the Pierce Brothers Chapel on Washington Boulevard. Clyde spared no expense, purchasing an expensive crypt in the Great Mausoleum at Forest Lawn, in the same area where Clark Gable, Carole Lombard, and David O. Selznick would eventually be interred. Her crypt is in a dimly lit columbarium off the Memorial Court of Honor where, just that spring, Forest Lawn founder Hubert Eaton had unveiled a massive stained-glass reproduction of Da Vinci's *Last Supper*. Less than a week had passed since her admittance to the hospital.

Some lives trace a rocket's smooth parabola; others are jagged as sawteeth. Harold Lloyd's was a rocket—by the time he realized he was plummeting, his apogee was years in the past. Keaton's was a sawtooth, and he knew it; he felt the shear force tearing him apart when he walked out of Nicholas Schenck's office, drunk, MGM's newest employee. Anyone who knew how Clyde saw his own life's trajectory died decades ago. Nineteen thirty-one might have been the moment of weightlessness where the tangent quietly flatlines, or the sickening jolt of an abrupt dive, a discontinuity in the derivative. Clyde had always been more like Buster than Harold, so maybe he felt it. Probably he felt it. The only thing certain is that after that terrible October, Clyde Bruckman spent the rest of his life in gravity's sway.

THE WASH-OUT

The first consequence of Lola's sudden death was an immediate and irrevocable rift between Clyde and the Hamblin family. They'd been close while she was alive: In the late twenties, when Al Hamblin was fired from one of his studio jobs as part of a mass layoff, the executives—who realized the same afternoon that they hadn't kept anyone on staff who knew where anything was—knew to go looking for him at the Bruckmans'. In 1930, Lola's brother George and his wife even briefly lived with them in the house on Elm Street. But things soured once she was gone. Richard Hamblin, Albert's son and Clyde's nephew, who heard about Lola and Clyde from his father years later, put it in biblical terms:

> They thought in some way he was responsible for her blood. The kindest way I can put it—because he would not have put it this kindly—was that in some way Clyde was responsible for her death.

Albert would later tell his son he believed Clyde had poisoned his wife. This seems unlikely: If there was evidence to support it, it vanished years ago. There's no way to know now why Lola was in the hospital to begin with, but her death certificate is unambiguous about her death being caused by complications from surgery. There was no coroner's inquest or other indication that anything about her death was suspicious at the time. What does seem clear is that Clyde's drinking was out of hand by that fall and it was causing problems in his marriage. Anyone looking for someone to blame for her sudden death would not have had to look far. Lola, the lost beauty of the family, remained a presence with the Hamblins for years after her death. But Clyde did not; after her funeral, they never spoke to him again. And in February, Harold Lloyd needed him to start making *Movie Crazy*.

Stories about the progression of alcoholism all follow the same monotonous template: strings of minor failures punctuated by catastrophic moments where the pawl snaps into a new tooth and the ratchet permanently tightens. *Movie Crazy* was one of Clyde's catastrophes. Filming began on February 27, 1932, and not a moment too soon: it had been seventeen months since Lloyd had worked. Conscious that his footing was a little unsteady, Lloyd went all out on story, hiring playwright Vincent Lawrence at considerable expense to write the script. Lloyd was also determined that the film would be visually striking, the *Los Angeles Times* reported that March as cameras rolled:

> Lloyd has been using a great variety of camera equipment for this production. Its middle name will be "travelling shots." On the set yesterday a huge crane and dolly moved hither and yon with a smooth dexterity and speed, swinging and carrying the camera about.
>
> "We have never done anything like this before," said Harold. "Most of the pictures we have produced have been made with a

toothpick and match as far as our technical equipment went. But we're becoming very arty in this instance."

Crane work had been around at least since Griffith's *Intolerance*, but involved one-off construction of moving platforms. It had only been in 1928 that Universal managed to build a camera crane that could be moved from stage to stage, and it was still a rare visual flourish in 1932. Lloyd was fascinated with its possibilities; on another visit, a reporter observed him careening around the set on the platform, testing it out.

Clyde is missing from both stories, except for a note in one mentioning how long he'd been with the studio, and there's a reason. According to Harold Lloyd, he and Vincent Lawrence directed almost all of *Movie Crazy* themselves because Clyde was drunk. Here's how Lloyd told it in 1968:

> Even in pictures where I directed practically the whole thing, I didn't take the directing credit. In a talking picture called MOVIE CRAZY [1932], I got one of the gag men to direct and he had a little trouble with the bottle and we practically had to wash him out and I had to carry on. The writer in it—I kept him right at my elbow, a man by the name of Vincent Lawrence, a very fine playwright who had written many shows for Broadway, and I always had the advantage of his advice.

There's no question Clyde directed at least some of the film—there are photographs of him on set. But there's no way of knowing how much, because Harold Lloyd's papers don't include the film's production files.

And there was another reason besides the bottle that Clyde was distracted during the filming of *Movie Crazy*—one that also helps to explain the bitterness of his rift with the Hamblin family.

On Saturday, March 26, during the film's production, Clyde was quietly married in a civil ceremony in Ventura County to Gladys Marie Meals, nine years his junior.

His new wife had been born Gladys Marie Prevost on October 3, 1903, in the Chocktaw Nation Indian Territory—later Oklahoma—in a town with the grimly descriptive name of Coalgate. Her parents, Joseph and Jeanne Prevost, were French immigrants from a mine-rich area near the Belgian border. In the United States, they'd first lived in an Illinois coal-mining settlement with a large French population, then moved to Coalgate when the Oklahoma Territory opened up. In 1912, when Gladys was nine, the family moved to Santa Ana, away from the mines. In California, Joseph worked in a lumberyard; his wife and eventually his children, including Gladys, worked in an orange-packing plant. Difficult work—Joseph lost several fingers—but easy living compared to Oklahoma coal mining.

By 1923, Gladys, who, like Lola, had grown into the family beauty, left orange packing and became a clerk at a local jewelry store in Santa Ana. She made her way to Los Angeles, and on Thanksgiving Day of 1926, she married a doctor named Robert Meals at what would be their first home, 1247 North Genesee Avenue, by Fairfax and Fountain. Meals was young, handsome, and more than a little bit of a daredevil. In 1928, after being turned down by two other hospitals, he removed his own appendix at Queen of Angels using only a local anesthetic. He gave three reasons for doing so: his appendix had to be removed anyway, he had a theory that general anesthesia posed more danger than the operation itself, and, probably most of all, he wanted "to test my mental discipline, a control that I believe every surgeon should have." The stunt got his face in the papers across the country, in some cases on the front page, and his fortunes continued to improve. By 1932, Robert and Gladys had moved to a new five-bedroom home on Kilkea Drive near Melrose and Crescent Heights; his practice was located in the brand-new First National Bank Building at 6777 Hollywood Boulevard.

There's no record of how Clyde and Gladys met, but they might have known each other socially. Not surprisingly for a daring young surgeon with an office between the Chinese Theatre and the Pantages, Dr. Meals moved in Hollywood circles. They also had at least one professional connection: Dr. Meals had delivered Clyde's nephew, Richard Hamblin—Queen of Angels again—in 1930. The record goes blank until March 3, 1932, when Gladys was granted a divorce from Dr. Meals in Carson City, Nevada, on the grounds of extreme cruelty—a catch-all category in the days before no-fault divorce. Three weeks later, she and Clyde were married. Perhaps Lola had been right to suspect an affair the previous fall. In any event, Clyde's hasty marriage closed the door permanently on any chance of reconciliation with the Hamblins. Dr. Meals, for his part, dealt with the split by spending the summer learning to fly airplanes, remarrying a year later. But however Gladys and Clyde's relationship began, it stuck; they remained married until his death.

There can't have been time for a honeymoon besides that weekend in Ventura Country, unless, of course, Clyde was off the rails enough that he didn't return to continue working on *Movie Crazy* at all. Despite a story in *Variety* in mid-April about Lloyd's lengthy production schedules—or maybe because of it—the film wrapped by early May, marked by a flurry of stories about how quickly Lloyd had worked. Clyde was at least on payroll during the cutting and early tests, first in San Francisco and then in Los Angeles, but on June 11, Harold Lloyd cut him loose. This was probably more of a cost-cutting measure than a firing: Lloyd had taken *himself* off the payroll on May 31, and in August would cut the pay of his highest-ranking employees, including his own brother. Regardless, Clyde found himself unemployed throughout the summer of 1932, as *Movie Crazy* neared its September release.

Whoever was behind the camera, *Movie Crazy* is easily Lloyd's best talkie. Lloyd, like Keaton before him, wanted to make his version of *Merton of the Movies*, and Vincent Lawrence's script manages to extract the heart of the story without outright stealing it. Lloyd, playing a film-obsessed bumpkin who mistakenly believes he is destined for great things in Hollywood after accidentally sending in someone else's headshot, gives a charming performance. Having some familiarity with and affection for the milieu—as opposed to, say, San Francisco Tong Wars or the Hawaiian shoe trade—makes an enormous difference. There's nothing in Lloyd's earlier talkies like the screen test sequence, for instance, which has been imitated so often since that it has become a cliché. Harold blows take after take of a simple scene in increasingly hilarious ways; rather than show him attempting to film it, we see him watch the resulting footage, complete with abrupt cuts, clapboards, and a prop man who keeps running on set as soon as each take ends to sweep up. The structure works, too: instead of *Feet First's* barely connected acts or *Welcome Danger's* utter chaos, the story flows smoothly from one event to another. And the cranes that so fascinated Lloyd were put to excellent use, particularly in a show-stopping tour of a soundstage that opens the film's final sequence. The camera begins with a long shot showing the entire set, a multi-story boat cutaway, before swooping into a medium shot of the director on the boat's lower level, then flying away to medium shots of the rest of the crew as the director confirms they're ready to film—the sound man one level up, a spotlight operator on a high catwalk, special effects crews manning wind machines and tanks of water—before finally circling back to the director. It's a functional map of the playground where the film's final gags will take place, and it's as fluid and smooth as anything for decades to come.

The film opened in September to the best reviews Lloyd had gotten in years. Martin Dickstein at the *Brooklyn Eagle*, who'd questioned the entire premise of Harold Lloyd in a talking picture after enduring *Welcome Danger*, conceded that Lloyd had "avoided the mistakes of his early talkie days," and said he hadn't heard more laughs during a movie in years. Virtually every review singled out an ingenious sequence where Lloyd mistakenly ended up wearing a magician's coat at a party, causing chaos as eggs, mice, and birds escaped from its hidden compartments. (The *Los Angeles Times* ran a short article consisting, in its entirety, of a summary of this sequence, under the headline "Lengthy Comedy Scene Keeps Audience Roaring.") But audiences were not as easily swayed as critics, and Lloyd had sailed past the top of his parabola years ago. *Motion Picture Herald* had a regular feature with reports from exhibitors on the performance of various films; that December, they offered grim accounts of Harold Lloyd's popularity with their patrons. A theater owner in Missouri offered a harsh but accurate assessment:

Too long between Lloyd pictures. Lloyd has been forgotten. Box office flop.

Movie Crazy grossed a scant $675,194 domestically—nearly a 40 percent drop from *Feet First*. It did slightly better in foreign mar-

kets, but not enough to make up for the American audience abandoning him. Lloyd was trying harder, working faster, and making
better films, yet still the downward slope steepened.

But neither the film's artistic successes nor its box-office failure
was really Clyde's to share. He only had his name on it. Here's
Lloyd again, in 1968:

> I still gave the directing credit to this other boy, the gag man, for that
> film. I felt it helped them. I didn't see that it was going to add to my
> prestige, and certainly from a monetary standpoint it wasn't going to
> help me anymore, and it did help them.

Another directing credit Clyde didn't earn. But *The General*
had been an agreed-upon exaggeration with Buster Keaton, a
reward for finding the film's story to begin with as well as a reflec-
tion of the work he'd done as an assistant director in Oregon.
Having his name on *Movie Crazy* was a reminder of his failure, and
Harold Lloyd's pity.

Whatever happened during filming of *Movie Crazy*, Lloyd kept
it quiet until long after Clyde was dead. Although he'd never
direct Harold Lloyd again, he had no problem finding directorial
work elsewhere. In November, Clyde signed a short-term contract
with Mack Sennett: one short film, with a shooting schedule not
to exceed six days, and the option to hire him for two additional
films at $1,000 per week. He was back in the Fun Factory, which
had hardly changed since he'd last worked there in 1925. It was
there he'd meet his last great collaborator, W. C. Fields. For Clyde,
no one could have been more professionally congenial or person-
ally ruinous.

THE HUMAN FISH

Mack Sennett hadn't actually been the first person to hire Clyde to direct a film after *Movie Crazy*, but Clyde had entered the stage of his career—and his drinking—where his résumé started gathering asterisks. Earlier in the fall of 1932, he seems to have briefly returned to RKO—home of *Everything's Rosie*—where he was to direct the next film in their Masquers' Comedy series of two-reelers. On his last visit to RKO, he'd been saddled with Robert Woolsey; this time, he'd be working with people he knew: James Finlayson and Max Davidson, both of whom had fled Roach Studios as Laurel and Hardy eclipsed them. In late October, without giving a reason, RKO announced that they'd replaced Clyde with Mark Sandrich. Although Sandrich would eventually become one of Rogers and Astaire's greatest directors, the film he replaced Clyde on was *Thru Thin and Thicket, or Who's Zoo in Africa*, in which, per the IMDb, "Famed white hunter Trader Cohen leads the Chuzzlebottom expedition into darkest Africa." So Clyde leaving would have been all to the good, if it hadn't been the beginning of a pattern.

His first assignment at Sennett was a step up from the Chuzzlebottom expedition, but not much of one. That summer Los Angeles had hosted the Olympic Games, and one of its stars was a swimmer named Helene Madison. Madison—who had already broken the world records for freestyle swimming at every distance between a hundred yards and a mile—won gold medals in all three of her events before announcing she would retire at the top of her game. Sennett, in a bit of stunt casting, signed her that fall. Clyde's job was to write and direct a short film to see if she could act as well as she could swim.

She could not. The AP ran a rather ominous production photo that included no cameras or sets but instead showed Clyde going over the script with her. That script, titled *Help! Help! Helene!*, was structured so that Madison could spend as much time in the water as possible, both saving swimmers from drowning and incorporating footage of one of her Olympic races. With little rehearsal or training besides posing for the AP photo, Clyde and Helene shot from Tuesday, November 15 to Saturday, November 19; the film, retitled *The Human Fish*, was released at the end of 1932 to resounding indifference. Even a positive report from a theater owner in rural Nebraska was backhanded: "What the famous Olympic swimming champ lacks as an actress she makes up as a swimmer." But it was an easy $1,000 for a film that almost no one saw, and Sennett picked up Clyde's option. His next assignment would have a star with a better track record: W. C. Fields.

Clyde's newest collaborator occupied a wholly unique place in motion picture history. Roger Ebert aptly called him "the most improbable star in the first century of movies." He played one character on screen and in life: a misanthropic drunk, trying hard to maintain a certain nineteenth-century dignity while under constant assault from the world around him.

Fields was on roughly his fourth career by the time Clyde worked with him. Born in Philadelphia in 1880, he'd begun in vaudeville as a juggler, making his way to New York by absconding with the receipts from a phony benefit show he'd put on, with advertising funded on what he'd later describe as "the pay-if-you-can-catch-us plan." In New York, he'd risen through the minstrel shows and burlesques, touring with a number of companies before joining the *Ziegfeld Follies* in 1915. The *Follies* landed him *Pool Sharks*, his first short film, that same year. Having begun his career as a genuine con artist, he became a Broadway star by playing one: a patent medicine salesman in 1923's *Poppy*, which Robert Woolsey would borrow liberally from years later. *Sally of the Sawdust*, D. W. Griffith's silent adaptation of *Poppy*, was his entry into feature films. By 1932, his comedic persona was fully formed. Coming from the stage, he'd made a smoother transition into talkies than many, and arranged a lucrative contract that year to make short films for Mack Sennett. In November, while Clyde was making *The Human Fish*, he'd finished the first of these, *The Dentist*—an excellent film, despite being exceptionally violent and misanthropic even for W. C. Fields. Sennett picked up the option on Fields's contract at the same time as Clyde's and, probably thinking they'd be comedically simpatico, paired them together.

But by 1932, the two men also shared an increasingly all-consuming hobby. Fields had rarely touched a drink in his juggling days, but while touring with the *Follies* he'd picked up the habit as a way to fuel dressing room socialization, and by the 1930s, he was drinking heavily enough to make Buster Keaton look like a piker. Prohibition made the subject a little publicly touchy, but it didn't really slow him down. Drinking was part of Fields's persona, expected of him, and he played the role to the hilt. Biographer James Curtis points to this 1935 interview, after alcohol was legal again:

> I'm an advocate of moderation. For example, I never drink before breakfast. During the morning, I have 15 or 20 highballs. Then comes lunch. But I don't eat lunch. Bad for the waistline. I drink it instead—oh, say, a gallon of cocktails. In the afternoon, which is longer than the morning, I have possibly 30 or 40 highballs. With dinner, I have ten or twelve bottles of wine or something to drink. In the evening, I like a case of sherry or maybe 50 to 60 highballs.

Even the comic version is a little sick-making, but the facts, according to Norman McLeod, who directed him in 1934's *It's A Gift*, were positively unimaginable:

> After breakfast he downed a solid glass of bourbon with one-half inch of water in it. He said he didn't want to discolor the bourbon. He had four or five of these until noon. He drank on the set. He was one of the few actors I knew of who was allowed to drink on the set. Then he had lunch. After lunch—he always ate big meals—he began imbibing again at 2:30. He would have four or five more bourbons until 5 p.m. At 5 p.m. he started on martinis. He'd have five or six martinis—he made a very good martini—before dinner. He was never drunk unless he consumed liquor after dinner. If he did, he went back to bourbon.

This was not a man anyone with a drinking problem would be well advised to have as a coworker. But Clyde was able to hold things together over the five days of shooting around Thanksgiving of 1932. It helped that they were making a film that would not only withstand a certain amount of incompetence, but positively reward it.

The work at hand was an adaptation of "The Stolen Bonds," a sketch Fields had performed on stage that sent up the shoddy writing, acting, and set construction of theatrical melodramas. For the film adaptation, retitled *The Fatal Glass of Beer*, Clyde and W. C. Fields made things even shoddier, adding an interminable parody of a temperance song and a terribly executed rear-projection sequence. The resulting film had what William K. Everson described as "a reckless lack of finesse" that was, for once, exactly the right approach. The sets are unimaginably cheap, Fields's singing is punishingly awful, there's barely any story, a group of Indians in full headdresses appear for reasons that are never explained, and the single funniest joke is about Fields eating his dog. The standout sequence from a filmmaking point-of-view has Fields announce that he is going to "milk the elk," before going outside and attempting conversation with rear-projected stock footage of stampeding animals, which is: (1) out of focus, (2) lit completely differently than he is, (3) shot from the wrong angle, (4) at a completely different scale, and (5) edited with abrupt, unexplained cuts. It's an absolute garbage fire of a movie, popping and fizzing with contempt for its audience, its subject, and the arts of theater, filmmaking, and presumably elk-milking. In other words, it's a masterpiece. Fields, in a letter to Sennett, who saw and hated an early cut, summed up its appeal:

You are probably one hundred percent right. "The Fatal Glass of Beer" stinks. It's lousy. But, I still think it's good.

Incredibly, the finished movie is *less* deliberately terrible than Fields wanted it to be; his plan was to have the camera stay on him for the entirety of his awful song about temperance. Sennett insisted on cutting away to shots of George Chandler as his son, illustrating the perils of alcohol as Fields sang about them. In some accounts, these were reshoots Sennett made Clyde make after viewing the original version, but the cutaway scenes appear in the shooting script from November 17, so it seems likely this was more of an editing dispute.

Some critics seemed to get the joke when the film was released: *Film Daily* called it a "Top-Notch Comedy," although the reviewer may have been thinking of a different film, since the review also praises the "clever process work" of the elk-milking section. Audiences, in contrast, overwhelmingly agreed with *Variety*: "No real laffs and hardly a snicker." *Motion Picture Herald*'s "What the Picture Did for Me" feature—practically the only place to find a good word about *The Human Fish*—was exceptionally harsh. One theater owner reported "Two reels of film time and 18 minutes of time wasted," and another was harsher still: "This is the worst comedy we have played from any company this season. No story, no acting and as a whole has nothing." Like the ostensibly negative four-word review of *The Dentist* in the same issue ("Inexplicable. Rank. Uncalled for."), complaining about the film's lack of story, wasted time, or bad acting seems like a case of missing the forest for the horribly photographed trees. But as with *The General*, albeit for very different reasons, it would take years for audiences to appreciate *The Fatal Glass of Beer*.

More than eleven years earlier, in the summer of 1921, Clyde had worked on his first masterpiece, *The Playhouse*. It had been a carefully planned and executed clockwork toy, all elaborate special effects and precise timing: virtuoso work. With *The Fatal Glass of Beer*, he made his last masterpiece, a shambling wreck of a film, bursting at the seams with bad ideas, badly executed. It's the cinematic equivalent of being cornered at a bar by a drunk whose manic, conspiratorial monologue somehow manages to be fascinating and hilarious. It sometimes *does* happen, but much less often than heavy drinkers come to believe. The hangovers are vicious.

TOO MANY HIGHBALLS

Clyde's follow-up at Sennett was a story that may have had some personal resonance for him: over the next decade he remade it three times, with three different stars. In December of 1932, he wrote the first version with W. C. Fields in mind: *His Perfect Day*.

His perfect day, according to Clyde, was pretty straightforward. In every version of the story, the hero, who shares a home with his brother-in-law and mother-in-law, schemes to ditch his family, ditch his job, and spend the day watching sports. Fields took the story and rewrote it to his own specifications, but Sennett, unhappy with the fiasco that was *The Fatal Glass of Beer*, made his own pass on the script, which Fields didn't appreciate, as he expressed in a letter in which he asked to be released from his contract:

> I worked on the last story ten full days to make it a story that would fit my style of work. You changed it to fit someone else, added an indelicate Castor Oil sequence, and sent it to me with the curt message that if I did not like it in the changed form you would give it to Lloyd Hamilton.

Neither Sennett nor Fields was bluffing, and Lloyd Hamilton got the part. Hamilton, who had been a big star in the teens and early twenties, specialized in playing a pudgy baby-face, but he drank nearly as much as Fields and held his liquor much worse. In 1927, he'd been at a speakeasy when a boxer died under mysterious circumstances; though he had nothing to do with the death, the ensuing scandal torpedoed his career. He'd drunk his way to homelessness in the late twenties, sleeping on the beach, before taking one of the era's dubious quick cures—these usually included morphine and phenobarbital—and temporarily sobering up. While Fields's comedic persona to some degree depended on his ruined face, Hamilton's manchild act didn't really work now that his face was lined and weathered, and he knew it. Dorothy Granger, his co-star in his first Sennett short, remembered him as a "very quiet and extremely sad man."

So Lloyd Hamilton was probably not the ideal star for *His Perfect Day*, especially once it had been retitled *Too Many Highballs*. Among the comic set pieces were Hamilton getting (mistakenly) arrested for drunk driving and being forced to take the cure, both of which are much funnier if you know nothing about him. The film was better received than *The Fatal Glass of Beer*, though it had a similarly slapdash approach to production value. One exhibitor reported that it was "quite a favorite here," despite being "noisy and cheap." But Hamilton looked terrible; his biographer, Anthony Balducci, points to a critic who specifically mentioned that his "disturbing appearance . . . spoiled the fun." He went on to die of a drinking-related hemorrhaging ulcer in January of 1935.

Sennett had apparently seen enough of Clyde's directing, and bounced him back to the gag room. He spent the spring of 1933 writing two-reelers as unmemorable as their titles: *Uncle Jake*,

Roadhouse Queen, Daddy Knows Best, and *The Big Fibber.* The biggest star in any of them was Billy Gilbert, and his best roles were still years ahead of him. The work of a Sennett writer hadn't changed much with the coming of sound. Scripts still began as treatments designed with plenty of room for improvisation while shooting, as in this one from *Uncle Jake,* which Clyde wrote with Felix Adler:

> They go on the picnic at which through a routine of gags they have a terrible time . . . Finally a bear comes up and eats all their food, and they have to go back home, hungry. The Uncle is always very optimistic about everything, and laughs all the trouble off.

They also created a separate sheet of "notes and gags for picnic," which, compared to the kinds of visual gags Clyde had designed at Sennett back in 1925, could charitably be described as "less elaborate." The ellipses here are in the original:

> At picnic . . . can get gags with skunk . . . hornet's nest . . . ants . . . animals coming in and eating food . . . etc.

Etc. The actual shooting scripts had to be more detailed than the silent ones, at least when dialogue was involved, but they also demonstrate that sound was still thought of more as a special effect than as an integral part of the film. Dialogue was written as it is in a modern screenplay, but all other sound was annotated separately for the technicians when a rough draft was converted to a shooting script. So the rough draft of *Daddy Knows Best,* which Clyde wrote with Felix Adler and John A. Waldron in February, has a shot like this:

> EXT STREET (NIGHT) Corner.

> FULL SHOT Standing Pan
> We see the young people in the roadster coming down the street, the kid playing the ukulele and they are all singing and laughing . . .

In the shooting script, the shot was rewritten to move sound effects into their own column, making things easier for the sound technicians.

> 6. – EXTERIOR: RESIDENTIAL STREET (NIGHT).
> PANNING STREET SHOT
> Showing the roadster
> containing Peggy, Billy and the
> other young folks coming down the
> street, the Boy still playing the
> ukulele and they are all singing . . .

And then, in the right column:

> SOUND: KIDS SINGING AND LAUGH-
> ING . . . UKULELE . . .
> SOUND OF AUTO AND AUTO
> "ATTENTION HORN"

But besides providing a glimpse into the workflow of early sound cinema, Clyde's second round in the gag room at Sennett has little to recommend it. Sennett was in serious financial trouble by this time: 1932 had been a bad year financially, and Clyde's movies hadn't helped. In January of 1933, Sennett's distributor, Paramount-Publix, once the richest studio in town, went into receivership, throwing things into further disarray. (Clyde's movies with Harold Lloyd hadn't helped there, either.) By May,

Sennett was looking into stunts like dubbing over his old silent films as a way to cut costs; in December, he declared bankruptcy.

In the meantime, Clyde continued adding asterisks to his résumé. That summer, Hal Roach announced Clyde had been hired to direct the first of a new series of comedies pairing Thelma Todd and Patsy Kelly. It's unclear whether Clyde quit or was fired, but Gus Meins ended up directing the first film, *Beauty and the Bus*, as well as the rest of the series. Later in the summer, despite the *Movie Crazy* fiasco, Harold Lloyd hired him back again to work on his new film, *The Cat's Paw*.

Lloyd had fled to Europe with his family for a six-month vacation as the disappointing box-office results for *Movie Crazy* came in. He returned in March 1933 with a new distribution contract at Fox, determined to reinvent himself for Depression-era audiences. After so many years starting with gags, he'd come to the conclusion that talkies depended on having better source material. Hiring a playwright for *Movie Crazy* hadn't been radical enough; this time, he bought the film rights to a novel, *The Cat's Paw*, by Clarence Buddington Kelland. *Variety* reported that he'd rehired Clyde to direct once again, but if this was ever true, it wasn't true for long. Clyde started on July 10 at a reduced rate of $600 a week (Lloyd was cutting costs across the board); his payroll card has him in the scenario department, not as a director. In two months' time, he wasn't in any department at all—Lloyd let him go on September 2. On September 25, he rehired him; this time he lasted three months before Lloyd cut him loose again on December 23. Whatever the reasons, Clyde got no credit for his weeks of work on the film, and it seems likely that Lloyd had him in mind when he wrote a letter telling Sidney Kent at Fox that he'd spent January

. . . lining up a production organization which, by the way, is many
times more efficient than any we have previously assembled. This,
I'm sure, the picture will reflect since we have gotten away from
the old formula, and seat-warmers whose knowledge was limited to
what they had previously done.

Clyde didn't work again until April, when *Variety* reported he'd
been signed to MGM. They paired him with Joe Sherman and
set the men to work on an adaptation of Cortland Fitzsimmons's
novel *Death on the Diamond.* This seemed like the perfect assignment for Clyde: it's a murder mystery in which someone is killing
off the members of a baseball team, and one of the main characters
is a sportswriter. It was the chance to do something other than
comedy, set in a milieu he knew perfectly. Clyde and Sherman
wrote the outline and first draft together, but he was off the project by the end of May; the final script was credited to Sherman,
Harvey Thew, and Ralph Spence. Another asterisk.

That June, unemployed once more, he turned forty. Prohibition
had ended in December, a few weeks before Harold Lloyd had
canned him. Since then Clyde, who was nervous when he had
nothing to do, had spent more time unemployed than working.
And now he could find a drink anywhere he looked.

In November he finally found a new job, this time at Columbia.
Jules White, who headed the shorts department, hired him to
direct the Three Stooges in *Horses' Collars,* their fifth short there.
The Stooges had started in vaudeville with Ted Healy in the 1920s.
Their initial act, billed as Ted Healy and his Stooges, had featured
brothers Moe and Shemp Howard with Larry Fine. Healy would
invite the Stooges on stage with him before berating them and
slapping them around. After Shemp was replaced by another
Howard brother, Curly, they'd made several films at MGM. In the

spring of 1934, fed up with Healy's abuse, Larry, Curly, and Moe had split with their old mentor to make two-reelers at Columbia. Though Clyde would write for the Stooges often once he became unemployable everywhere else, this time around he only worked with them for four days.

The earlier Stooges shorts at Columbia were slapdash affairs, but Clyde managed to out-slapdash them all. Ray McCarey's *Three Little Pigskins*, which immediately preceded it, is positively lavish by comparison. McCarey's film opens in a gangster's apartment, uses location shooting around Yucca Street in Hollywood where the Stooges end up working as publicity men, returns to the apartment for some slapstick including several falls down a dumbwaiter shaft, then finally returns to Gilmore Stadium for a football match with college players as extras. In terms of production values, it's not *The General*, but it's also not *Horses' Collars*. Clyde's film has only three locations: an office where the Stooges have been hired as detectives in what seems to be the present day (although the Stooges are dressed Sherlock Holmes–style), an Old West saloon introduced without so much as stock footage of a train, and, finally, the saloon owner's office, which appears to have been created by decorating a generic set with Native American rugs. The highlight is a sight gag where Curly has painted eyes onto his eyelids so he can nap unnoticed. It also features one of the first gags Clyde reused: a bit where Curly fights a henchmen while sharing a coat with the villain, each wearing one sleeve. Harold Lloyd had done this in *Welcome Danger* (and, according to Clyde, the gag wasn't even original then; Lloyd had knowingly lifted it from *Horse Shoes*). Clyde also reused a conceit from an earlier Stooges short (later reused in other Stooges films): Curly becomes an invincible fighter whenever he sees a mouse. (Their second Columbia film, *Punch Drunks*, has a similar gag, although it's the song "Pop Goes the Weasel" that sets him off.) But while in *Punch Drunks* Curly's secret weapon is the point of the film (Curly uses it to launch a boxing career), here it's just a *deus ex machina*.

Both the plot and the shoddy production values come to a head in a sequence where the Stooges are strung up. Moe and Larry are hanging from poorly rigged harnesses that pull their costumes so severely they appear to be hunchbacked. Clyde seems to have approached the film as carelessly as he had *The Fatal Glass of Beer*, but although the sets and production values are a joke, this time around they aren't *the* joke. Sloppy in concept and execution, *Horses' Collars* doesn't seem to have been made by a man in complete control of his facilities. The film was released that January and went over fine, but the only reason it wasn't the worst Stooges short to that point was that their debut outing, *Woman Haters*, had for some reason been delivered entirely in rhyming couplets.

Most of Clyde's carelessness in *Horses' Collars* can be explained by his struggle with the bottle, but it's also true that he—correctly—saw the film as a step down from Keaton and Lloyd. In a deposition a decade later, asked if he remembered the stars of one of the Stooges shorts he'd written, he replied, "There were three stooges if you want to call them stars." Still, Columbia was happy enough with his work to hire him to direct three more Stooges films. But they weren't so happy that they paid him as much as he'd been making in his heyday, and his year of scatter-shot employment was starting to eat into his finances. The mortgage on his Beverly Hills home had been manageable in 1927 when he was fresh off *The General*, but he'd barely worked at all in 1934. In January of 1935, he put the house up for sale with a classified ad promising "A steal. 4 bedrms., 3 baths, libr., game rm., 2 servants rms." Even as a steal, the height of the Great Depression was the wrong time to try to sell a four-bedroom home with servants' quarters. A few weeks later, he listed it again through real estate agent Ed Winchell, as one of the week's "Winchell's Bargains that Sell." It didn't. But then it suddenly didn't have to. The day before his second Three Stooges short was to begin shooting, he suddenly got the opportunity to go back to features, and for enough money that he was able to take his house off the market. Del Lord, one of the best and most prolific of the Stooges directors, replaced him at the last minute, and Clyde went to Fox. It was the only time Fox ever hired him, but they were desperate.

A week into shooting an adaptation of Ben Hecht and Rose Caylor's play *The Man-Eating Tiger* for Fox, director Melville Brown walked off the set and quit. According to *Variety*, he was "dissatisfied with the treatment of the story, and claiming that the principal parts are miscast." Clyde was once more brought in on cleanup duty, fixing another director's mess.

To say he didn't succeed this time around is too kind—the film, released in the summer of 1935 as *Spring Tonic*, is an outright catastrophe. It's hard to tell what casting or story could have saved things, but Melville Brown's assessment seems to have been correct. Claire Trevor stars as a runaway bride who flees her dull fiancé for a country lodge, where she contends with bootleggers and an escaped tiger. Lew Ayres is insufferable as her fiancé and ZaSu Pitts is utterly wasted as her maid. The film's best laughs, such as they are, come from Walter Woolf King as the Latin guitarist who romances her—basically a wan version of the Erik Rhodes character in the Rogers/Astaire musicals. The most interesting thing about it is that compared to the usually sexless films of Keaton and Lloyd, *Spring Tonic* is positively kinky. Ayres finally fixes his marriage thanks to advice from an extraordinarily butch tiger tamer played by Dietrich-manqué Tala Birell. "I never let Mina forget that I am her master," Birell tells Ayres, before he literally cracks a whip and orders his suddenly enthusiastic bride home. But out-of-character sexual undertones weren't enough to convince audiences or critics to overlook the shoddy craftsmanship. *Variety*'s review was typical:

> This picture has every appearance of being ad libbed by the cast while the director's back was turned. Everyone rolls his own for a total of inanity. All the hokum and horse-play of the Sennett era, plus a free translation of the Selig cat epics, are conglomerated here for a gag men's picnic and zero entertainment.

It seems likely that Clyde's reputation as a heavy drinker was starting to get out at this point, because although the film may have been made while his back was turned, most of it doesn't seem ad-libbed—certainly not compared to his work with Keaton or Lloyd. If anything, it sticks too closely to its not-very-good script. The "gag men's picnic" line, however, must have stung, because Clyde was continuing to reuse gags from his earlier films. He inserted two gags from *The Navigator*, having ZaSu Pitts recreate Keaton's struggles with canned food and, bizarrely, reusing a creepy bit where a portrait swinging by a window is mistaken for a prowler. In both cases, the seams show. Even less successfully, Clyde made a baffling reuse of a bit from *Welcome Danger*—both Lloyd and Pitts end up with an accordion attached to their posteriors, frightening them when they sit down—a gag that couldn't have played very well the first time around. None of these reach the level of outright plagiarism, but by the same token, they're such tiny jokes that it's unclear why Clyde bothered to reuse them. What's clear is that as his drinking got worse and worse, Clyde was losing faith in his ability to create new material.

But as it happened, he didn't have to create new material. In the time between finishing *Spring Tonic* and its catastrophic release, W. C. Fields brought him back to Paramount to direct him in a feature. They'd finally get to make *His Perfect Day*, the story Clyde had written for him at Sennett. Paramount first announced it under the title *The Plot Thickens*; less than a week later, it was *The Flying Trapeze*. Without Sennett to interfere, Sam Hardy and Fields, working under the name "Charles Bogle," worked up a screenplay—or most of one, anyway. Filming began on April 27 under its third new title: *Everything Happens at Once*.

What happened next is something of a vexed question. Fields continued to drink on set, and although Clyde had managed to hold things together on *The Fatal Glass of Beer*, a feature shoot proved to be his undoing. The script wasn't finished, so Fields and Hardy wrote nights and mornings, shooting during the day as the production slowly caught up with them. For Clyde, that meant lots of waiting around for script pages to be finished, and it can't have been hard to find a way to pass the time. As early as the second day of shooting, the assistant director noted that they'd failed to accomplish what they'd set out for the day, and in the "Reason for Delay" field wrote: "MR. BRUCKMAN NOT BACK ON SET UNTIL 3:00 P.M. AFTER LUNCH." A few weeks later, the bottom fell out.

On Monday, May 13, 1935, Clyde had an unplanned, unannounced three-day weekend. The assistant director's report records this as "LATE START DUE TO MR. BRUCKMAN'S ABSENCE ON ACCOUNT OF ILLNESS," but it seems clear that Clyde's "illness" was alcoholism. Fields and Hardy were caught unguarded by his disappearance—*Variety* called it a "flu attack"—and Fields had to take over directorial duties rather than lose the day. In W. C. Fields's grandson Ronald Fields's account of the film, Fields and Hardy were the film's sole directors from then on. But after May 13, Clyde seems to have at least showed up at work. He's still listed as the director on each day's assistant director report, and it's his signature on the retake request forms. What's more, the assistant director had no qualms about recording Fields's every absence, late arrival, or long lunch hour; it's a parade of entries like "MR. FIELDS ILL, NOT ON SET UNTIL 11:05 A.M. HE WAS ALSO ONE HOUR & THIRTY MINUTES LATE RETURNING FROM LUNCH," and "MR. FIELDS NOT ON SET UNTIL 10:45 A.M. NOT FEELING WELL SO WENT HOME AT 3:40 P.M." Despite the script and drinking problems the production didn't grind to a halt—shooting continued six days a week, except for Memorial Day, until wrapping on June 4. When the production did two days of reshoots later in June, it was definitely Bruckman and not Fields behind the camera.

But there's a difference between showing up at work and being sober enough to work at a studio, and directing isn't really a career where unannounced absences are possible. It didn't help matters that the finished film wasn't well received by preview audiences.

The preview audiences were wrong. Despite its troubled production, *Man on the Flying Trapeze* is one of Fields's best features. This time around, the protagonist of *His Perfect Day* has the perfectly Fieldsian name of Ambrose Wolfinger, and it's wrestling, not boxing, he longs to see. It's funnier the less you know about Clyde self-destructing during filming: both men were very familiar with the patterns and habits of alcoholics, and it's a little painful to watch Fields sneak into the bathroom under the pretense of brushing his teeth in order to steal a drink from a hidden bottle. But Fields is in fine form throughout, muttering the sort of throwaway lines only he could pull off. One of many highlights comes after he's told his boss that he has to leave work because of his mother-in-law's sudden death. His boss consoles him, "It must be hard to lose your mother-in-law," and he replies, "Yes, it is, it's very hard. It's almost impossible." Clyde restaged the rear-projection tomfoolery that made *The Fatal Glass of Beer* so memorable, this time with Fields pursuing a rolling spare tire across a railway bridge, leaping ungracefully to the side to avoid a passing train. It couldn't be any more obviously stock footage and a treadmill, and it kills. (Keaton, of course, would have used a real train.) It's one of the rare comedies that becomes funnier each time it is seen, as more of Fields's throwaway lines and perfectly-timed deliveries reveal themselves.

But it was created by two men in thrall to the bottle, and although Harold Lloyd kept Clyde's meltdown a secret, Paramount did not. When filming was complete, Fields made a not-so-secret attempt to dry out at Soboba Hot Springs in the San Bernardino Mountains. Clyde took a month's vacation on Vancouver Island. This may have also been an attempt to sober up—*Variety* did not normally cover his travels but this time mentioned it twice, first reporting his return to Los Angeles after a "four weeks idler," and then a week later, noting he was "back at grind after month on an island."

But Clyde wasn't back at the grind. When he left for Vancouver Island, he was a director, and when he came home, he wasn't. Clyde's directorial career had begun as one of Buster Keaton's pranks, occasionally proceeded as a salvage operation, launched the careers of Laurel and Hardy, and produced a handful of verifiable comedic masterpieces. Now it had ended, drowned in a bottle over an impromptu three-day weekend. Perhaps its best epitaph is the explanation Ambrose Wolfinger offers at the end of *Man on the Flying Trapeze* when confronted with the baffling wreckage of his perfect day: "Things happened."

San Bernardino High *Tyro* staff photos of Clyde in 1910, 1911, 1912, and 1913. *The Tyro*, June 1910, June 1911, June 1912, June 1913. Courtesy of the Arda Haenszel California Room, Norman F. Feldheym Central Library, San Bernardino, California.

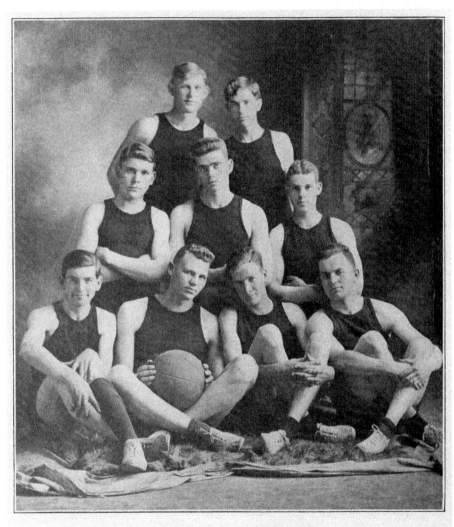

BASKETBALL TEAM

The 1911 San Bernardino High Basketball Team. Clyde is lower left. *The Tyro*, June 1911. Courtesy of the Arda Haenszel California Room, Norman F. Feldheym Central Library, San Bernardino, California.

"THE IMPORTANCE OF BEING. EARNEST"

With the cast of the 1913 San Bernardino High production of *The Importance of Being Earnest*. *The Tyro*, June 1913. Courtesy of the Arda Haenszel California Room, Norman F. Feldheym Central Library, San Bernardino, California.

CLYDE BRUCKMAN

"He attempts to get the general love and good will of his fellow students."

Senior photo/Baby photo. *The Tyro*, June 1913. Courtesy of the Arda Haenszel California Room, Norman F. Feldheym Central Library, San Bernardino, California.

Ad for Lyons and Moran Star Comedies, *Motion Picture News*, June 22, 1918.

Buster Keaton's gag men during the production of *Three Ages*, 1923. From left to right: Buster Keaton, Clyde Bruckman, Joe Mitchell, Jean Havez, and Eddie Cline. From the collections of the Margaret Herrick Library, Academy of Motion Picture Arts and Sciences.

Hal Roach conferring with his directors. "See the whip? Now, think up something funny!" Thus are Roach M-G-M comedies made. . . . However, this much IS true: From left to right, they are Fred Guiol, Bob McGowan, Roach, Leo McCarey, Hal Yates, James Parrott, and Claude Bruckman.

"Claude Bruckman" with Hal Roach and staff, *Exhibitor's Herald and Moving Picture World*, January 7, 1928.

Harold Lloyd and crew during the production of *Welcome Danger*, 1929. From left to right: Unidentified, John L. Murphy, Unidentified, Malcolm St. Clair, Walter Lundin, Harold Lloyd, William F. Fraser, Clyde Bruckman. © 2011, The Harold Lloyd Trust. From the collections of the Margaret Herrick Library, Academy of Motion Picture Arts and Sciences.

Harold Lloyd and Barbara Kent on board the SS
Malolo during the filming of *Feet First*, 1930. Clyde is
to the right of the camera. © 2011, The Harold Lloyd
Trust. From the collections of the Margaret Herrick
Library, Academy of Motion Picture Arts and
Sciences.

The Double Feature Octopus. *Motion Picture Herald*,
February 13, 1937.

Crane setup on *Movie Crazy*, 1932. Clyde is to the right, near Harold Lloyd, looking down. © 2011, The Harold Lloyd Trust. From the collections of the Margaret Herrick Library, Academy of Motion Picture Arts and Sciences.

Clyde's publicity photo for Paramount during the production of *Man on the Flying Trapeze*, 1935. The original caption read:

HE GOT THE JOB – Clyde Bruckman got the assignment of directing W. C. Fields' latest Paramount picture, temporarily titled "Everything Happens At Once." Bruckman is a veteran in handling comedy on the screen.

Courtesy of Universal Studios Licensing LLC. From the collections of the Margaret Herrick Library, Academy of Motion Picture Arts and Sciences.

Clyde on location filming *Man on the Flying Trapeze*, 1935. The original caption read:

BUSINESS – W. C. Fields works out a piece of business with a member of his technical crew as he waits for something or other on the set of his current picture for Paramount, "Everything Happens at Once."

Courtesy of Universal Studios Licensing LLC. From the collections of the Margaret Herrick Library, Academy of Motion Picture Arts and Sciences.

SLAPSTICK

With no directorial jobs in sight, Clyde returned to Columbia, the studio he'd abruptly left to make *Spring Tonic*. They took him back, but not as a director, adding him to the writing staff in September of 1935. He'd work there off and on for the rest of his life.

Columbia, founded by Harry Cohn in 1924, had begun as a Poverty Row studio, but in the early thirties began a concerted effort to become more respectable. In 1934 they'd received their first Best Picture nomination (called "Outstanding Production" at the time) for Frank Capra's *Lady for a Day*, and the next year Capra's *It Happened One Night* became the first picture to sweep the awards, winning for Outstanding Production, Actor, Actress, Directing, and Writing (Adaptation). In 1933 the studio had begun production of its own two-reelers, but Harry Cohn, busy with features, let the short subject division operate under what might kindly be called a policy of benign neglect. Edward Bernds, who worked there for years, recalled that

> . . . we, the short subjects people, were ignored by the Columbia hierarchy. We were even separated from the main lot, housed in a shabby

old building. . . . We knew the shows were good, but the Columbia bosses never bothered to look at our stuff, and when we shipped the films to New York, they disappeared into a silent void.

The man presiding over the factory shipping films off into the void, and Clyde's new boss, was Jules White. White had started out as a child actor, but his first big success came when he co-created the Dogville comedies with Zion Myers in 1929. These were two-reel parodies of other films, starring dogs dressed up as people: *So Quiet on the Canine Front*, *Dogway Melody*, and the like. The dogs wore harnesses so they could be puppeteered around dog-scale sets on their hind legs, they were fed taffy so they'd move their lips, and their voices were dubbed in later. (The original plan, as pitched by Zion Myers and Mark Sandrich at a Coffee Dan's at four in the morning, had been to use horses—dogs were Jules White's idea.) Harry Cohn hired White to run the Columbia short department in 1933; he quit after a month but was lured back in 1934. Mack Sennett's bankruptcy had left a lot of experienced two-reeler directors, actors, and crew out in the cold, so White was able to build a talented crew quickly and cheaply. Del Lord, one of the better Stooges directors, who'd taken Clyde's place when he'd gone to Fox, was selling used Buicks when White brought him to Columbia. Clyde, in disgrace after *Man on the Flying Trapeze*, must have seemed like the same kind of bargain.

The Columbia shorts department seems to have been a pretty congenial place for functional alcoholics to work, which is to say it was a terrible place for functional alcoholics to work. Jules White had an elaborate system for managing Clyde's frequent collaborator Felix Adler's drinking, as he explained to David Bruskin in the 1980s:

JULES: . . . on Sundays, Felix and I used to write a script. He'd usually get loaded Saturday night, so I'd have to pull him out of there. We'd go to the office and sit from morning until night, Saturday and Sunday, and get a script ready for me.

DAVID: Did the scripts usually have to be in Monday morning?

JULES: Not necessarily, but Felix would work better on the weekend.

DAVID: Did he work better sober or drunk?

JULES: It didn't bother him to inhale. He didn't get blithering drunk.

DAVID: Was he funnier when he had a few?

JULES: No, because writing comedies is not just funny. You can make them cry easier than you can make them laugh. Felix had fun drinking, but he didn't do this all the time. When I needed him, he'd lay off. He wasn't drunk from a week until next month. He would work very diligently, and as a human being, he was a very sweet, lovable man. A great comedy writer.

If Clyde needed this kind of management yet, White didn't mention it. On October 1, 1935, he handed in his first script, for a Three Stooges short called *Three Little Beers*. Two weeks later, as Del Lord directed it, White picked up Clyde's option. He was a Stooges writer now.

Writing for Larry, Curly, and Moe required a drastic change in tone. Keaton responded to tribulations with stoicism; Lloyd, with optimism. Laurel and Hardy were boneheaded, but looked out for each other; even W. C. Fields, a genuine misanthrope, was smart, and would usually just as soon be left alone. The Stooges were something else, a perfect storm of stupidity and viciousness. A Keaton or Lloyd stunt relied on miraculous escapes; the paradigmatic Keaton stunt was the moment in *Steamboat Bill Jr.* when the brick façade of an entire house collapses on Keaton's head, with a window precisely placed so that Keaton emerges without a scratch. For the Stooges, the house never missed and the House always won. Although the Stooges jump time periods and locations from short to short—the Old West, medieval times, high society—each story is positively rudimentary. Screenplays for Stooges shorts exist to put Larry, Curly, and Moe in situations where they can whale on their surroundings and each other; everything else is filler. By this time Clyde had a little experience with houses collapsing on his head, and he embraced the new style immediately, as *Three Little Beers* shows. The Stooges are new men at a brewery, which gives them the opportunity to drop barrels on heads from great heights; asked to deliver beer to a golf course, they end up playing, which lets them hit people in the heads with golf balls, do laundry in the ball-washer, and destroy the grounds. That's it; that's the plot.

Clyde's scripts for Columbia are finally formatted like modern screenplays: sound had fully entered the production pipeline. But if the format had entered the modern era, the content was mired in the past. In the finale, the Stooges accidentally dump a truck's worth of beer barrels on a steep hill and run to avoid them, which Keaton had done only a few years earlier in MGM's *What! No Beer?* (The barrels were themselves a reworking of a gag with rolling boulders in *Seven Chances*, which Clyde had helped write.) For once, the Stooges version of the gag is better than the original, but the reused gags Clyde had fallen back on were becoming central to his work.

This wasn't a secret, and at Columbia it was practically a matter of policy. Even before the Stooges started reusing their own material, they freely took other people's, and although Clyde would eventually be brought down by the practice, at least at first he wasn't even the worst offender. Nineteen thirty-five's *Uncivil War-riors*, written by Felix Adler and directed by Del Lord, features a scene in which the Stooges get past a guard by telling him they are searching for Charlie, who "walks like this," then imitate his silly walk until they are far enough away to run. This would become a running gag in the Stooges shorts, but it wasn't theirs to begin with—it's lifted from *Feet First*. That same year, in *Restless Knights*, written Felix Adler and directed by Charles Lamont, Adler steals a chase scene from *Welcome Danger*, of all places. And in *Pardon My Scotch*, written by Andrew Bennison and directed by Del Lord—again, these are all just from 1935—Curly briefly recreates Charlie Chaplin's dance of the bread rolls from *The Gold Rush*, one of the most famous gags ever filmed. Reusing gags wasn't something only the Stooges did, either: Chaplin took the bread roll dance from Fatty Arbuckle and Buster Keaton's 1917 short *The Rough House*.

In fact, given the shoddy preservation status of most early film, to say nothing of vaudeville, it's difficult to point to any particular appearance of a gag as original. Curly mistakenly eats a powder puff in Clyde's *Three Sappy People*, just like Robert Woolsey in Clyde's *Everything's Rosie*, just like Harold Lloyd in Clyde's *For Heaven's Sake*. But Harry Langdon also eats a powder puff in 1924's *Picking Peaches*, as does Larry Semon in 1922's *The Show*, neither of which Clyde had anything to do with. (Semon's version is slightly different in that he knows he is eating a powder puff and finds it delicious; film historian Anthony Balducci has written a detailed family tree for this bit, tracing the origin of the "forced to eat something inedible for reasons of politeness" aspect to a mothballs-in-a-candy-box bit in Harold Lloyd's 1922 film *Grandma's Boy*.) Perhaps some long-forgotten vaudevillian came up with the idea. These aren't exactly homages and they aren't exactly plagiarism, but they were common practice and neither Clyde nor Columbia were the only offenders.

Clyde wrote two more Stooges shorts in early 1936: *Half Shot Shooters* (the Stooges ruin artillery practice!) and *Whoops, I'm an Indian!* (the Stooges ruin Native American culture!) but in the summer, Harold Lloyd hired him back once more. *The Cat's Paw*, made with Lloyd's new, efficient, Clyde-Bruckman-free production organization, had failed utterly at the box office. So Lloyd had pivoted again, making *The Milky Way* at Paramount on salary instead of self-producing. Paramount had bought the play with Lloyd in mind, and paired him with their best comedy director, Leo McCarey, who'd risen far since he'd worked with Clyde in the early days of Laurel and Hardy. But McCarey could do nothing to slow Lloyd's decline. *The Milky Way* was a critical success but a box-office flop.

So over the summer of 1936, Lloyd buckled down and tried a different tack: writing his own material. Working with Francis Cockrell, Lloyd hammered out a treatment about a commoner who married into nobility that was 15,000 words long *after* it had been "whittled down." Lloyd hoped to have the film in front of cameras by November 1, and was having a custom stage built at General Service Studios (Hollywood Center Studios today) for use by the production. In hopes of speeding the process, he rehired Clyde, Felix Adler, and Eddie Moran, and set them to work with Francis Cockrell and Grover Jones turning the lengthy treatment into a screenplay. Somewhat ominously, given Clyde and Felix's taste for liquor, they set to work at the Bel-Air Bay Club in Pacific Palisades, a private club with an ocean view and plenty to drink. Clyde's pay had dropped to $450 a week, and he only lasted two weeks before being let go in another one of Lloyd's "temporary layoffs."

This time it really was temporary. Clyde spent October writing another Stooges short—*Grips, Grunts, and Groans* (the Stooges ruin a wrestling match!)—and returned to work with Lloyd on October 26. November 1 was out, but Lloyd still hoped to begin shooting in early December. His distribution deal with Paramount required him to make two films a year, and he was already falling behind. But as Clyde and the rest of the staff rushed through revisions, they were overtaken by history.

Rumors about British King Edward VIII's relationship with Wallis Simpson had been circulating for months, but when news broke on October 14 that Simpson was divorcing her second husband, everything became public. On October 17, the *Washington Post* reported that the King would marry Simpson "at any cost," including abdication. A Harold Lloyd film about an American marrying into royalty suddenly seemed uncomfortably close to reality. By November 14, when Lloyd let Clyde go again, the United Kingdom was in an all-out crisis. Lloyd may have been planning to wait to see how everything shook out, but only days after Edward VIII's abdication in December, the *Los Angeles Times* reported that no one in Hollywood would touch the story for fear of offending audiences across the United Kingdom. It was too delicate, and in the age of talkies, foreign receipts across the English-speaking world were becoming too important. Harold Lloyd's office, contacted for the story, claimed that everything was proceeding as planned on his new film, but within days announced he'd abandoned it "out of deference to the people of the British Empire."

Clyde began 1937 by returning to Columbia, writing *3 Dumb*

Clucks in January (the Stooges ruin their father's wedding to a gold-digger!) In February, he and Mark Kelly, the one-time sports-writer who'd replaced him at *Examiner*, were signed by Paramount to write the screenplay for a film called *Cuckoo College*, from a story by Ted Lesser. Jack Benny was attached to star, Leo McCarey to direct, but the film never happened. It was most likely a casualty of McCarey's masterpiece *Make Way for Tomorrow*, which did poorly enough on its release that May that Paramount immediately loaned McCarey out to Columbia—the main studio, not the short subject ghetto where Clyde was working. It was Paramount's loss: McCarey made *The Awful Truth* at Columbia, for which he won the Academy Award for Best Director. On his return, he asked Paramount to let him out of his contract. If audiences had embraced *Make Way for Tomorrow*, the follow-up to one of the most sublime films ever made about mortality might have been called *Cuckoo College*. But it wasn't to be.

Once more, Clyde picked up a Stooges assignment at Columbia, *Cash and Carry* (the Stooges ruin a treasure hunt!). In the summer, Lloyd had finally picked himself up from the Wallis Simpson fiasco and was ready to work on his next film for Paramount, *Professor Beware*, already months behind schedule. Clyde went on payroll again on June 29, 1937, the day before his forty-third birthday. His pay card shows he was initially hired at $400 a week; this was then hand-corrected to $450, and production manager John L. Murphy signed off and wrote "OK," so perhaps Clyde had to request the already-lowered rate he'd been getting in 1936. After several more months of work on the screenplay, a story about an Egyptologist on a cross-country flight from the law, production started in late November. On December 1, the company made its way to Kernville, California, for location shooting. Lloyd had hired Elliot Nugent to direct, but Clyde was assigned second unit work—probably the last time he was behind a camera.

The press releases put out during the production of *Professor Beware* show Lloyd's beleaguered public relations man, John Summer, gamely trying to put a positive spin on what seems like a miserable experience for everyone involved. There are the usual puff pieces: the film company introducing the latest dances to the grateful residents of Kernville; Harold Lloyd talking about his favorite comedies (one of them was Clyde's *The Battle of the Century*). There's also the tidbit that December sunsets plus shooting at the base of a hill meant the light was unusable after 3:30 in the afternoon, so work began at 5:30 every morning. Then on December 9, the rains came. Summer issued a release reassuring the public that the production would still be on schedule. As the rain continued, he found a story of Hollywood ingenuity: the rain-bound production had jerry-rigged a sound stage in a garage, using blankets and tarps to muffle the sound of rain on the roof. The release ends on an up note: the cast

> . . . performed in the garage-studio with the same effectiveness they would have in the most modern stage in Hollywood.

Summer also found a nice modern-technology angle when the company, unable to get accurate local weather reports, enlisted the help of an army air force pilot stranded in Scovern Hot Springs who had access to military weather bulletins. But he couldn't find an upside in the story of half the cast coming down with the flu (assistant cameraman Eddie Adams had to be rushed by ambulance all the way to Los Angeles). Or the story about a wildcat taking refuge from the rain in actor Lionel Stander's cabin at the Mountain Inn. By the time Harold Lloyd's trailer reportedly caught fire, it must have seemed like a wrath-of-God situation, and the production returned to shoot interiors in Van Nuys on December 16. Although *Professor Beware* continued shooting until the beginning of March, Clyde was done on January 8, except for a two-week stint in mid-February for a return trip to Kernville. (It rained.) At least this time, unlike 1933, Harold Lloyd hadn't let him go two days before Christmas. He might have had a self-serving reason to keep him through the New Year: as another of the press releases reveals, this time around Clyde had managed to use his sportswriting connections to get Lloyd tickets to the Rose Bowl.

But perhaps the real story in the *Professor Beware* press releases is what became of them—outside of the nearby *Bakersfield Californian*, which used a small amount of the material in their regular "Kernville" column, almost no one ran any of them. The *Washington Post* published the story about the Army assisting with weather reports, and the *Daily Tribune* of Ames, Iowa, unaccountably ran an undated two sentences about Lloyd's Kernville trip in April of 1938 (it must have been an exceptionally slow news day, even for Ames, Iowa), but for the most part the releases were shipped off into the void. The public just didn't seem to care that much about what Harold Lloyd was up to anymore.

Their indifference was confirmed when *Professor Beware* was released that summer. The film is neither very bad nor very good; it's ostensibly one of Lloyd's stunt comedies, but the most impressive stunt—a bit with Lloyd and two hoboing companions sprinting backward across the top of a moving train to avoid an oncoming tunnel—is clearly done with stuntmen and rear projection. Lloyd was already using stuntmen by *Feet First*, but the execution here is graceless: It's more reminiscent of W. C. Fields chasing a tire across a railroad bridge than it is Keaton's train acrobatics in *The General*. There are highlights: Raymond Walburn is very funny as a con artist Lloyd meets on his journeys. (He claims to be a judge; asked what sort of judge he is, he replies, "Erstwhile.") And Lloyd's performance has none of the obvious problems of his early sound work—although, by 1938, the year of *Bringing Up Baby*, an adequate performance in the role of awkward professor wasn't really adequate at all. Audiences couldn't be bothered, and *Professor Beware* was an indisputable flop. Lloyd, having put his own money into the production when Paramount's initial funds were spent, took a personal loss of $100,000. When the film wrapped, Lloyd was still planning to finally ramp up production to the two films a year he'd been eternally promising, immediately hiring Delmer Daves to start writing his next vehicle. The box-office receipts put an end to that; he wouldn't release another film until 1947.

And so Clyde went back to Columbia and, as it happened, to Buster Keaton.

BONFIRE

Although they'd remained friends, Clyde hadn't worked with Buster Keaton since *The Cameraman*, and the intervening years had not been kind. As MGM took more and more control of his career, he'd also lost more and more control of his personal life and his drinking. In 1930 he'd transitioned to sound with *Free and Easy*, a backstage comedy made by people suffering under the misapprehension that audiences had been waiting all these years for Keaton to sing and dance. Misapprehension is actually the wrong word; as with Lloyd's *Welcome Danger*, the film was a financial success despite being no good, as were those that followed. It was difficult for Keaton to convince anyone at MGM they were putting him in increasingly terrible movies (they were) when they kept making money. He told Rudi Blesh later about the frustrating paralysis he felt when MGM assigned him projects that didn't serve his talent:

> "I knew before the camera turned on the first scene that we had the perfect foundation for a stinker. And by now, I couldn't tell anyone

anything. They had the one answer for it all. 'What's happened to Keaton? Nice guy, but he's slipping.'

"So—I slipped. I did what so many others have done. I started to drink. And that's when I blew it."

His home life with Natalie Talmadge was no better, and his drinking didn't help. Talmadge put up with the scandal when her husband got into a brawl in his MGM bungalow with a young actress but was less forgiving when Keaton, after a fight, took their two sons on a trip to Mexico she'd opposed. She contacted the D.A.'s office in San Diego and had him stopped at the border, accused of kidnapping. Buster told the papers the point of the trip had been "to show who wears the trousers around our house." She filed for divorce in the summer of 1932, charging him with neglect, and was given custody of their sons. She reportedly told the judge that as a husband, Buster was an excellent comedian.

Natalie also got custody of the Italian Villa and a yacht Buster had recently purchased. Keaton, in the kind of joke that can seem funny to someone who is drunk and angry, responded by buying a custom bus—it had belonged to the head of the Pullman company—equipped with sleeping berths, a kitchen, and a club room. Keaton referred to it as "the land yacht," parked it on the MGM lot, and moved in. *Movie Classic*, a fan magazine with an editorial voice that resembled the *Professor Beware* press releases—putting a bright face on terrible things by adding exclamation points—ran a picture of Keaton dressed as an admiral with his land yacht, and reported one of his favorite pranks with the vehicle was shanghaiing other actors with early calls the next day and taking off for San Francisco or Agua Caliente. "Most of them wish Buster had never heard of a land yacht!" they cheerily wrote. Along similar lines, a piece about the land yacht's very existence—a bitter, public joke about the boat he'd lost to his ex-wife—credits Keaton with inventing "a new kind of divorce—the divorce in which the ex-husband can still kid the ex-wife. And he's making it awfully, awfully hard for Natalie to forget him!"

Having drunk his way out of one marriage, Keaton drank his way into another, marrying Mae Scriven, the nurse he had hired to keep him from drinking, while the two were on a blackout bender in Ensenada in January of 1933. Shortly thereafter MGM finally fired him; he'd taken his Mexican honeymoon in the middle of a film production without telling anyone. He dealt with the news by getting even drunker, eventually getting lost in Kingman, Arizona, where his mother found him doing pratfalls for an audience of tramps gathered around an open fire. The sheriff threw him out of town.

He eventually found his way to Educational Pictures, a rock-bottom studio specializing in two-reelers. There he made some of the worst films of his career. His second marriage failed in 1936; Educational Pictures failed in 1937. In 1938, he was given a job at MGM at the urging of his old coworkers. They hired him as a gag man, working for $200 a week. Even after leveraging a job at Fox to get a raise, his rate was only $300 a week—$150 less than Harold Lloyd was paying Clyde.

So Keaton could be had for a price. When Clyde, back at Columbia, where he'd just finished writing *Three Sappy People* for the Stooges, suggested this to Jules White, he jumped at the chance:

One day Bruckman came to me and said, "Buster Keaton hasn't worked for a couple of years. He's not money hungry and you can make a good deal if you're interested in him." If I was interested in him? I was thrilled at the prospect of having him work for us.

He was also thrilled at the prospect of getting Keaton at a bargain price, as he explained when discussing his hiring process to David Bruskin:

I'd pick up the stars who had refused to work for me when times were good. Now, they'd take whatever salary I offered. . . . I had great respect for them, and I was also sorry that there was such a thing as the top of the ladder.

Keaton, of course, was nowhere near the top of any ladder by this point. White suggested that Clyde help broker the deal, since he "felt Buster would be more comfortable" this way. There was a specific reason Keaton would have been more comfortable with Clyde, however, and it wasn't their longstanding friendship. White and Keaton had crossed paths before, when he was hot off the Dogville Comedies at MGM. He and Zion Myers had directed Keaton in *Sidewalks of New York*, his most financially successful film there, and Keaton had hated them both. As Dogville Comedies producer Harry Rapf's son Maurice Rapf put it, "White was being moved up from dogs to people and they gave him Buster Keaton. You can't blame Keaton for being offended." It wasn't just a question of politics, either: White and Myers had directed Keaton as they had their canine stars. According to Keaton, they

. . . alternated telling me how to walk, how to talk, how to stand, and how to fall—where and when, how fast or slow, how loud or soft. I was Trilby with two Svengalis—MGM had gone to the two-platoon with unlimited substitutions.

But Keaton couldn't afford bad blood, and besides, his old

friend was there. Clyde brokered the deal, announced in March of 1939. Keaton would be paid $1,000 per short, a fortune compared to his work as a gag man, and he and Clyde set to work. Clyde handed in the first script Keaton would make at Columbia, *Pest from the West*, only a few days after the contract was announced.

One reason the script may have been completed so quickly is that it was nothing more than a reworking of *The Invader*, a disastrous film Keaton had made in England in 1935, in which Keaton played a millionaire visiting Mexico who falls for a local. The Columbia version has the distinct advantage of being forty minutes shorter, and has a few good sequences—a scene in which Keaton must dance with Lorna Gray with his feet stuck to the floor offers a glimpse of his old gift for physical comedy—but it was shot in four days and looks it. Keaton would go on to make ten shorts for Columbia between 1939 and 1941 before swearing off two-reelers forever; Clyde wrote seven of them. (He received screen credit for *She's Oil Mine*, although only Felix Adler's name is on the screenplay.)

These are not examples of Buster or Clyde's best work, and some of them, particularly *Mooching Through Georgia*, are positively terrible. But landing Keaton put Clyde in Jules White's good graces, and he began to get other assignments: more Stooges shorts, but also an Andy Clyde film and an assignment creating a new character for Noah Beery Jr. in the summer of 1939. The result, *Glove Slingers*, which he wrote with L. A. Sarecky according to the screenplay even though he didn't receive screen credit, turned into an eleven-film series. Clyde got screen credit for the sequel, 1940's *Pleased to Mitt You*, which contains a variation on the powder puff gag he'd already used so many times before. This time around it's a feather-stuffed cushion mistaken for a cake, and the routine has been stretched to an excruciating four minutes. The best response to these shorts is baked right into *Pleased to Mitt You*: "Isn't this funny?" Doris Donaldson's character says after a particularly bad joke. "It's corny," scoffs John Kellogg. He's the villain, but he's not wrong.[1]

That fall, Clyde and Felix Adler finally found a subject well suited to the Stooges' particular brand of humor. Over the summer, Charlie Chaplin announced that he had begun work on *The Great Dictator*, and in August, after working in secret, he'd released the first stills. The production was budgeted at more than two million, all of it Chaplin's. As it happened, Moe Howard looked a little like Hitler, and embodying inchoate rage was basically his entire comedic range. Given Columbia's fast, cheap aesthetic, Clyde and Felix had a chance to beat Chaplin to the punch. They took it.

By late October, they'd written a script, and *You Nazty Spy!* was in theaters by January of 1940. Chaplin wouldn't release his film until that October. *The Great Dictator*, as everyone knows, is a masterpiece; *You Nazty Spy!* is . . . something else. The Stooges are paperhangers pushed by arms dealers (Ixnay, Onay, and Amscray) into staging a coup in the country of Moronika. Moe plays Hitler (Moe Hailstone), Curly plays Goering (Curly Gallstone), and Larry plays Goebbels (Larry Pebble), rising to power under the populist slogan "Moronika for Morons." After battling a spy named Mattie Herring and sending a peasant to a "Concentrated Camp," they are accidentally eaten by the lions Moe has procured to throw people to. Although *The Great Dictator* is the better-made film, the Stooges' moronic barbarity was unquestionably a

---

1. Clyde must have disagreed; he used the feather gag again in *The Naughty Nineties* and *Three Hams on Rye*.

more fitting approach to take to the Nazis. Chaplin couldn't help imbuing Adenoid Hynkel, his version of Hitler, with some of his own grace and beauty, as in the famous scene in which he delicately bats an inflated globe around the room. What's more, *The Great Dictator* is ultimately optimistic about humanity, as can be seen in its climactic radio address:

> We are coming out of the darkness into the light! We are coming into a new world; a kindlier world, where men will rise above their hate, their greed, and brutality. . . . The soul of man has been given wings and at last he is beginning to fly. He is flying into the rainbow! Into the light of hope, into the future!

Needless to say, subsequent events of the 1940s did little to validate Chaplin's prediction. *You Nazty Spy!* got nowhere near the attention given Chaplin's film, but it arrived first, and it made enough of a stir to merit a sequel, *I'll Never Heil Again*, which Clyde and Felix wrote in March of 1941. In this version, they took direct aim at Chaplin, restaging his globe dance as a brutal touch-football match between Hailstone, Gallstone, and Pebble and representatives of the rest of the "Axle Powers." (In a detail that somehow made it past the Hays Office, this is pronounced "Ax-hole Powers.") It's racist, imbecilic, mean-spirited, and completely lacking any redeeming graces—the perfect embodiment of the cruel and stupid political forces that were busy transforming the world into an abattoir. Moronika for Morons.

But whatever credit Clyde deserves for being ahead of the political curve when it came to Nazis is colored by the fact that he also wrote *The Yoke's on Me*, one of the Stooges' most reprehensible efforts. Like most of the country, Clyde had abandoned his father's Republicanism: In 1944, he'd join a "Writers for Roosevelt" group, but as early as the script for 1937's *Cash and Carry*, he and co-writer Elwood Ullman gave Roosevelt a cameo (in an Oval Office with a desk facing away from the door so that only the back of his head is on camera) to help a crippled orphan obtain money for a necessary operation. In *The Yoke's on Me*, written in October of 1943, Clyde added an unnecessary subplot involving Roosevelt's most shameful action as president: the internment of Japanese-American citizens, which had begun in the spring of 1942.

The setup isn't out of the ordinary. The Stooges flunk a draft board medical examination and decide to help the war effort by becoming farmers. But on the farm, in addition to the expected tomfoolery with farming implements and livestock, they are beset by escapees from a nearby internment camp: buck-toothed stereotypes whose treacherous sabotage plan includes wearing jack-o'-lanterns on their heads. For reasons too stupid to explain in detail, the Stooges end up killing all of them with a gunpowder-laced ostrich egg. The gag is bad, but the topper is appalling—instead of cutting away from the explosion, the Stooges wander through a barn strewn with Japanese corpses. Or rather, Japanese-American corpses, since Roosevelt's detainees were citizens. The worst thing about the subplot is, there's no good reason for it to have been there to begin with: *The Yoke's on Me* is essentially a farming story. And Clyde, who'd been thrown in jail for being German during World War I, might have known better.

In the meantime, Clyde's financial situation had become desperate. The house on Elm Drive, once a symbol of his status as a director, had become an albatross. He'd briefly tried to sell it in 1935 before landing *Spring Tonic*, and had sporadically tried to sell it in the ensuing years, listing it for a few days in November of 1936, and then again from August through October of 1937. In the fall of 1940, the listings started to run almost daily. It didn't sell, so Clyde started the New Year with a new real estate agent and more creative listings. One day it was "a VERY REAL BUY," the next it was "THE HOUSE OF IDEAS / For 100% comfort." Even that didn't work, and in April Clyde placed his own ads, practically begging to have it taken off his hands: "WANT reasonable offer or accept some trade." That did it. On April 27 and 28 of 1941, Clyde and Gladys had a sad little auction at their home. As the ads explained, "HOUSE SOLD. MUST VACATE." They sold the piano, most of the books, a Widicomb bedroom set, and even the carpet. But despite outward appearances, this was a positive step. Clyde and Gladys had barely been managing to pay the interest on the mortgage in Beverly Hills: Westwood, where they lived briefly on Malcolm Avenue before settling at 1826 Prosser, was a neighborhood they could afford, especially if Clyde could land steadier work than Columbia. The solution, oddly enough, turned out to be musicals.

SONG AND DANCE MAN

In the summer of 1941, Clyde got one last shot at cinematic respectability. Barring an incredible stroke of luck (or, unlikelier still, the miraculous revival of Keaton or Lloyd's career), there was little chance of returning to the prestige pictures he'd worked on in his heyday. But there was a middle ground between that and the Stooges' slapstick ghetto: B-pictures. These had grown increasingly important over the course of the 1930s, to the point that they were slowly but surely throttling the short subject departments, including Columbia's. The problem—and for Clyde, the temporary solution—was double features.

The practice of showing a second cheaper, shorter feature on a single bill had begun, paradoxically, because studios were doing too much to promote their A-features. Studios still owned their own theater chains—the antitrust case that forced them to divest wouldn't be settled until 1948—and at a studio-owned theater, the main feature would often include not only a short and news-reel, but a live stage show. Independently owned theaters didn't have the means for this sort of foofaraw, and, under no obligation to limit themselves to any one studio's product, began booking cheap features to compete. Studios loathed the practice, which meant splitting box-office receipts and associating their prestige films in the public's mind with the cheaper product they were shown with. The studios waged a PR campaign against the practice with the same restraint and calm with which they'd later approach VCRs and internet piracy: they branded it "the double feature evil," and, in a 1937 *Motion Picture Herald* editorial, depicted it as a giant octopus strangling audience and exhibitor alike.

In fact, the tentacles were wrapped around the short subject studios. With two features on the same bill, there was little time to show a twenty-minute short film, and demand began to drop. Mack Sennett's bankruptcy had mostly been caused by losing his distribution deal with Paramount due to the larger studio's financial woes, but no one else wanted Sennett shorts either. Al Christie folded his studio into Educational Pictures; Educational went out of business. Hal Roach saw which way the wind was blowing and began a transition to features in 1936. That left Columbia, which had entered the field late, in 1933, but had both an A- and B-feature unit to support the shorts department.

Actually, they mostly had a B-feature unit: they only made a few A-features each year, which were used to force exhibitors to block-book the cheaper fare. As Harry Cohn supposedly put it, "I want one good picture a year, and I won't let an exhibitor have it unless he takes the bread-and-butter product, the *Boston Blackies*, the *Blondies*, the low-budget westerns and the rest of the junk we make." Clyde had been working at the very bottom level of this hierarchy. But in the summer of 1941, he managed to briefly climb up a rung, working with Warren Wilson on the story for one of the studio's most successful B-franchises: *Blondie*. Chic Young's comic strip had debuted in 1930; Columbia made the first *Blondie* film late in 1938. By 1941, not even three years later, they were making the tenth. (Columbia eventually made twenty-eight *Blondie* films before losing the rights to the strip in 1950.) The films, which starred Penny Singleton and Arthur Lake, were made quickly and cheaply, but compared to the Stooges' shorts they were lavish.

It's not really clear how Clyde talked his way onto *Blondie Goes to College*, since the B-picture unit was in a different facility a few miles away and producer Robert Sparks didn't work in shorts. But however it happened, Sparks hired him, Lou Breslow wrote a screenplay from the story Clyde and Warren Wilson worked out, and, if the resulting film isn't exactly good, it's also not terrible. (It might have more aptly been titled *Blondie Goes to "College,"* however, because the story features a climactic crew race that will be familiar to anyone who's seen Buster Keaton's *College*.) Larry Parks, Janet Blair, and Lloyd Bridges all have supporting roles, but the highlight is probably double-talk comedian Cliff Nazarro as a college professor delivering an incomprehensible lecture. *Blondie Goes to College* was released in January of 1942 to more or less indifferent reviews, and Clyde continued working on shorts.

And double features continued to choke the remaining life out of the department. That spring the *Los Angeles Times* noted with surprise that two-reel comedies were still being made at all, especially since "the faithful standbys go on doing the same old things in the same old way." Hugh McCollum, interviewed for the piece, lamented his inability to get new talent interested in appearing in two-reelers:

Most "legitimate" players are leery of their reputations and shy away from the lowly banana peel. "We could 'build' people like Alan Mowbray, Joan Davis, and Una Merkel, for instance," he added, "but they won't let us—too scared."

But those functions had been taken over by B-pictures; it was clear Clyde was working in a cinematic dead letter office. In 1943, he found a way out. His *Blondie* cowriter, Warren Wilson, had moved on from Columbia and landed at Universal, in a unit that specialized in B-musicals. He brought Clyde along with him to write the script for a musical called *Honeymoon Lodge*.

The film, which Edward Lilley would direct, is by design no great piece of screenwriting; the plot only exists to string together musical numbers. And they're definitely B-picture musical numbers: Ozzie Nelson and Harriet Hilliard—at the time more famous as bandleader and singer than as film personalities—do several songs, and there's an entirely unmotivated performance of an Ink Spots cover at a railway station. But the plot is different from anything Clyde had written before, and seems more personal. *Honeymoon Lodge* is closer to screwball comedy than it is to the Stooges (or, indeed, to Keaton or Lloyd): the characters are actual humans instead of comic archetypes. Stars David Bruce and June Vincent play a playwright and his wife; their arguments over Bruce's late-night smoking while writing feel like something Clyde might have experienced, as opposed to, say, ruining a high society party with a pie fight. Of course, biographical parallels do nothing to improve the film, which is mediocre. But after years of writing slapstick routines that would have fit right in at Keystone, Clyde was finally attempting to change with the times.

Even with a mediocre film, being on the right side of the Double Feature Evil was an immediate step up. *Honeymoon Lodge* played at the Pantages, probably the nicest theater to show Clyde's work in years, even if it was bizarrely paired with Edward Dmytryk's anti-Japanese propaganda film *Behind the Rising Sun*. And *Honeymoon Lodge* gave him something he hadn't had since drinking away his directorial career: respectability. *Variety* reported on production details of Columbia shorts but rarely stooped to reviewing them. Reviews for *Honeymoon Lodge* were basically of the "mostly harmless" sort (*Variety* raved that it "pleasantly accomplishes goal it reaches for—wholesome entertainment"), but his name was back in the conversation. And although these films didn't have stars, while the Columbia shorts were a home of last resort for down-and-out actors, the Universal B-musicals were a testing ground for talent the studio thought might make the jump to the A-list. So when Universal brought him on board the regular writing staff, he had a job with a future, for the first time in years.

Clyde's $275 a week from Universal wasn't in the same league as what he'd been making in his heyday; it wasn't even what Harold Lloyd paid him for *Professor Beware*. But it was still a tremendous amount of money: $3,667 a week in 2015 dollars, and being paid weekly instead of by the script meant a stable income. Between 1943 and 1945 he worked on nine films at Universal: *So's Your Uncle* and *Swingtime Johnny* in 1943; *Week-End Pass, Moon Over Las Vegas, Twilight on the Prairie*, and *South of Dixie* in 1944; *She Gets Her Man, Under Western Skies*, and *Her Lucky Night* in 1945. His level of involvement varied from one film to another; for the Andrews Sisters vehicles *Swingtime Johnny* and *Her Lucky Night*, he was the only writer, although Warren Wilson received story credit. For other films like *So's Your Uncle*, he was brought in to punch up other writers' scripts with gag material. As was routine for him by now, some of these gags were old ones. For *So's Your Uncle*, he inserted the Magician's Coat gag he'd created for *Movie Crazy*. This wasn't a simple matter of eating a powder puff: Clyde rewrote the entire sequence, shot for shot. Still, the principle was the same, and neither he nor anyone at Universal anticipated any trouble. In fact, he'd already used it at Columbia, for the Stooges short *Loco Boy Makes Good*. But as he'd soon find out, now that he was finally out of the two-reel ghetto, people were watching.

None of these were great films, but Universal was happy with the work he was doing, and in 1944 they began using him on bigger pictures. Though he wasn't credited, he worked on *In Society* for Bud Abbott and Lou Costello, two of Universal's biggest stars. That fall, he was assigned to *She Gets Her Man*, a comedy murder mystery for comedienne Joan Davis, whom Universal was making a big push for. Clyde's plot was byzantine but moved quickly, and Davis knocked it out of the park. As *Variety*'s review made clear, the film could have been a springboard to the A-list for both the star and writer:

> Universal has a winner here which it will sell strictly as an A production . . . Star offers one of her topnotch performances in this driving comedy character part setting her up definitely as big-time performer after a long series of B picture appearances.

After so many years in freefall, Universal seemed like a place where Clyde—at fifty years of age—might begin to climb once more, or at least coast to a soft landing. Naturally, Harold Lloyd threw him an anvil.

SPECIAL DAMAGES

Clyde's ruination began in March of 1945, when Harold Lloyd and his business manager, Jack Murphy, went to the movies. The film was *So's Your Uncle*—although Lloyd had been tipped off that the film used portions of his work, he was horrified to see the entire Magician's Coat sequence from *Movie Crazy*. A stolen punch line would have been one thing, but this was a lengthy part of the film in which every carefully worked-out payoff was duplicated, a sequence of gags Lloyd had so expertly executed the first time around that the *Los Angeles Times* had dedicated an entire article to it. Adding insult to injury, Lloyd thought the movie was terrible. Soon after, he watched *She Gets Her Man*, where he discovered a routine from *Welcome Danger*, and *Her Lucky Night*, which had a gag that went all the way back to *The Freshman*. All these films had one thing in common: they were written by Clyde Bruckman.

Furious, Lloyd called his attorney, Harold A. Fendler, who had defended him in a previous copyright suit. After going through the necessary formalities of notifying Universal and asking them to stop showing the films, Lloyd filed three lawsuits in the U.S. District Court on the same day, April 4, 1945, against Clyde, Universal, and parties to be named later. These suits would ultimately expand the copyright protections for motion pictures—as hard as they fought him, Universal ended up indirectly benefitting from Lloyd's litigiousness. But the lawsuits had no silver lining for Clyde, who would emerge with his career—foundering since *Man on the Flying Trapeze*—reduced to an unsalvageable wreck. And they didn't do Harold Lloyd much good, either.

The first case covered the sequences in *So's Your Uncle* that had been taken from *Movie Crazy*. Lloyd wanted $200,000 in general damages, $200,000 in special damages, covering the money he felt he had lost in potential revenue from remaking or rereleasing *Movie Crazy*, plus another $40,000 in attorney's fees. In addition, Lloyd requested that all prints and the original negatives of *So's Your Uncle* be impounded by the court and destroyed. For the gags in *Welcome Danger* taken from *She Gets Her Man*, Lloyd sought $150,000 in general damages, $150,000 in special damages for remake and reissue rights, $25,000 in attorney's fees, and, again, destruction of all prints and negatives. And for ripping off *The Freshman*, the most financially successful of the films, in *Her Lucky Night*, Lloyd asked for a whopping $500,000 in general damages, $500,000 in special damages, $50,000 in attorney's fees, and—one more time—destruction of all prints and negatives. Total bill: $1,815,000.

It was not the first time Lloyd had dealt with copyright law, but it was the first time he'd been the plaintiff. In January of 1926, Harold Lloyd had been sued by short story writer H. C. Witwer for $250,000 over claims that *The Freshman* had been based on his 1915 short story "The Emancipation of Rodney," which he'd shown to Lloyd as early as 1923. That initial case was dismissed when it became apparent that Witwer no longer owned the copyright to his own story because he'd sold it to *The Popular Magazine* (one of Clyde's venues back in his short fiction days—they'd even had a story in the same issue). Witwer bided his time and let *The Freshman* rack up profits until April of 1929, when he bought back his copyright and sued Lloyd for $2,300,000, nearly ten times as much. Most sources say Fendler successfully defended this case on appeal, but the decisions themselves seem to indicate otherwise. Lloyd lost the original case outright in 1930—though Witwer had died by the time a decision was reached, his wife carried on the legal battle—and was ordered to hand over every dime of *The Freshman*'s profits since three years before the filing of the lawsuit. Fendler managed to have the financial part of the decision overturned on appeal in 1933, but the Ninth Circuit upheld the original court's ruling that Witwer's copyright had been infringed: all negatives and prints of *The Freshman* were to be handed over to the U.S. Marshals to be destroyed. That might have been less expensive for Lloyd than the lower court's holding, but it would have been a disaster for film history. It's unclear if any prints were actually destroyed—the petition for writ of certiorari to the Supreme Court was dismissed per stipulation of counsel, which probably means Lloyd came to some sort of settlement with the Witwer estate. In any event, he had a clear enough copyright to *The Freshman* by 1945 that he felt comfortable suing to protect it. But the main result of the Witwer case was that Harold Lloyd was justifiably wary of waging a long, expensive legal battle with no promise of victory.

Unfortunately for him, Universal was extremely comfortable with drawing out the proceedings, hoping Lloyd would run out of money. Clyde was named separately in the suit and had his own lawyers, but the two legal teams worked closely together, and from the very beginning did everything they could to stall. Lloyd's cases involving *Movie Crazy* and *Welcome Danger* were both assigned to Judge Benjamin Harrison; *The Freshman* went to Judge Harry A. Hollzer. For any point of law, Clyde's attorneys would file one motion in all three cases, then Universal's attorneys would file a slightly different one, leaving Fendler to respond six times. (At one point, the two judges had to issue parallel orders to *re-file* a motion that had been mistakenly sent to the wrong courtroom.) And both legal teams filed motions contesting *everything*—including a demand that Lloyd's attorneys explain, in detail, why they hadn't somehow attached prints of *Movie Crazy* and *So's Your Uncle* to their original complaint. Fendler responded incredulously (and in triplicate):

> It is obvious that it is "impracticable" to attach ten thousand feet of valuable, highly inflammable celluloid film to a complaint or to file the same where there are no facilities to store it.

Fendler gave nearly as good as he got, however, asking Universal to produce a list of every single showtime at every single theater *So's Your Uncle* had ever played, right before the July 4 holiday. Lloyd and Fendler made one critical misstep early in the case: Lloyd was angry enough about what he viewed as his stolen property that he arranged for U.S. Attorney Charles H. Carr to see the films to investigate criminal charges. Carr thought it might be worth pursuing, and Lloyd, mistakenly thinking it would improve his bargaining position and possibly force a settlement, let Clyde and Universal both know there was a chance they'd be charged with a crime. This turned out to be perversely convenient for them, because Lloyd was simultaneously serving them with subpoenas to be deposed for the civil case.

The right to remain silent in a civil deposition can only be invoked if the deponent fears criminal consequences—which is remarkably easy to demonstrate if the opposing litigant is talking to the U.S. Attorney and threatening criminal consequences. So on April 28, only a few weeks after the initial complaint, Clyde, producer Warren Wilson, and Universal executive Edward Muhl arrived promptly at their appointed locations downtown, were sworn in, politely answered their first question—"What is your name?"—and then declined to answer anything else on the advice of counsel. (Their attorneys filed motions to quash the subpoenas the same morning, after scheduling Muhl and Bruckman's depositions at different locations to thin Fendler's staff as much as possible so that no one would be available to respond to the motions.)

For Lloyd, it was very important that depositions be taken immediately. According to one of his filings, it was customary when studios were sued for copyright infringement to hire literary experts to scour the public domain, find alternative sources their writers might have drawn from, and brief their witnesses to claim to have used these in depositions. Only by deposing Clyde before anyone had time to prepare him could Lloyd be sure of untainted testimony. Universal, of course, claimed to have never heard of anyone doing anything of the sort. But Lloyd had good reason to believe otherwise: His company had taken almost exactly the same shady approach in 1934, when a writer named Morgan Wallace accused Lloyd of stealing the plot of *The Cat's Paw* from his play *Congratulations*.

The similarities between *The Cat's Paw* and *Congratulations* seem to have been a meaningless coincidence, but after losing so much time and money fighting Witwer, Lloyd wasn't taking any chances. Through his general manager, Creed Neeper, he hired a literary expert named Roden to prepare a report to see if the case had any merit. When Roden reported the play and film were "practically identical," Neeper set up a lunch under false pretenses to see if he could coax him into changing his report without outright coaching him, as he explained in a letter to William Fraser:

> I do feel that there is a chance Mr. Roden didn't mean to make the statement quite as strong as that, being for the moment influenced by a desire to do further research work. I feel it would be a good thing for me to have lunch with him tomorrow and in the course of conversation ask him if he thinks the word "identical" is the correct word to use in that statement. If he says "yes" to make no further comment. If he qualifies the statement verbally and indicates his desire (on his own account) to change the report, I shall offer no objection to his doing so.

There's a world of passive-aggression in Neeper's report of their lengthy lunch: "He is a very sociable fellow and we became well acquainted." When Roden stood by his original assessment, Lloyd hired him to produce a second report tracing possible public domain sources for both play and film, just as he would claim Universal was planning to do years later. The idea wasn't to lie in depositions so much as it was to argue that the elements *Congratulations* and *The Cat's Paw* shared had already entered the public domain and couldn't be protected by copyright. But Neeper knew coaching an expert witness wasn't playing fair. Many of his letters—preserved all these years—have closings along the lines of this:

This letter would not be a good thing to have in your files. I hope you will destroy it. I shall not retain a copy.

Wallace dropped his case when it became apparent that Lloyd was going to force him to go to court. There's no evidence Lloyd knew what his employees had been up to back in 1934, but in 1945, someone at the company was worried Universal would attempt suspiciously similar legal shenanigans. Things were acrimonious enough that they devolved into a fistfight between opposing counsel before the *Welcome Danger* and *Movie Crazy* cases reached their first hearing on May 14. Judge Harrison was furious, and opened the meeting by expressing his opinion that evading the depositions bordered on contempt of court:

> It looks like horseplay, so far as the court is concerned. I want to say, frankly, if the parties do not answer the questions the Appellate Court is going to have a chance to settle it, because I am going to send somebody to jail.

Lloyd and Fendler eventually got the U.S. Attorney to assert that he was no longer actively pursuing an investigation, and Clyde, Edward Muhl, writers Leonard Lee and Maurice Leo, and director Jean Yarbrough were finally deposed on June 5 in a bungalow at Universal. By then, Lloyd had given up on the *Welcome Danger/She Gets Her Man* case for the time being. The issues of law were substantially the same, the judge was the same, and it was clear that Universal was going to use the same maneuvers to stall and derail things, so on May 28 Fendler asked that the charges be dismissed without prejudice (reserving the right to refile the case after the first had been tried).

But if Universal was able to slow Lloyd down in the first two cases, they were able to nearly stop him completely in the third. As part of the pre-trial agreements—once it became apparent that neither judge wanted inflammable nitrate prints sitting around the courthouse—both sides agreed to make prints of the films in question available to the opposing side. (Universal, unsurprisingly, seems to have delighted in requesting these prints on short notice.) But during one of the many, many screenings of *The Freshman*, Universal's attorney Guy Knupp noticed that the print he'd been provided did not have any on-screen notice of copyright, at the time required by law. If he could show that it had not been included when the film was in theaters, Lloyd didn't have a case. The flurry of motions, affidavits, and eight-by-ten glossies of frames from *The Freshman* that followed are a strange mix of legal wrangling and film archive history.

It turned out that the print Knupp had screened was Harold Lloyd's personal copy, a work print that didn't necessarily match the theatrical version. Lloyd swore that Pathé had added copyright titles when making theatrical prints, but he couldn't prove it without a print, and there weren't any. Universal demanded to see the original negative. Lloyd agreed, but then discovered to his horror that it had been among the films destroyed in a huge nitrate fire in Bound Brook, New Jersey; his personal print might be the last remaining copy. Finally a surviving 16mm print surfaced at the Museum of Modern Art. Just as Lloyd had said, Pathé had included the correct copyright information all along.

Having wasted months on the search for film prints, the lawyers merrily moved on to their fallback position: even if the eventual theatrical release had included a copyright notice, Harold Lloyd's print had been publicly screened first without it, thus invalidating the copyright. They dug up everyone they could find—theater managers, projectionists, old employees, even newspaper editors—to make the case that the work print had been used in "test" screenings that were nevertheless advertised and required purchase of a ticket: in other words, not test screenings at all, but commercial exhibitions. This sort of nonsense delayed the proceedings so long that the judge literally died of old age; Judge Hollzer had a heart attack on January 3, 1946, and died from complications a week and a half later. But by then, Judge Harrison had reached his decision in the parallel case.

In fact, Harrison made up his mind as soon as he watched the films. He didn't have Hollzer's patience for legal wrangling ("I will be frank with you. I think you are just seeing how much work you can make [for] everybody," he told Universal's lawyers), and shepherded the case to trial on September 10, 1945. The opening day's arguments, like so many conversations in Los Angeles, were mostly devoted to a discussion of traffic—how long would it take the judge to reach the Valley to watch *Movie Crazy* and *So's Your Uncle?* He set out the next day, watched both movies in a screening room on the studio lot, and by the next morning the issue was mostly settled in his mind.

> ". . . it is clear to the court . . . that just anybody seeing these pictures would say that one is directly taken from the other...as far as the two pictures are concerned, there is just no use, as a factual matter, arguing with me about that, because there are too many detailed incidents in the sequence in both pictures that clearly indicate that one is copied from the other.

But no one was arguing that Clyde hadn't copied the Magician's Coat sequence. The precise nature of Universal's case was exactly what made it so emotionally brutal to both Harold Lloyd and

Clyde Bruckman, and, ultimately, why it was so professionally devastating. It came in several parts:

- Gags like the Magician's Coat sequence, which did not include plot or dialogue, were not protected by copyright at all—they were properly regarded as "stage business" and, like a dance or magic routine, copyright prohibited anyone reusing Lloyd's actual footage, but not from performing the routine themselves.

- Even if an infringement had occurred, Lloyd had no claim to damages for remake or reissue rights for his films, because they were out of fashion and worthless, and Lloyd himself was old, forgotten, and no longer a star.

- Even if Lloyd were able to remake the films successfully, *Clyde's* work was worthless, because the gags he'd reused were so old, common, and out-of-style that the success or failure of Lloyd's remake would not depend on those sequences.

- Even if *So's Your Uncle* had reduced the value of *Movie Crazy*, it couldn't have reduced it that much, because Clyde had used the same gag in the earlier Three Stooges short *Loco Boy Makes Good* without Lloyd noticing or filing suit, and, in any event, the damages should be properly paid by Columbia, not Universal.

- Even if court rejected all of the other arguments, Lloyd himself had knowingly reused gags in all of his previous films, including *Movie Crazy*, and could hardly ask the court to protect him from his own business practices.

Judge Harrison was interested in none of this, having more or less made up his mind while the projectors were running, but he allowed Clyde and Universal to present their case for the benefit of appellate courts. At one point, facing another lengthy memo from Universal, he expressed his frustration with the case:

I am free to receive any memorandum that counsel wishes; and I hope that however I decide this case it is appealed so that both sides can have the opportunity to spend all the money they want to. As I have expressed myself before, you have decided to wash your linen in public, and I think you should be perfectly willing to pay the bill. And so, as far as I am concerned, I will help you to make your record and I am going to take that into consideration if I grant judgment for the plaintiff in fixing attorney's fees.

And so the case dragged on, through brutal and humiliating depositions and testimony. After the standard questions about his name and position with the Harold Lloyd Corporation, here's how Universal and Clyde's lawyers treated Harold Lloyd—who'd spent the 1930s in desperate denial about his faded popularity—at his deposition:

> Q The plaintiff corporation, I take it, is inactive at the present time?
> A No. It has never been inactive.
> Q It has never been inactive? Well, what are its present activities?

After some flustering from Lloyd about movies he planned to make in the future, the attorneys got to the nut-cutting:

> Q Has the Harold Lloyd Corporation produced a picture within the last year?
> A No.
> Q Did it produce a picture in 1944?
> A No.
> Q Did it produce any in '43?
> A No.
> Q '42?
> A No.

Q When did it last produce a picture?

From there, they moved right along to asking pointed questions about his age. This continued at trial; the first question in the cross-examination was, "Mr. Lloyd, you are 51 years old, I believe?"

Clyde had it even worse. As Lloyd testified at trial, he wasn't even aware of *Loco Boy Makes Good* before he was deposed. For his part, Clyde was not aware that Maurice Leo, his ostensible co-writer on *So's Your Uncle*, had been forced to use Clyde's gags over his own objections until Leo was deposed:

> . . . I was not too enthusiastic over it because I thought it was dated and old-fashioned, but [producer/director Jean Yarbrough] seemed to think that, despite that fact, he wanted to use it and he was the producer and so I used it.

Jean Yarbrough testified to the same effect, recalling that Leo had called Clyde's work "old and hokey." Clyde seemed hurt and baffled that he was being accused of anything; asked why he'd thought he could reuse the Magician's Coat sequence, he responded:

> I felt so honestly because in the 25 years I have been in the business it has been common practice for comedians to borrow, one from the other, various routines. And comedians have always done that. If they hadn't, I think we would all have been out of business a long time ago. And I know we also did that at Mr. Lloyd's, to be perfectly frank.

To that effect, Clyde filed an offer of proof listing no fewer than seven gags in *Welcome Danger* that had been stolen from other films, including Buster Keaton's *The Navigator*, Monty Banks's *Horse Shoes*, and Laurel and Hardy's *Leave 'Em Laughing* (in other words, mostly gags taken from other films Clyde had worked on, although, given the complicated production history of *Welcome Danger*, it wasn't clear if they'd been stolen before he came on board). According to Clyde, Lloyd was well aware of this, and had even secured a print of *Horse Shoes* to study how a particular effect had been achieved. Lloyd denied everything, but it didn't matter anyway, because Judge Harrison saw the whole issue as immaterial—if other people felt Harold Lloyd was reusing their gags, that was a matter for their own lawsuits, not this one. In any event, there was no question that Universal had known what it was doing; Bruckman and Yarbrough agreed that Clyde had specifically suggested they use a gag from *Movie Crazy*.

And so the trial—in essence decided the minute the judge watched *So's Your Uncle*—dragged on until December 17, 1945, including a recess to watch Three Stooges shorts. The court heard from expert witnesses ranging from literary agents to a professional magician there to discuss historical vaudeville routines, and plenty of time was devoted to amateur film criticism from both the witness stand and the bench. One witness testified under oath that *Loco Boy Makes Good* was "one of the worst pictures I have ever seen. I would not understand why any exhibitor would want to show it." On being told that *So's Your Uncle* had played in fewer theaters than most Universal releases, Judge Harrison observed, "I could rather believe that after seeing the picture." ("Yes," conceded Universal's lawyer.) Harrison doesn't seem to have been a Three Stooges fan either ("Gentlemen, I have viewed the Columbia short called *Three Wise Saps*. I feel the record should show that I saw that picture under stipulation of counsel . . ."), but he did have kind words for *Movie Crazy*, telling Lloyd during his testimony, "I would say you were good all the way through."

And in the end, nobody got what they wanted. As he'd said he planned to immediately after seeing the films, Judge Harrison ruled that gags were protectable under copyright and that Clyde had infringed Lloyd's rights by reusing the Magician's Coat sequence. But throughout the trial, he'd scoffed at the value Lloyd assigned to remake rights—"the figures that come out of Hollywood sound like the national debt and they do not register very strongly with this court"—and only awarded him $40,000 in damages, plus $10,000 in attorney's fees. This was barely more than Lloyd had requested for his attorneys alone. Lloyd felt Harrison had been unfairly prejudiced against Hollywood accounting, Clyde and Universal felt that he'd erred in extending copyright protection to gags, and both parties appealed to the Ninth Circuit. Lloyd and Fendler took advantage of their free time while the appeal was pending, filing two suits against Columbia over the Three Stooges shorts they'd discovered during Clyde's deposition. All three outstanding cases, including the one inherited by Judge Jacob Weinberger after Judge Hollzer's death, were put on hold while the courts waited for the Ninth Circuit to rule.

It took more than a year, but on May 12, 1947, the decision came down. Judge Albert Stephens wrote the opinion, affirming Harrison's ruling and expanding copyright protections for motion pictures. In the case of *Movie Crazy* and *So's Your Uncle*, Clyde had reused too much and too exactly:

> Here, we find 57 consecutive scenes lifted almost bodily from the Lloyd product, not just the reproduction of an isolated single incident or event . . . we find no evidence that they had ever previously appeared in like combination, arrangement or form.

However, they found no evidence that Harrison had erred in

assessing the damages—Lloyd would get $50,000 and court fees, full stop. On the strength of the Ninth Circuit ruling, the other cases were rapidly settled out of court.

But Clyde was ruined long before Lloyd saw dime one. From now on, his gags were not only hokey and old fashioned, but legally suspect. In August of 1945, before the trial had even begun, he handed in his last screenplay for Universal, a draft of Abbott and Costello's *Hang The Noose High*, which was promptly shelved. (Abbott and Costello bought it from the studio in 1947 to produce elsewhere, but Clyde wasn't credited in the final film; his gags were probably removed.) Clyde's history with Universal went back to the days of Lyons and Moran, but he never worked for them again. No more features, no more premieres, no more stars—only Stooges. As Harold Fendler had promised in the case's first hearing, "It is one of these bitter end situations." But there was a cost for Harold Lloyd, too, as he admitted in one of his depositions:

Mr. Bruckman, up until the time that this particular incident happened, has been a very close friend of mine, I always considered.

WAXWORKS

In November of 1945, down and out with Universal, Clyde returned once more to Columbia. On the sixteenth, about a month before Judge Harrison ruled, he handed in his first Columbia script since October of 1943. That script, *Andy Plays Hookey* (working title *Wilbur Goes Wild*), seems like a conscious act of self-destruction: It's nothing more than a two-reel, condensed version of Clyde's Waterloo, *Man on the Flying Trapeze*. Even if Judge Harrison had found that gags in Clyde's pending cases were not protected by copyright, he was reusing the entire story—and not even from a script he was credited for. In fact, although Clyde came up with the original idea back when it was called *His Perfect Day*, W. C. Fields, Sam Hardy, Paramount Pictures, and Mack Sennett all had various degrees of moral or legal claim to the story. (No lawsuit seems to have come of it.)

Jules White seemed unbothered by the reused gags and lawsuits. Although Lloyd filed his suits against Columbia in 1946, Clyde worked there steadily that year, handing in a screenplay each month between April and August, and another in November—six in all.[1] (The release dates for the films don't always correspond to the dates on the scripts, because White stockpiled them to film later.) His name was on four films released in 1946, but he had nothing to do with at least one of them, *Uncivil War Birds*, a remake of Keaton's dreadful Columbia short *Mooching Through Georgia*. Clyde got a story credit, but Jules White's name is on the script. The best work he did all year was on the Stooges short *Three Little Pirates*, but not all of the work was his. The film's most famous sequence, the "Maharaja" routine, was part of the Three Stooges stage act, and, according to Edward Bernds, who directed the short, Clyde simply transcribed the routine from Moe Howard's rendition.

By now the Stooges were having troubles of their own. Okuda and Watz called 1946 the year of "the worst Stooge comedies to date," with the single exception of Clyde's *Three Little Pirates*. By the time *Uncivil War Birds* was filmed, Curly had suffered the first of a series of minor strokes, and his delivery is noticeably wavering. *Three Little Pirates* was the last full performance he gave as a Stooge; on May 19, 1946, during the filming of *Half-Wits Holiday*, he had a major stroke and his career came to an end. The Stooges—and the Columbia Shorts department—were heading toward the downslope.

There was one last burst of activity. In 1947, Columbia geared up production as the Stooges, now with Shemp Howard, began a spring vaudeville tour. White was hiring more writers than he had for years, and he needed Clyde. He was in third position for freelance work; according to White, the lineup was "Felix [Adler] or Jack [White, Jules's brother] or Clyde, in that order." But as

---

1. *Three Little Pirates* on April 4, *Fright Night* on May 28, *Out West* on June 27, *Honeymoon Blues* on July 31, *Scooper Dooper* on August 21, and *Nervous Shakedown* on November 13.

Clyde's name was irrevocably linked to the plagiarism cases, he drank more and more, and as Edward Bernds recounted to Ted Okuda, his work got worse and worse:

"Bruckman's scripts were very sloppy. I would frequently have to revise his work, as there were so many unconnected pieces. Some of his scripts were totally incomprehensible."

In 1947, though, Columbia needed material to sell the new Stooges lineup, and Clyde wrote five scripts for them.[2] His career was down, but didn't seem over.

In 1948, the bottom fell out. One script for Columbia, *Three Hams on Rye*; no other work all year. The house on Prosser, which had once seemed like a way to get his expenses under control, was now out of reach; he sold it in January. In the 1920s, Clyde and Lola had moved westward across the city as their fortunes improved; now Clyde and Gladys moved further west, this time in defeat: an apartment near UCLA, and then another, their last, at 934 6th Street in Santa Monica, with nowhere to go but the ocean. The commute to Universal would have been brutal—but then Clyde no longer had to go to Universal.

In fact, Clyde no longer had to go anywhere or do much of anything. His nephew Donald Swisher remembers him during these years as an excellent host, but someone who always needed to be occupied; the second his guests finished eating, he'd immediately wash the dishes to keep himself busy. Addictions rapidly expand to fill idle hours, and in those years Clyde had nothing but time.

In late 1949 he got his last shot. Like the arrival of sound in the late 1920s, the beginnings of television served as a sort of career

2. *Should Husbands Marry?* on January 29, *Brideless Groom* on February 26, *Pardon My Clutch* on April 23, *Tall, Dark, and Gruesome* on June 11, and *Wedlock Deadlock* on August 25.

reset button: No one knew how best to use the new medium, and as with any frontier, even people at the bottom suddenly had opportunities for rapid advancement. Strangely enough, when Clyde's chance came, it was because of Harold Lloyd.

With the exception of the legal victories that finished Clyde's career, the 1940s had been almost as unlucky for Lloyd as they'd been for Clyde. In 1944 he'd experimented with radio, hosting a *Lux Radio Theatre* knockoff called *The Old Gold Comedy Theater*. It didn't even last a year. The film he was making with Preston Sturges during the lawsuits, *The Sin of Harold Diddlebock*—the first movie he'd made since the disaster of *Professor Beware*—not only failed at the box office, but had a humiliating rerelease in which Howard Hughes recut it to include a talking horse. He'd never get a chance to make another feature. Toward the end of the decade, he and his agent, Ben Pearson, were talking about the new medium of television when it suddenly occurred to Lloyd that his old rival Buster Keaton would be perfect for it. ("All those sight gags!") Lloyd suggested to Pearson that he reach out to Buster via Clyde.

Buster Keaton had spent the 1940s in a much happier fashion than his bad years in the 1930s. In 1940 he'd married Eleanor Norris, a dancer more than twenty years his junior. The marriage turned out to be good for him, and he'd gotten his drinking more or less under control. Unhappy with the quality of the Columbia films he'd been making, he arranged a return to MGM as a gag man, and rode out the decade there, contributing to many films and making the occasional on-screen appearance. He'd gotten along well with Red Skelton, less well with the Marx Brothers, and hadn't been in charge of anything to call his own in years.

So just as he had a decade earlier at Columbia, Clyde was able to deliver Buster to a new home. Clyde met with Pearson at his offices in Santa Monica and promised to put together a pitch for KTTV. The station, a joint venture between CBS and the *Los Angeles Times*, had been on the air for less than a year; the idea of having an established name on their broadcasts was appealing. Clyde's diminished state made an impression on Pearson, but not as much as Keaton's: when Buster came by the offices the next day, he requested $250 to get him through the upcoming week. Pearson apparently paid it, and they scheduled a meeting the next evening at Buster's house.

If Pearson's account of that night can be trusted, Buster's cameo in *Sunset Blvd.*—filmed that year—was more or less based on reality. In Buster's scene, screenwriter Joe Gillis introduces the depressing bridge games at faded silent film star Norma Desmond's house through a voiceover:

> The others around the table would be actor friends—dim figures you may still remember from the silent days. I used to think of them as her waxworks.

In the film, the waxworks were Buster, H. B. Warner, and Anna Q. Nilsson. The night Pearson visited Buster's house, they were Betty Compson, Norman Kerry, Florence Vidor, and Minta Dufree: figures too dim by then to rate *Sunset Boulevard* cameos. They played bridge in the living room to the sounds of Buster's mother, Myra, seventy-two that year, practicing the saxophone in another room. Amid that funhouse atmosphere, Pearson talked the show over with Buster and Clyde: thirty minutes, live, weekly. Clyde was hired to write, but the idea was that Buster would recreate the gags and stunts that had made him famous.

The Buster Keaton Show aired for the first time at nine o'clock on the night of Thursday, December 22, 1949. Donald Swisher recalls a family gathering around the holidays at which Clyde proudly showed everyone a TV show he'd been working on. Most likely it was this one. He was right to be proud; *The Buster Keaton Show* debuted to more critical acclaim than anything he'd done in decades. *Variety* was particularly effusive, singling out the "finely-tailored" script Clyde had co-written with Columbia Short department veteran Henry Taylor. Studebaker picked up the show's sponsorship immediately, and *Variety* wrote, "It looks like television has a new 'must-see' program, very likely to become a permanent fixture."

But the show turned out to be anything but permanent. For one thing, only Los Angelenos could see it; the transcontinental microwave relay that allowed live broadcasting nationwide wouldn't be completed until September of 1951. This was pre-syndication, so there was no real reason for KTTV to preserve it; only one episode survives on kinescope. But judging from that episode, Studebaker got their money's worth, both in terms of the frequent breaks to discuss the merits of the 1950 Studebaker, and the show itself. Buster is nearly as agile as ever, trading blows with stuntman Harvey Parry[3] in a boxing ring (and at one point juggling Indian clubs like Rudy Bruckman). The anything-can-happen quality of live television makes the reused gags seem fresher, and the laughter and applause of the studio audience is copious and genuine. It seems like a show that could have survived.

But a new job is no cure for alcoholism, and after years with nothing to do but drink, Clyde couldn't stop. Pearson reported

---

3. Parry, nicknamed the "dean of Hollywood stuntmen," had a career spanning almost the entire history of cinema; he was rumored to have doubled for Harold Lloyd in *Safety Last*, Clyde had directed him when the sequence was recreated in *Feet First*, and he was still working as a stuntman in 1980s films like *Better Off Dead*.

that he usually had a pint bottle in his jacket pocket by this time. He was unable to meet his deadlines for the minimal amount of writing the show required, so Harold Goodwin (and eventually Eddie Cline) ended up picking up the slack. Buster, too, was still having problems with the bottle. Costar Shirley Tegge remembered him showing up tipsy; Harold Goodwin related that he was drunk enough to fall over and cut his head in front of CBS executives who were thinking about bringing him to the network.

In April, the live show went off the air; in June, KTTV announced they would be producing a new version for syndication, shot on film. Clyde produced the show as well as writing several episodes—again, almost entirely using gags from old Keaton shorts. The revamped show aired beginning in the spring of 1951, both on KTTV and in other markets. Because they'd been shot on film, these episodes could easily be rerun or repackaged; in 1952 they were acquired by Crown Pictures International and rereleased under the title *Life with Buster Keaton*.[4] But without the studio audience for Keaton to play to, these episodes just feel like poorly produced Keaton shorts; the timing is off and Buster looks like an old man wearing a Buster Keaton costume. *Variety*, rapturous about *The Buster Keaton Show*, called the filmed version "only partially successful" and "disappointing." Although stories about the CPI acquisition say that more episodes were in the pipeline, they were never made. The day Buster filmed his final episode, he and Eleanor left for Paris for a circus appearance: a live audience, like the first version of the show. Clyde and Buster remained

4. Although reports of the Crown Pictures acquisition of *Life with Buster Keaton* and reviews of the show in 1952 treat it as something new, descriptions of the show in the *Los Angeles Times* story about the return of *The Buster Keaton Show* to KTTV make it clear that *Life with Buster Keaton* and the syndicated episodes of *The Buster Keaton Show* from summer 1951 were one and the same.

close friends, playing cards and drinking, but they never worked together again.

In November of 1952, Clyde returned to Columbia one last time. Perhaps based on his experiences in television, he wrote a Stooges short called *Goof on the Roof* (the Stooges ruin a friend's house while ruining the installation of a TV antenna!). When cameras started rolling on November 17, *Variety* reported that Clyde was directing—for the first time since his second-unit work on *Professor Beware*, and for the last time in his life. Maybe the reporter got it wrong, maybe Jules White changed his mind, or maybe Clyde drank his way out of another job, but when the film was released Jules White was credited as the director. Whatever happened, he never worked at Columbia again, though his name appeared on later shorts that were based on his earlier scripts. The Columbia Shorts department was on the decline, remaking old films with increasing regularity as budgets were slashed.

Clyde got his last job because Bud Abbott and Lou Costello were unhappy with their television show. It had premiered on December 5, 1952, and *Variety* reviewed it on the same page as their mixed review of *Life with Buster Keaton*. Their review of *The Abbott and Costello Show* was not mixed:

> Abbott & Costello have proved too often in the past that there's an audience for even the lowest type of their shenanigans, so it's impossible to write off this assault on the intelligence of TV viewers. . . .
>
> Show carries screen credit for a writer [Sidney Fields] but what his contributions were is difficult to determine. Preem stanza resembled the weakest of the old two-reel comedies which the Hollywood studios once turned out as filler material for theaters.

Variety was misremembering the two-reelers, but they had *The*

Abbott and Costello Show dead to rights. The first season had virtually nothing in the way of plot, meandering from one routine to another, usually reusing material from their films. After six shows produced by Alex Gottlieb, the duo brought in Lou's brother, Pat Costello, to produce and Jean Yarbrough, from Clyde's Universal days, to direct. After the twenty-six-episode first season, Yarbrough decided the show needed more structure and hired Clyde.

The second season began airing on New York's WNBT on Saturday nights at six o'clock on October 10, 1953. By December, the entire season had been filmed and was being offered in syndication as a fifty-two-episode package by MCA-TV. Clyde had written fifteen episodes, most of which reused material from Buster Keaton shorts he'd worked on decades before (and some he hadn't—one episode is a recreation of *One Week*, which Buster made before hiring Clyde). In March of 1954, *Variety* revisited the show, just beginning to air in syndication on KTTV. The review damns with faint praise, calling the new season "the comedy of least resistance," but compared to the first season, it's practically a rave. No points were awarded for originality, however: "Clyde Bruckman and [co-writer] Jack Townley must have trunks full of the stuff and they'll keep it coming as long as the buffoons can turn it to profit."

But they couldn't turn it to profit anymore. WNBT aired the last episode in New York on March 13, 1954, just eight days after the review; there was no third season. Although the show had a long life in reruns and syndication, Clyde would never work again. And if he wasn't a writer, what was he?

Of all the films Clyde Bruckman worked on over the years, none lays out the merciless logic of capitalism with as much clarity as *Day Dreams*, one of Buster's First National shorts from all the way back in August of 1922, the first summer Clyde worked for him. Buster's in love with a girl played by Renée Adorée. He proposes marriage, but her father opposes the match, so Buster makes a promise. "I'll leave for the city to make good. If I'm not a success, I'll come back and shoot myself." "Splendid, I'll lend you my revolver," the father replies. After about twenty minutes of increasingly humiliating professional failure—Buster fails as a veterinarian's assistant, he fails as an actor, he fails shoveling horseshit off the city streets—he returns to the girl's house, sad and bedraggled. He looks, in other words, like the opposite of Harold Lloyd's gladhanders and tryhards: *defeated*. Adorée seems more embarrassed for him than anything; she makes no attempt to intercede on his behalf. Her father sets the revolver on an end table, and he and his daughter retire to another room so Buster can make good on his promise. They wince at the sound of the gunshot. Then Buster walks through the door. "I missed," he explains.

It's a miraculous recovery, the moment of unexpected, undeserved grace that defines comedy. But Clyde made comedies: he didn't live in one.

THE GENTLEMEN OF THE SANTA MONICA POLICE DEPARTMENT

In *The Sun Also Rises*, a character says his financial ruin happened two ways: "Gradually and then suddenly." Clyde's money went the same way. His last work for *The Abbott and Costello Show* was late in 1953; his career had been limping along since the lawsuits. Then on April 17, 1954, Clyde's mother, Bertha, died in Santa Ana. She was eighty-two and had been sick for a while; Clyde's nephew remembers that she'd had a nurse well before her death. But the hospital and funeral expenses were the final straw.

There was no work for Clyde all summer, so he wrote on spec. Two treatments he wrote for *The Danny Thomas Show* resurfaced in 2014 and were sold at auction for $2,752, but sixty years earlier, Clyde couldn't get a dime for them. His agent at this time was Antrim Short, an ex-actor who'd appeared in Columbia shorts before starting his own talent agency. Some sense of Short's place in the Hollywood ecosystem can be inferred from the times he made non-trade papers for his work: once for representing Barbara Price, "Miss San Fernando Valley 1951," once for suing his own client (Reed Hadley, "the fearless Inspector Braddock of 'Racket Squad,' "), and finally, once for representing accused wife-murderer L. Ewing Scott in an attempt to sell his life rights for a film adaptation. (Scott, who suggested from prison that Ronald Colman might be the right person to play him, was convicted; after maintaining his innocence for thirty years, he confessed to the crime in 1986.)

But even Lew Wasserman would have had a hard time selling Clyde Bruckman's work that year. By the 1940s, he had a reputation as an unreliable drunk whose gags were stale; after the lawsuits, he was a legal risk as well. And in the summer of 1954, he turned sixty.

By the fall, his situation was desperate. He paid a visit to Stan Laurel to see if Laurel and Hardy might be interested in following Keaton into the brave new world of television; they were not. He then made one last attempt to reinvent himself, this time as a writer of drama. George Stevens, Clyde's cameraman on his Laurel and Hardy shorts in 1927, was by now a successful director; in 1954 he was in preproduction on *Giant*. Clyde called him to see if he might want any help with the screenplay. When he couldn't get Stevens on the phone, he wrote him a letter, unconsciously echoing his twenty-two-year-old self, who had been careful to tell *The Editor* about all the stories he had "under way or out for consideration":

November 14, 1954

Dear George:

The reason I called you the other day regarding the possibility that you might have some sort of writing work I might be able to do on your forthcoming picture is because a recent series of reverses have left me in a desperate situation.

Unfortunately, over the years I have been established strictly as a comedy writer. But it so happens that as a newspaper man and magazine writer before entering picture work I wrote everything from character studies and human interest stuff to dramatic material. But after all my years with Keaton, Roach, Lloyd and W. C. Fields try and convince anyone of that fact. At the present time I have six outlines for situation comedy TV shows in the hands of my agent, Antrim Shot [sic]. Three are for Danny Thomas and three for the Stu Erwin show. Now I sit back and wait for action on these stories, but in the meanwhile I am writing other scripts for Antrim to submit to other TV shows.

Now this brings me to write you the most difficult request I have ever written in my life. The recent illness and death of my mother, with the accumulation of hospital and funeral expenses, has put me in the position of needing urgent financial assistance. So in desperation I am presuming on our old friendship to ask you if you could make me a temporary personal loan of one hundred dollars, a loan I will break my neck to repay as soon as Antrim completes a sale on one of my stories.

I don't know where else to turn, George, or else I would not ask this favor from you. It isn't an easy thing to do. But believe me if you do not feel you should grant this loan I will understand and still retain my high regard for you.

If that letter and request for a loan survived, it's safe to assume there were others that didn't, particularly since the letter makes it clear Clyde and Stevens hadn't been in touch in years. Stevens replied on the sixteenth, walking a delicate line of being encouraging while remaining noncommittal:

Dear Clyde—

Have your letter before me this morning and I am very unhappy to hear about the lack of activity coming your way, but I know only too well the artificial and unreasonable line that is drawn between the comedy field and the dramatic field in all of its aspects. With your magazine and newspaper experience, there is no reason why you should not swing over into the serious stuff when there is more of it to do. To me, work in that category has always been easier to do than work in the highly specialized comedy field.

I would have enjoyed having a talk with you when you called, even though there is no more work to be done here at this time. You probably know from Fred that we are right up to our ears under full steam trying to get a script out, and at the same time go along with the production development, and you know on this kind of schedule there just aren't enough hours in the day to keep up with things. When we get out from under this pressure, would enjoy having a visit with you and do hope things break in your favor shortly, as I know they will.

He enclosed a personal check for one hundred dollars. Clyde wrote back on November 25—Thanksgiving Day.

Dear George—

I wish to express my deep appreciation of your swell letter, and to thank you for your consideration in extending me a loan to help me over this rough spot.

As I explained before I have a considerable number of situation comedy scripts in the hands of my agent, Antrim Short, who has submitted them to the Danny Thomas and Stu Erwin TV shows for consideration. Now, as in all speculative writing, you wait for a decision. In the meanwhile I am taking your advice by developing several outlines that might appeal to the producers of dramatic shows. As you said in your letter it is easier to do work in more serious stuff than in the cockeyed comedy field. During my newspaper days I ran across enough true dramatic situations and stories to give me a good backlog of material for that type of writing. I'm certainly going to give it the old college try even though at first it might seem to be a haze-ridden road leading to an uncertain future. Also, as you said in your letter, I would enjoy having a visit with you when you are out from under the pressure of your present picture.

Because I had considerable experience as a liquor store salesman during the holiday seasons of the past few years I am trying to land such a job to help out, doing my writing on the side. If, by the way, you have any friends in the liquor store business who could use a good (plug) man kindly have them contact Bruckman.

It's the familiar mixture of grandiose plans and toxic self-pity of the clinically depressed—to say nothing of the idea that a sixty-year-old alcoholic who'd ruined his life by drinking would make a good liquor salesman during the holidays. If Stevens wrote a reply, he didn't keep it in his papers.

Clyde's plan to reinvent himself as a dramatist lasted, barely, through Christmas. On December 26, he sat at his typewriter to do his last piece of writing. Like his father, he'd carefully thought through how to wrap up his affairs. But while Rudy Bruckman had numerous business interests to straighten before his death, Clyde's only material concerns were his car, his watch, and his own body.

One of the characteristics of suicidal depression is an all-pervading sense of isolation, of a vast, unbridgeable gulf between the depressed person and his or her loved ones. You can see it in Rudy Bruckman's throwaway mention of "the wife and boy" in his suicide note. It's in Clyde's letter too, which offers no explanation for his death, and is addressed to the "Gentlemen of Santa Monica Police Department."

He apparently had second thoughts, and made one last attempt to save himself, waiting until the holidays were over. Nineteen fifty-five began on a Saturday; on Monday, January 3, Hollywood returned to work. Clyde met with Jules White at Columbia and asked for a job. But White owed Felix Adler a favor at the time, and, as he explained in the 1980s, "I had no idea he was that desperate."[1] With nowhere else to turn, Clyde made his final decision. He crossed out the date on his typewritten note, corrected it to the third, and sealed the envelope. But it wasn't until the next day that he got up the nerve to drive to Bess Eiler's, a Santa Monica restaurant that had relocated to a brand new building at 2001 Wilshire Boulevard that September.

Between 3:00 and 3:15 that afternoon, Walter Brown, the bartender, heard what he thought was a car backfiring on Santa Monica Boulevard. It took ten minutes before he connected the noise with the customer who'd gone into the men's room but hadn't come out. Unable to get any response from the stall, he eventually got a stepladder and saw what had happened.

The police found Clyde's letter in his jacket pocket. He left no reason, no explanation, and no words of goodbye to his wife or friends. Instead, he was detached, dispassionate, and entirely concerned with logistics.

> Gentlemen of Santa Monica Police Department:
>
> You will find a 1948 blue Dodge sedan—license number 8N 33537 parked nearby. This car belongs to my wife, Gladys Bruckman, who resides at 934-D 6th Street, Santa Monica. The keys to the car are in my pocket.
>
> I will be very grateful if you contact Eleanor Sevland at the Douglas Aircraft Co. on Ocean Park Ave. The phone number is Ex. 43241

---

1. White remembered hearing about Clyde's death the morning after he turned him down, which would mean they'd met Tuesday morning—but it seems more likely they met on Monday, the third, since Clyde would presumably not have dated his note and sealed the envelope with a meeting pending for the next day.

and her Extension No. is 473. I would prefer that she or her husband, whose phone number is Dickens 19168 break the news to my wife because they are our closest friends.

Also I would like to have Mel Sevland contact Dr. Marvin Mack, who is Mel Sevland's close friend, and see if Mr. Mack can arrange to have my body accepted by the Los Angeles Medical Association or some medical school for clinical examination because I have no money to provide for my burial. Perhaps they can store some parts of me in their medical banks. The rest they can burn up or dispose of as they see fit.

The gun I used I borrowed from my pal, Buster Keaton. I told him I was making a trip and would feel safer having a gun in the glove compartment while on this trip. Would you be kind enough to call him at York 7804 so he can pick up his gun at your police department.

Thanks for your courtesy, gentlemen.

Clyde Bruckman

He added a handwritten postscript to the letter before sealing it, but it wasn't an attempt to reach across the gulf—he'd simply forgotten a detail:

P.S.: Mel Sevland is a teacher at Santa Monica High School and he can be reached there in the event he is not at his home—phone number Dickens 19168.

If Clyde's exit was impersonal, it was, in its way, considerate: Gladys didn't have to find the body or clean up after him. The police respected Clyde's wishes and had Mel Sevland break the news. His car was taken to a local garage to be returned to Gladys; his body was taken to the funeral home of Moeller, Murphy, and Moeller. Buster even got his gun back.

Clyde's suicide made the AP wires and was picked up nationally, mostly because of the Keaton connection. The *Los Angeles Times* called him a "Film Writer" and didn't mention he'd covered baseball for them. At the *Examiner*, he was a "Film Veteran," not their former sports editor. And *Variety*, which had run Harold Lloyd's lawsuit front page above-the-fold in 1945, only gave Clyde a forty-seven-word obituary on page four. They got the facts of his death right, but every single word about his life was inaccurate:

> Bruckman most recently worked as a writer at Columbia. In silent-film days he wrote and directed comedies starring Harold Lloyd, W. C. Fields and Buster Keaton.

Two days after Clyde's death, Columbia released its latest Three Stooges short, *Fling in the Ring*. According to the opening credits, it was written and directed by Jules White. The film lifts the plot, the gags, and, in fact, most of the footage from *Fright Night*, another Stooges short Clyde wrote in 1947. He has never been credited.

MAGIC LAMPS

In the early 1950s, when everything was nearly over, Clyde and Buster were talking with Rudi Blesh about *The Navigator*, their first great feature-length success. This was the movie where they learned to build a comedy by stripping things away—no extraneous gags, nothing unmotivated, just two people on a dead boat, adrift in the blue. Buster explained to Blesh how the process of subtraction let *The Navigator* go deeper than the romantic mix-ups that characterized the films that preceded it:

> "Only then, you see, we'll have a bigger problem—no two bit problem who marries who, but just staying alive on a derelict ship."
> "Life," said Bruckman.

The conversation turned from the haunting early scenes—the empty ship, the man and woman always just barely missing each other—to the finale. The boat is overrun by cannibals. Buster and Kathryn McGuire attempt to steal a canoe, but fail. With no hope of rescue and their pursuers fast approaching, Buster throws their sole lifebuoy away. All is lost. The couple embrace and sink beneath the surface of the water together. This was, Clyde told Blesh, "the real end" of the film. Buster agreed.

Then—a miracle. The duo rise back into frame, borne upward by a submarine surfacing beneath their feet. But by the time he talked to Blesh about the film, Clyde saw this as a copout.

"The story really ended when you two dove in and sank," said Bruckman.

"Oh," said Buster "it was in the books for us to die all right. But not in the jokebooks. We were making a comedy, remember?"

Buster was right, of course. In 1924, they were making a comedy: The doctrine of miraculous recovery was a professional and personal credo. They all believed, in those years, that if they swam too far from shore, if they tired and sank beneath the waves, a submarine would rise beneath their feet and carry them home. The bullets from the borrowed gun would always miss their target, the train that pursued them would crash into the valley below. One by one, they all learned the real ending.

Jean Havez went first; his heart gave out in 1925, when Buster's star was still rising. On Christmas Day of 1946, W. C. Fields's drinking caught up with him. Joe Mitchell got Alzheimer's and died of pneumonia in 1950. That same year, Monty Banks, who'd had so much trouble with driving, collapsed in a train on the way to Capri. He'd been contemplating directing a drama about Leonardo da Vinci. Oliver Hardy had a stroke in 1957; Eddie Cline drank himself to death in 1961. Two years later, Clyde's frequent collaborator Felix Adler died of cancer. And in 1965, it was Stan Laurel's turn.

That left longtime rivals Buster Keaton and Harold Lloyd. Buster lived long enough to enjoy a brief career resurgence in the

1960s. He took virtually every job he was offered, from Stanley Kramer's *It's a Mad, Mad, Mad, Mad World* to Alka-Seltzer commercials to Samuel Beckett's *Film*. He may have died in 1966 waiting to feel the submarine beneath his feet; when he was diagnosed with terminal lung cancer, his wife told him he had bronchitis.

If Keaton was overexposed by the time of his death, Lloyd, once so eager to be liked, had the opposite problem. He'd hung on to his money and his mansion, but he kept his films out of circulation—no one offered him what he thought they were worth—and was gradually forgotten. In their heyday, the rivalry that mattered had been Chaplin and Lloyd—Keaton was a distant third place. But Chaplin and Keaton's films found new audiences. Lloyd's didn't, and in the popular imagination it became Keaton vs. Chaplin. Greenacres fell into disrepair, and Lloyd became obsessed with high-fidelity audio, cataloguing and recataloguing his enormous record collection and rigging up custom stereo systems until, according to Tom Dardis, "the living room became a hazardous labyrinth of criss-crossing cables." He died in March of 1971. By 1975, even the Stooges were gone.

Gladys Bruckman outlived almost everyone. She blamed Buster for loaning Clyde the gun; in the aftermath, she moved to Santa Ana, far from Hollywood, far from Clyde's memory. The girl who'd married a daredevil surgeon and left him for a movie director spent her later years working at Virginia's Gift Shop at Knott's Berry Farm. She died on June 9, 1983. Only Jules White—the man who'd reused Clyde's reused gags—lived longer. After White's death in 1985, nothing was left of Clyde Bruckman but a half-remembered legend: a silent-era plagiarist. A drunk.

Part of the legend is true: he was an alcoholic. But plagiarism is a crime of envy, and Clyde almost always stole from himself. He was recreating his best work, films no one had seen in years, in an era before revival screenings. Alcoholism and fear of failure were certainly factors. His directorial career had begun as a favor and continued as a prank, and by the time he started stealing, he had a well-developed case of impostor syndrome. But Clyde robbed his own past, again and again, because more than anything else he wanted to return to it. He wasn't a thief; he was a frustrated time traveller. Here's something else he told Rudi Blesh:

"I often wish," he said, "that I were back there, with Buster and the gang, in *that* Hollywood. But I don't have the lamp to rub."

Everyone's life is the story of learning that particular lamp doesn't exist. But let Clyde have it. Go past the man with the neatly typed note in the bathroom stall, past the loans and the television shows and the lawsuits, past MR. BRUCKMAN'S ABSENCE ON ACCOUNT OF ILLNESS and Queen of Angels Hospital, past flasks and bottles and crystal decanters and years and years of monotonous failure. Here's where the lamp takes Clyde Bruckman. He's thirty years old, living with Lola, the woman he married at twenty-two, back when they were practically kids. Mack Sennett wants him at the Fun Factory and Harold Lloyd wants him to help with this college movie, but for now he's working for Buster Keaton. He feels good. His mind's at ease, and working. He and Jean Havez and Eddie Cline and Joe Mitchell and Buster are at each other's houses 'til all hours, cooking late-night meals, throwing anything they can think of at the wall, writing jokes that will outlive them all by decades, inventing the cinematic language of comedy. He can't put down this book he's been reading, about a train.

On warm afternoons they play baseball.

ACKNOWLEDGEMENTS

This book began because of time zones and my well-documented inability to get up early in the morning. Crankily convinced that east-coasters would have beaten me to any obvious pitches for essays about *Sherlock Jr.* for the Movie of the Week feature at *The Dissolve*, I settled on something that hit the Internet trifecta for unprofitability: obscure, long, and depressing. Endless thanks are due to Keith Phipps for taking a chance on a long shot and saying yes. Thanks also to Scott Tobias, Tasha Robinson, Genevieve Koski, Noel Murray, and Nathan Rabin for their help seeing the original article through to publication, and supporting and promoting it, and to Joy Burke for her great artwork. I'm grateful to Alex Kane for wading through the morass of the manuscript and improving it throughout. Finally, I owe thanks to Thomas Elrod for seeing the potential for a book, and supporting it with thoughtful editing, tireless work, and above all, patience.

Special thanks are due to Jeff Hamblin, Richard Hamblin, and Donald P. Swisher, who gave generously of their time and shared their memories of Clyde, Lola, and Gladys.

This book would not exist without all the talented archivists and librarians who helped immensely with the research: Jenny Romero, Sue Kane, Faye Thompson and everyone else at the Margaret Herrick Library, Ned Comstock at the University of Southern California, Ruth Geos at the San Francisco Law Library, Lynn Nashorn and Matthew Law at the National Archives at Riverside, Charles Miller at the National Archives at San Francisco, Bernie Hogya at The Stan Laurel Correspondence Archive Project, and Paul D. Garrity at the San Bernardino Public Library. Special thanks to Lisle Foote for sharing the manuscript of her book about Buster Keaton's collaborators, in the halcyon days when it seemed my research would be complete before it was published.

I also owe a debt I can't repay to everyone who suffered through rough drafts of my work over the years and encouraged me to keep writing anyway.

Finally, heartfelt thanks are due to my family for their love and support: Mom, Dad, Lindsay, Emily and Ellen. My father deserves special thanks for helping me decode ancient docket sheets, filings, and memos. Above all, thank you to my wife, Yasmin. No more late nights writing, for a while.

Notes

No End of Credit

1. "An Acknowledgement": "An Acknowledgement," *Exhibitors Trade Review*, September 27, 1924.

1. at the bottom of page A3: "Correction," *New York Times*, September 21, 1989.

2. a brief history of pie-throwing in movies: Dan Barry, "In Comedy, Some Weapons Are Sweet," *New York Times*, July 12, 2015.

2. a 1999 Chris O'Donnell vehicle: "The Bachelor (1999): Full Cast and Crew," *Internet Movie Database*, http://www.imdb.com/title/tt0120596/fullcredits.

2. an episode of *The X-Files*: Dean A. Kowalksi, " 'Clyde Bruckman's Final Repose': Reprised 2009," *The Philosophy of the X-Files*, ed. Dean A. Kowalski (Lexington: University Press of Kentucky, 2009), 189–208.

2. Bruckman was planning to sue: Roman Lynch, "Scrabble Champ Misspells 'Cat' and Goes on Rampage," *Weekly World News*, March 7, 2005.

3. an almost mythical creature: Tom Dardis, *Harold Lloyd: The Man on the Clock* (New York: Viking, 1983), 209.

3. he was not very funny, and he drank too much: Tom Dardis, *Buster Keaton: The Man Who Wouldn't Lie Down* (New York: Charles Scribner's Sons, 1979), 104.

3. Pearson had never even met him before: Dardis, *Keaton*, 259–261.

4. his own writing lacked the qualities that could be considered "great.":

Ted Okuda and Edward Watz, *The Columbia Comedy Shorts: Two-Reel Hollywood Film Comedies, 1933–1958* (Jefferson, NC: McFarland and Company, 1986), 33.

4. his most valuable employees: Dardis, *Harold Lloyd*, 122.

4. he was considered too unreliable to hire: Contract between W. C. Fields and Universal Pictures, August 1938, W. C. Fields Papers, Margaret Herrick Library, Academy of Motion Picture Arts and Sciences.

4. "the two best I ever had were Jean Havez and Clyde Bruckman.": Buster Keaton, interview by Kevin Brownlow, *Buster Keaton: Interviews*, ed. Kevin W. Sweeney (Jackson, MS: University Press of Mississippi, 2007), 176.

4. His first job in the motion picture industry: "Lyons and Moran Increase Staff," *The Moving Picture World*, February 15, 1919.

5. They were not word guys, at all: Buster Keaton and Charles Samuels, *My Wonderful World of Slapstick* (New York: Doubleday, 1960), 130–131.

6. the bathroom stall of a restaurant and bar in Santa Monica: Deputy Chief C. Brown, Santa Monica Police Department, "Death (Suicide): Bruckman, Clyde Adolph," Report Number 55-117, January 4, 1955.

6. "dated and old fashioned,": Joseph L. Lewinson, "Further Memorandum for Defendants on Liability and Damages," filed November 14, 1945, Case 4361, Box 751, Civil Case Files 1938–1950, Records of the District Court of the United States for the Southern District of California, Central Division, Record Group 21, National Archives at Riverside, Riverside, CA.

7. "master comedian and good citizen.": "The Official Academy Awards Database," *Academy of Motion Picture Arts and Sciences*, http://awardsdatabase.oscars.org.

7. "for his unique talents: Ibid.

7. a list that contained nothing he'd worked on: "The Sight and Sound Top Ten Poll: 1952," *British Film Institute*, http://old.bfi.org.uk/sightandsound/polls/topten/history/1952.html.

7. He didn't live long enough to see *The General* surpass Chaplin: "The Sight and Sound Top Ten Poll: 1972," *British Film Institute*, http://old.bfi.org.uk/sightandsound/polls/topten/history/1972.html.

Though they've traded places over the decades, *The General* received more votes than any of Chaplin's films in the most recent poll.

7. **or outrank Chaplin on the American Film Institute's list:** "AFI's 100 Funniest American Movies of All Time," *American Film Institute,* http://www.afi.com/100Years/laughs.aspx.

A Happy Life

11. **Clyde Adolph Bruckman was born on June 30, 1894:** "World War I Draft Registration Cards, 1917–1918," digital images, *Ancestry.com,* Clyde Adolph Bruckman registration, no. 20 (right side numbering), Draft Board 07, City of Los Angeles, California; citing *World War I Selective Service System Draft Registration Cards, 1917–1918,* NARA, microfilm publication M1509, no specific roll cited.

11. **Elgin, Illinois, in 1888:** Luther A. Ingersoll, *Ingersoll's Century Annals of San Bernardino County, 1769 to 1904: Prefaced with a Brief History of the State of California: Supplemented with an Encyclopedia of Local Biography and Embellished with Views of Historic Subjects and Portraits of Many of Its Representative People* (Los Angeles: L. A. Ingersoll, 1904), 743–744.

11. **a wave of migration and a real estate bubble:** Ibid., 161–174.

11. **They were married on December 23, 1889:** "Short Mention," *Daily Courier* (San Bernardino, CA), December 24, 1889.

11. **Bertha had four brothers and five sisters:** "In the Shadow," *San Bernardino Daily Sun,* February 28, 1907. The Smiths had 12 children, but only 10 were alive by 1907.

11. **only twenty-five thousand in the entire county:** California Department of Finance, "Historical Census Populations of Counties and Incorporated Cities in California, 1850–2010," *California State Data Center,* March 2013, http://www.dof.ca.gov/research/demographic/ state_census_data_center/historical_census_1850-2010/documents/ 2010-1850_STCO_IncCities-FINAL.xls.

11. **Their first son, Earl Ronald Bruckman:** Grave Marker, Lloyd S. Bruckman and Earl Ronald Bruckman, Mountain View Cemetery, San Bernardino, California.

12. born a scant seven and a half months after the wedding: "Short Locals," *Daily Courier* (San Bernardino, CA), August 12, 1890.

12. Rudy gave a demonstration of club swinging: "Society Gems: Mrs. W. E. W. Lightfoot Entertains 'Our Babies,' " *Daily Courier* (San Bernardino, CA), April 12, 1891.

12. in the 1904 Olympics: *Universal Exposition Saint Louis, 1904: Preliminary Programme of Physical Culture: Olympic Games and World's Championship Contests* (St. Louis, MO: St. Louis Universal Exposition, 1904), 21.

12. Rudy had trained in Illinois as a barber: Ingersoll, 743.

12. he bought his way into a partnership: "City Chat," *Daily Courier* (San Bernardino, CA), December 2, 1891.

12. the Bruckmans' second child, Lloyd, was born: Grave Marker, Lloyd S. Bruckman and Earl Ronald Bruckman, Mountain View Cemetery, San Bernardino, California.

12. "our popular young barber and champion club-swinger.": "Brief Mention," *Daily Courier* (San Bernardino, CA), April 25, 1891.

12. Just before Thanksgiving: "Around Town," *Daily Courier* (San Bernardino, CA), November 20, 1892.

12. For Christmas that year: *Daily Courier* (San Bernardino, CA), December 25, 1892.

12. two-month-old Lloyd Bruckman died: "Town Talk," *Daily Courier* (San Bernardino, CA), January 11, 1893.

12. Earl followed his brother less than a week later: "Sorely Afflicted," *Daily Courier* (San Bernardino, CA), January 17, 1893.

12. until a club-swinging demonstration: "The Advertising Bazaar," *Daily Courier* (San Bernardino, CA), December 6, 1893.

12. Rudy planned extensive renovations: "Signs of Prosperity," *Weekly Courier* (San Bernardino, CA), January 13, 1893.

12. moving to a temporary location: "The News in Brief," *Weekly Courier* (San Bernardino, CA), March 24, 1893.

13. he got involved in politics: "Judge H. C. Gooding's Able Argument," *San Bernardino Weekly Sun*, October 24, 1896.

13. he lost in the third round: "Republicans of the City Meet In Council," *San Bernardino Daily Sun*, February 28, 1897.

13. Cole promptly lost to the Democrat: "San Bernardino County," *Los Angeles Herald*, April 15, 1897.

13. the astonishing score of 24 to 62: "Political Baseball Game," *San Bernardino Daily Sun*, March 31, 1897.

13. Rudy joined not just the Odd Fellows: "Widely Known Man Takes Life," *San Bernardino Daily Sun*, November 8, 1912.

13. served as the founding president: "Athletic Club Organized," *San Bernardino Daily Sun*, March 19, 1897.

13. managed a local baseball team: "The News in Brief," *San Bernardino Daily Sun*, May 11, 1897.

13. "Daughters of the Nile.": "Fine Dancing and Costumes," *San Bernardino Weekly Sun*, May 11, 1895.

13. the M. & O., a saloon on Third Street: "Murray Takes a Partner at the M. & O.," *San Bernardino Daily Sun*, March 19, 1898.

13. The bar's name had come from Murray: "Short Mention," *Daily Courier* (San Bernardino, CA), January 18, 1890.

14. the top 3 percent of American households: Claude S. Fischer, *America Calling: A Social History of the Telephone to 1940* (Los Angeles: University of California Press, 1992), 144.

14. and a dachshund: "Mistaken Identity," *San Bernardino Daily Sun*, November 29, 1900.

14. A childhood photo: "Lot 234 of 641: An Archive of Clyde Bruckman Material, Julien's 90210 Exclusive Spring Online Entertainment Auction (#3314)," *Julien's Auctions*, http://www.julienslive.com/view-auctions/catalog/id/118/lot/49087/.

14. His tenth birthday party: "Society," *San Bernardino Daily Sun*, July 1, 1904.

14. Beam's definition of *obstreperous*: "Negro Shot," *Los Angeles Herald*, July 15, 1895.

14. Charges against Beam were dismissed: "City News in Brief," *San Bernardino Weekly Sun*, July 20, 1895.

14. fights routinely ended in jail time: "Five Days for a Smash," *San Bernardino Daily Sun*, September 9, 1903.

14. attacked each other with axes: "Court Notes," *San Bernardino Weekly Sun*, November 27, 1903.

14. a blood clot lodged in his brain: "Whacks with a Club on a Miner's Head," *Los Angeles Times*, October 31, 1903.

14. Beam's victim died, and he was arrested: "Miner Dies from Effect of Bartender's Beating," *Los Angeles Times*, November 2, 1903.

14. charges dropped on a technicality: "Peter Beam Set Free," *Los Angeles Herald*, June 28, 1904.

14. he got out of the saloon business: "Saloons Transferred," *San Bernardino Daily Sun*, June 11, 1905.

14. who then sold to Rudy in 1906: "A Tax Levy for Repair of Streets," *San Bernardino Daily Sun*, June 5, 1906.

15. The complaint sworn against him by the town marshal: Statement of John C. Ralph, July 30, 1894, San Bernardino County Historical Archives.

15. Ordinance no. 165: San Bernardino Ordinance no. 165, July 3, 1894, San Bernardino County Historical Archives.

15. donating prizes for the town's May Day horseraces: "Fair Skies for Race Events," *San Bernardino Daily Sun*, May 1, 1907.

15. Clyde's bicycle was stolen: "Bicycle Thieves Are Busy," *San Bernardino Daily Sun*, November 2, 1907.

16. "probably the work of boys: "Missing Bicycles Found by Police," *San Bernardino Daily Sun*, November 3, 1907.

16. Clyde joined the Boys' Brotherhood: "Social," *San Bernardino Daily Sun*, June 8, 1907.

16. He loved fishing and camping: Clyde A. Bruckman, "Advice from a Veteran Hiker," *Los Angeles Times*, June 14, 1914.

16. "would have been sent home had they stayed much longer.": "A-Plenty of Grub at Camp," *San Bernardino Daily Sun*, July 9, 1907.

16. His first published comedy writing: Vernon Brydolf, "High School News," *San Bernardino Daily Sun*, November 25, 1909.

16. "An Indian never forgets, Dick,": Clyde Bruckman, "The Love of Man," *The Tyro*, November 1910, Arda Haenszel California Room, Norman F. Feldheym Central Library, San Bernardino, California, 5–9.

16. He played basketball that year: Merritt B. Curtis, "The High School," *San Bernardino Daily Sun*, January 13, 1911.

16. leading the "yell section" at high school games: Merritt B. Curtis, "High School," *San Bernardino Daily Sun*, November 16, 1910.

16. he was elected class treasurer: Merritt B. Curtis, "The High School," *San Bernardino Daily Sun*, May 24, 1911.

17. "to where the girls abide,": *The Tyro*, June 1911, Arda Haenszel California Room, Norman F. Feldheym Central Library, San Bernardino, California, 98.

17. Witnesses to the crash thought: "Local Man in Fatal Auto Accident," *San Bernardino Daily Sun*, June 13, 1911.

17. a fishing trip to celebrate his seventeenth birthday: "Personal," *San Bernardino Daily Sun*, July 8, 1911.

17. a hayrack party with his classmates: "Last Merry Makings," *San Bernardino Daily Sun*, September 14, 1911.

18. "The murder scene in Shakespeare's Macbeth is like an old maid's: Clyde A. Bruckman, "Stars Win in Great Game at Urbita," *San Bernardino Daily Sun*, January 23, 1912.

18. Rudy was beginning to become paranoid: "Widely Known Man Takes Life," *San Bernardino Daily Sun*, November 8, 1912.

18. "When it becomes necessary to set forth our athletic feats,": *The Tyro*, June 1912, Arda Haenszel California Room, Norman F. Feldheym Central Library, San Bernardino, California, 95.

18. "My boy . . . I am proud of you: Ibid., 58–62.

19. Clyde was to be enrolled in a boys' school: "Personal," *San Bernardino Daily Sun*, June 7, 1912.

19. he filed a story with the *Daily Sun*: "Bruckman Takes In The Big Game," *San Bernardino Daily Sun*, June 20, 1912.

19. He returned home alone in September: "Personal," *San Bernardino Daily Sun*, September 12, 1912.

19. was elected class president: Fessenden Haskell, "High School," *San Bernardino Daily Sun*, October 10, 1912.

19. his parents returned at the end of October: "Personal," *San Bernardino Daily Sun*, October 29, 1912.

19. "a child could almost have solved.": "Widely Known Man Takes Life," *San Bernardino Daily Sun*, November 8, 1913.

19. the equivalent of nearly $75,000 in 2015: "US Inflation Calculator," http://usinflationcalculator.com.

19. he went into the alley behind his bar: "Widely Known Man Takes Life," *San Bernardino Daily Sun*, November 8, 1913.

20. Paul Maher's account: E. P. Fuller, "Inquest on Rudolph Bruckman, San Bernardino, Deceased, Held on 8th day of Nov., 1912," San Bernardino County Historical Archives.

20. And this is A. A. Garner: Ibid.

20. I hope they will have a happy life: "Widely Known Man Takes Life," *San Bernardino Daily Sun*, November 8, 1912.

20. Nearly two hundred people attended the funeral: "Hundreds Pay Tribute to the Dead," *San Bernardino Daily Sun*, November 10, 1912.

20. were re-buried next to their father: Grave Marker, Lloyd S. Bruckman and Earl Ronald Bruckman, Mountain View Cemetery, San Bernardino, California.

21. the Sunbeam Saloon was sold to a local baseball player: "Vernon Player to Buy Sunbeam Saloon," *San Bernardino Daily Sun*, December 14, 1912.

21. He appeared in the minor role of a servant: *The Tyro*, June 1913, Arda Haenszel California Room, Norman F. Feldheym Central Library, San Bernardino, California, 99–100.

21. a ceremonial students-vs.-faculty game: "Faculty Team Subdued by Seniors," *San Bernardino Daily Sun*, June 8, 1913.

21. "Los Angeles.": Fessenden Haskell, "Plans of the Graduates," *San Bernardino Daily Sun*, May 31, 1913.

The Sportswriter

23. a candy pull at Thousand Pines: "Summer Jollity at Thousand Pines," *San Bernardino Daily Sun*, July 27, 1913.

23. The 1914 phone directory lists Bertha: *Los Angeles City Directory 1914* (Los Angeles: Los Angeles Directory Company, 1914), 642.

23. The building was constructed in 1911: "New Property Leased," *Los Angeles Times*, February 16, 1913.

23. a news report from when she left Los Angeles: "Personal," *San Bernardino Daily Sun*, November 25, 1917.

23. a common location for suicides: E.g., "Bullets Stop Nerve Fears: High Diver Makes Leap into Eternity," *Los Angeles Times*, July 15, 1910; "Gruesome Find," *Los Angeles Times*, January 27, 1913; "Dies in Lake," *Los Angeles Times*, August 26, 1913.

23. Several high-end apartment buildings began construction: E.g., "Will Front on Westlake Park," *Los Angeles Times*, January 26, 1913; "Metropolitan Type," *Los Angeles Times*, September 21, 1913.

23. Clyde reported on a football game: Clyde A. Bruckman, "0 to 0 Battle on Bovard Field," *San Bernardino Daily Sun*, October 7, 1913.

24. he was hired to cover the upcoming baseball season: "Clyde Bruckman on Los Angeles 'Times,' " *San Bernardino Daily Sun*, February 24, 1914.

24. it was firmly in last place when Clyde was hired: *The Typographical Journal* 43, no. 1 (July 1913), 225.

24. The first one ran on April 4, 1914: Clyde Bruckman, "Foul Tips," *Los Angeles Times*, April 4, 1914.

24. "refreshments will be placed at third base in considerable bulk,": Harry A. Williams, "Where Tiger Players Will Pass the Winter," *Los Angeles Times*, October 19, 1914.

24. "who want to learn a few pointers from the intellectual gentlemen: Ibid.

24. the *Times* lineup featured De Witt Van Court: E.g., De Witt Van Court, "Eddie Campi Appears Even Faster than Ever," *Los Angeles Times*, November 3, 1913.

24. an ex-boxing coach who'd trained heavyweight champions: Bill Potts, "First 75 Years the Hardest," *Los Angeles Times*, September 21, 1935.

24. a chain smoker and cat fanatic: Randy Skretvedt, *Laurel and Hardy: The Magic Behind the Movies* (Beverly Hills: Moonstone Press, 1987), 52.

25. "a cane with a silver knob.": James Richardson, *For the Life of Me: Memoirs of a City Editor*, (New York: G. P. Putnam's Sons, 1954), 210.

25. cold-cocked Walker in the jaw: Ibid.

25. a large portrait of the ex-boxer in white tie: E.g., James J. Corbett, "In Corbett's Corner," *Los Angeles Examiner*, June 8, 1918.

25. the man who got Clyde his job: "Bruckman Is Named as Sporting Editor," *San Bernardino Daily Sun*, April 23, 1920.

25. a graduate of San Bernardino High: "Bruckman to Pilot Van Loan in Hills," *San Bernardino Daily Sun*, July 7, 1914.

25. so he could golf year-round: Trey Strecker, introduction to *The Collected Baseball Stories*, by Charles Emmett Van Loan (Jefferson, NC: McFarland and Company, 2004), 1–2.

25. he promoted Beanie Walker: Earl E. Buie, "They Tell Me," *San Bernardino Sun-Telegram*, January 7, 1962.

25. Ring Lardner's short stories: Strecker, 2.

25. the fortunes of long-forgotten teams: "1914 Pacific Coast League," *Baseball-Reference.com*, 2014, http://www.baseball-reference.com/minors/league.cgi?id=96e2b294.

26. "with slaughter-house rules: Clyde A. Bruckman, "Kores Stops Long Battle," *Los Angeles Times*, August 8, 1914.

26. "Ty Lober spread wreck and ruin: Clyde A. Bruckman, "Ty Lober Is Loose Again," *Los Angeles Times*, August 5, 1914.

26. In June he took Beanie Walker and De Witt Van Court: "Beanie Walker's Bunch Here on Fishing Trip," *San Bernardino News and the Free Press*, June 11, 1914.

26. "extensively German in his thought processes: Charles E. Van Loan, "C. E. Van Loan Writes About Mountain Trip," *Los Angeles Times*, August 4, 1914.

26. "Ay-dolf owns a cabin: Ibid.

27. his prized 1914 Cadillac: "Van Loan, The Baseball Author, Becomes Autoist," *Los Angeles Times*, September 28, 1913.

27. the front left wheel slid onto the soft shoulder: "C. E. Van Loan, Noted Writer, Hurt as Auto Falls 30 Feet Near Skyland," *San Bernardino Daily Sun*, July 17, 1914.

27. Van Loan returned to Los Angeles within a week: "Van Loan Comes Home," *Los Angeles Times*, July 30, 1914.

27. to trade barbs in the pages of the *Los Angeles Times*: Charles E. Van Loan, " 'Brick Through Glass House,' Says Van Loan," *Los Angeles Times*, August 7, 1914.

27. Even the Cadillac was fine: "Van Loan's Machine Undamaged by Fall," *San Bernardino Daily Sun*, July 26, 1914.

27. "I don't want to see an automobile again.": "C. E. Van Loan, Noted Writer, Hurt as Auto Falls 30 Feet Near Skyland," *San Bernardino Daily Sun*, July 17, 1914.

27. "unsafe for the average driver": Clyde Bruckman, "Highway Variety Is Found In Mountains," *Los Angeles Times*, July 26, 1914.

27. his last *Times* byline: Clyde Bruckman, "Southpaws Make Great Fielding Pitchers," *Los Angeles Times*, August 21, 1914.

28. he hit an eighth-inning home run: Bill James, "Glories Beat Squirts 14–2," *Los Angeles Times*, October 20, 1914.

28. the players all received professionally printed invitations: Bob Ray, "The Sports X-Ray," *Los Angeles Times*, April 7, 1935.

28. "It would have been a perfect evening: Ibid.

29. her family followed him in 1913: "Mrs. Bruckman Last Rites Held," *Los Angeles Examiner*, October 10, 1931.

29. Al was in the film industry: Jeff Hamblin, e-mail message to author, July 21, 2015.

29. she had been a telephone operator: 1912 *Kansas City Directory* (Kansas City, MO: Gate City Directory Co., 1912), 730.

29. took the same job in Los Angeles: *Los Angeles City Directory 1914* (Los Angeles: Los Angeles Directory Company, 1914), 1141.

29. she was working in the mechanical department: *Los Angeles City Directory 1915* (Los Angeles: Los Angeles Directory Co., 1915), 970.

29. They were married the summer after: "Clyde Bruckman Takes a Bride in Los Angeles," *San Bernardino Daily Sun*, August 1, 1916.

29. "a charming blonde,": "Clyde Bruckman and Bride Visit San Bernardino," *San Bernardino Daily Sun*, September 6, 1916.

29. Clyde and Lola delayed their honeymoon: Ibid.

29. "Safety first," " 'Bruckie' Picks Horse for Safety but Misjudges Brute," *San Bernardino Daily Sun*, September 6, 1916.

29. abandoning both animal and vehicle: Ibid.

29. The newlyweds moved to a home: *Los Angeles City Directory 1917* (Los Angeles: Los Angeles Directory Co., 1917), 449.

29. **He'd been writing baseball stories:** *The Tyro*, June 1912, Arda Haenszel California Room, Norman F. Feldheym Central Library, San Bernardino, California, 58–62.

29. **he sold one to** *The Saturday Evening Post*: "Clyde Bruckman Takes a Bride in Los Angeles," *San Bernardino Daily Sun*, August 1, 1916.

30. **"If he's done anything with his habits:** Clyde A. Bruckman, "Reverse English," *Saturday Evening Post*, October 21, 1916.

30. **"There was one bet they overlooked:** Ibid.

30. **as more stories ran in** *The Blue Book Magazine*: "Chronological List," *The Fiction Mags Index*, http://www.philsp.com/homeville/fmi/d520.htm#A16112.

30. **and** *The Red Book Magazine*: "Clyde Bruckman Now Real Author," *San Bernardino Daily Sun*, April 24, 1917.

30. **"I am twenty-two and hopeful.":** Clyde A. Bruckman, "Contemporary Writers and Their Work: A Series of Autobiographical Letters: 122: Clyde A. Bruckman," *The Editor*, January 25, 1918.

30. **Bertha left Los Angeles for Denver:** "Personal," *San Bernardino Daily Sun*, November 25, 1917.

30. **he published six stories:** "Chronological List," *The Fiction Mags Index*, http://www.philsp.com/homeville/fmi/d520.htm#A16112.

30. **He was ineligible for the draft:** "World War I Draft Registration Cards, 1917–1918," digital images, Ancestry.com, Clyde Adolph Bruckman registration, no. 20 (right side numbering), Draft Board 07, City of Los Angeles, California; citing *World War I Selective Service System Draft Registration Cards, 1917–1918*, NARA, microfilm publication M1509, no specific roll cited.

30. **"it having developed that he is harmless:** "Seeing San Bernardino in Five Minutes," *San Bernardino Daily Sun*, June 8, 1918.

30. **he seems to have gone immediately to a baseball game:** C. A. Bruckman, "Babe Borton's Circuit Whack Downs Solons," *Los Angeles Examiner*, June 8, 1918.

31. **One contemporary report:** "Six Million Die From Flu," *Los Angeles Times*, December 20, 1918.

31. **the CDC currently suggests at least fifty:** Jeffery Taubenberger and

David Morens, "1918 Influenza: The Mother of All Pandemics," *Emerging Infectious Diseases*, January 2006, http://wwwnc.cdc.gov/eid/article/12/1/05-0979_article.

31. businesses, theaters, schools, and churches were closed: "Fighting 'Flu' In Los Angeles," *Los Angeles Times*, October 13, 1918.

31. at noon on December 2 the theaters reopened: " 'Funless' Season Ends Today," *Los Angeles Times*, December 2, 1918.

31. the Chinese was nearly a decade away: "Biblical Story Wins Applause," *Los Angeles Times*, May 29, 1927.

31. "four-system lighting effect.": " 'Funless' Season Ends Today," *Los Angeles Times*, December 2, 1918.

31. a $7,000 ventilation system: A. H. Giebler, "Installs $7,000 Ventilating System," *The Moving Picture World*, December 14, 1918.

31. Clyde's mother travelled from Denver: "Seeing San Bernardino in Five Minutes," *San Bernardino Daily Sun*, December 7, 1918.

31. she decided to move back to Los Angeles: "Seeing San Bernardino in Five Minutes," *San Bernardino Daily Sun*, February 12, 1919.

31. a house-to-house quarantine: "Quarantine Regulations," *Los Angeles Times*, December 18, 1918.

31. had closed for a month at the height of the pandemic: A. H. Giebler, "Universal Opened on November 18," *The Moving Picture World*, December 14, 1918.

31. his brothers-in-law at Famous Players-Lasky: Jeff Hamblin, e-mail to author, September 28, 2014.

32. who had been moonlighting for Hal Roach: "Hal Roach Reorganizes," *Los Angeles Times*, May 22, 1923.

32. the opportunity to do a new kind of writing: "Lyons and Moran Increase Staff," *The Moving Picture World*, February 15, 1919.

32. terrible news arrived from Philadelphia: "Charles E. Van Loan Dies," *Los Angeles Times*, March 3, 1919.

Missing Reels

33. new distributors and producers lined up: Richard Lewis Ward, *A His-*

tory of the Hal Roach Studios (Carbondale, IL: Southern Illinois University, 2006), 6–7.

34. The new firm began buying movie theaters: Bernard F. Dick, *Engulfed: The Death of Paramount Pictures and the Birth of Corporate Hollywood* (Lexington, KY: University Press of Kentucky, 2001), 9–13.

34. He had to submit each individual film: Ward, 13–14.

34. A reel ran between ten and fifteen minutes: Ibid., 7.

34. fronted with several single-reel shorts: Ibid., 3.

35. "More Plots and Fewer Pies.": "Mabel Wants 'More Plots and Fewer Pies' in Films," *Washington Times*, May 6, 1916.

35. Lyons had been at Carl Laemmle's: "News From the IMP Californian Company," *The Implet*, March 30, 1912.

35. Moran started working for Al Christie: "Three of a Kind," *The Moving Picture News*, April 20, 1912.

35. in the merger that formed Universal: "The Universal Film Manufacturing Company," *Motography*, August 3, 1912.

35. in Al Christie's *Hearts and Skirts*: "Hearts and Skirts," *The Cinema News and Property Gazette*, February 12, 1913.

35. that October: "Calendar of Independent Releases," *The Moving Picture World*, September 28, 1912.

35. "the unheavenly twins.": "Brevities of the Business," *Motography*, December 5, 1914.

35. "the mainstay of the Nestor-Universal Comedy Company,": "Lyons and Moran Stay With 'U'; Christie With Horsley," *Motion Picture News*, June 3, 1916.

35. They were on a grueling schedule: Ibid.

35. they celebrated making their fiftieth film together: G. P. Harleman, "Doings at Universal City," *The Moving Picture World*, May 5, 1917.

35. they'd made nearly 250: "Lyons And Moran Complete Their 250th Production," *The Moving Picture World*, May 17, 1919.

35. the studio had given them their own release label: "Lyons and Moran Back with Universal in One-Reelers," *The Moving Picture World*, March 30, 1918.

36. Fred Palmer: G. P. Harleman, "Activities at Universal Studios," *The Moving Picture World*, July 21, 1917.

36. C. B. "Pops" Hoadley: "New Bluebird Started," *Motion Picture News*, January 5, 1918.

36. "Captain Leslie T. Peacock.": G. P. Harleman, "Lyons and Moran Return from East," *The Moving Picture World*, December 22, 1917.

36. James Roots described their screen personas: James Roots, *The 100 Greatest Silent Comedians* (London: Rowman and Littlefield, 2014), 341.

36. According to *Moving Picture World*: "To Burlesque 'Flu' Epidemic," *The Moving Picture World*, December 14, 1918.

36. stories and experiences he'd had at the ballpark: Clyde A. Bruckman, "Contemporary Writers and Their Work: A Series of Autobiographical Letters: 122: Clyde A. Bruckman," *The Editor*, January 25, 1918.

36. including adapting Victor Hugo: "The Man Who Laughs," *The Film Daily*, May 6, 1928.

37. Clyde didn't leave the ballpark or the *Examiner*: "Seeing San Bernardino in Five Minutes," *San Bernardino Daily Sun*, February 22, 1919.

37. Lyons and Moran came up with many of the scenarios: Celia Brynn, "In Again, Out Again," *Picture-Play Magazine*, January 1920.

37. some were contributed by freelancers: William Lord Wright, "Hints for Scenario Writers," *Picture-Play Magazine*, February 1920.

37. or Clyde himself: "The Silent Drama," *The Cincinnati Enquirer*, June 14, 1919.

37. a style Al Christie had insisted on: Roots, 341.

37. he did this at night and in the early mornings: "Shadows on the Screen," *Buffalo Evening News*, June 17, 1919.

37. he alternated films with Melville Brown: "Engage Melville Brown," *The Moving Picture World*, April 5, 1919.

37. Word War I correspondent: William J. McGrath, "The Lost Express," *Motion Picture News*, September 15, 1917.

37. Frederick Bennett had come on board: "Short Stuff," *Wid's Daily*, July 13, 1919.

37. they released fifty-five one-reel shorts: These are listed variously in the

film catalogs for *The Moving Picture World* and *Motion Picture News* during this period, although only the four or five films in current release show up in each issue.

37. only credits Clyde for one of these: "Three in a Closet," *IMDb*, http://www.imdb.com/title/tt0334501/.

37. in which Eddie and Lee get addicted to Russian cigarettes: "Lyons and Moran Complete New Comedies," *Motion Picture News*, May 17, 1919.

37. "tea, cubeb cigarettes, malted milk, etc.": "Short Stuff," *Wid's Daily*, June 30, 1919.

37. a review of *The Smell of the Yukon*: "Universal Picture Company," *The Moving Picture World*, June 7, 1919.

38. As far as the plots go (not far): "Three in a Closet," *The Moving Picture World*, May 17, 1919.

38. a series of five-reel films: "Lyons and Moran Renew Contracts," *Exhibitors Herald*, December 20, 1919.

38. "comedy-drama": Ad for *Everything but the Truth*, *Motion Picture News*, June 12, 1920.

38. *Everything but the Truth*: "Movies Discover Clyde Is Clever," *Los Angeles Times*, June 6, 1920.

38. *Once a Plumber*: "The Liberty," *The Evening Herald* (Klamath Falls, OR), April 21, 1921.

38. both adaptations of stories by Edgar Franklin: "Universal Is Busy Titling," *Motion Picture News*, September 11, 1920.

38. "those who will perhaps appreciate it: "Lyons and Moran Slip in Their Third Feature Comedy," *Wid's Daily*, September 19, 1920.

38. "Seems as though patrons are loathe to accept: "What the Picture Did for Me," *Exhibitors Herald*, January 22, 1921.

38. Carl Laemmle got the message: "Lyons and Moran Again Producing Two-Reelers," *Exhibitors Herald*, January 22, 1921.

38. the team split permanently that summer: Clifford Knight, "Lee Moran to Star in a Series of Century Laughs," *Exhibitors Trade Review*, December 10, 1921.

38. Clyde pitched nineteen strikeouts: "Scribes Throw It to the Boobs," *Los Angeles Times*, September 9, 1919.

39. He began 1920 by covering the Rose Bowl: Clyde A. Bruckman, "Harvard Beats Oregon in Gridiron Classic," *The Washington Herald*, January 2, 1920.

39. while writing titles for *Everything but the Truth*: Harry Hammond Beall, "With the Procession in Los Angeles," *Exhibitors Herald*, April 10, 1920.

39. Beanie Walker was finally making enough writing: "Bruckman Is Named Sporting Editor," *San Bernardino Daily Sun*, April 23, 1920.

39. Sennett saw talent: "Comedian Has Long Struggle," *Los Angeles Times*, January 10, 1926.

39. shot in May 1920: J. C. Jessen, "News Notes from the West Coast," *Motion Picture News*, May 15, 1920.

39. and released on June 7: "Advance Information on All Film Releases," *Motion Picture News*, June 5, 1920.

39. Banks had just signed a deal with Warner Bros.: "Warner's New Comedies," *Wid's Daily*, April 29, 1920.

39. reused titles and tangled copyright registrations: David Levy, "Notes for an Essay on the Film Career of Monty Banks," *Early American Cinema*, http://early-american-cinema.com/articles/monty_banks.html.

39. Banks made his first four of these films: "Federated Announces Short Reelers," *Motion Picture News*, August 14, 1920.

40. credit Bruckman with writing all four of these two-reelers: Robert Farr, Joe Moore, Davide Turconi, "Monty Banks Filmography," *Slapsticon*, http://www.slapsticon.org/ mugshots/banksfilmo.htm.

40. Lola fell seriously ill and lingered near death: "Seeing San Bernardino in Five Minutes," *San Bernardino Daily Sun*, August 7, 1920.

40. the players had put together a $2,000 pool: "Probe of Coast League Games in 1919 Conducted," *San Bernardino Daily Sun*, October 19, 1920.

40. Clyde testified on November 15: "Babe Borton Heard in Baseball Scandal," *San Francisco Chronicle*, November 16, 1920.

40. Babe Borton and three other men were indicted: "Three Coast League Players Are Indicted," *Oakland Tribune*, December 11, 1920.

40. deliberately losing baseball games was not a crime: "Los Angeles Jury Drops Indictments," *Washington Post*, December 25, 1920.

40. The National Association of Minor Leagues: "Rumler, Borton, Dale, Maggert Expelled," *Oakland Tribune*, January 12, 1921.

40. Clyde wrote the titles for Lyons and Moran's *Once a Plumber*: "Universal Is Busy Titling," *Motion Picture News*, September 11, 1920.

40. as well as both scenarios and titles: Robert Farr, Joe Moore, Davide Turconi, "Monty Banks Filmography," *Slapsticon*, http://www.slapsticon.org/mugshots/banksfilmo.htm.

40. "ahead of his production schedule,": "Monty Banks Going Abroad October 28," *Exhibitors Herald*, November 6, 1920.

41. Clyde's last byline at the *Examiner*: Lisle Foote, *Buster Keaton's Crew: The Team Behind His Silent Films* (Jefferson, NC: McFarland and Company, 2014), 135.

41. ending his career as a sportswriter: C. A. Bruckman, "Angels to Tilt Lid on Baseball," *Los Angeles Examiner*, April 5, 1921.

41. *Variety* reported that Clyde had left the *Examiner*: Fred Shader, "Coast Film Notes," *Variety*, April 22, 1921.

41. The company had been founded by bankers: "Los Angeles Capital to Invade Picture Industry on Big Scale," *Exhibitors Herald*, February 14, 1920.

41. ARE *you* looking for comedies carrying *every week*: *Exhibitors Herald*, April 3, 1920.

41. Special Pictures ran into financial trouble: "Walgreen to Deliver 26 Films to Fed. At $1,500,000," *Variety*, February 25, 1921.

41. the Warner brothers took over: "Short Reel Deal," *Wid's Daily*, March 3, 1921.

41. He described his first full-time job: Rudi Blesh, *Keaton* (New York: The MacMillan Company, 1966), 148.

41. A *Peaceful Alley*: Robert Farr, Joe Moore, Davide Turconi, "Monty Banks Filmography," *Slapsticon*, http://www.slapsticon.org/mugshots/banksfilmo.htm.

42. released in September: "Monty Banks Making Personal Appearances," *Exhibitors Trade Review*, September 3, 1921.

42. "rescued from the financial scrap-heap,": Fred Shader, "Coast Film Notes," *Variety*, April 22, 1921.

42. suing for unpaid wages: "Director Brierly Sues," *Variety*, June 10, 1921.

42. "the fiasco of the Special Pictures Corporation.": "Bankers, Merchants Sued Through Fiasco," *Variety*, November 18, 1921.

42. he'd played first base for the Scribes: "Scribes Throw It to the Boobs," *Los Angeles Times*, September 9, 1919.

42. " 'Why don't you come over with Keaton?': Blesh, 148.

The Playhouse

43. "We want 'gags,' not story.": Harry R. Brand, "Writing Slapstick Comedies," *The Photodramatist*, November 1921.

44. Buster was a baseball nut and always had been: Keaton and Samuels, 154.

44. the *Los Angeles Times* covered their games: E.g., "Buster Keaton Nine Trounces Larry Semon's," *Los Angeles Times*, October 24, 1921.

44. Keaton's employment application looked like this: Blesh, 148.

45. "outfielder and writer": Ibid.

45. One of Keaton's stunt doubles, Ernie Orsatti: Feg Murray, "Another Walloping Wop," *Los Angeles Times*, January 16, 1929.

45. 'Nothing like baseball,': Blesh, 149.

45. "The Human Mop": Keaton and Samuels, 11.

45. "grotesque comedy.": Ad for "Keith's," *Boston Post*, May 28, 1903.

45. Fatty Arbuckle's *The Butcher Boy*: Keaton and Samuels, 90–92.

45. "you cannot make people laugh for five reels: "Arbuckle to Leave Keystone," *Motography*, October 7, 1916.

46. The deal was worth the exorbitant sum: "Zukor Signs Arbuckle," *New York Clipper*, February 26, 1919.

46. Keaton was moved into leading roles: Edwin Schallert, "Buster To Star," *Los Angeles Times*, March 26, 1920.

46. Schenck bought a studio at Lillian Way and Cahuenga: "Motion Picture Directory," *Screenland*, November 1923.

46. rechristening it the Keaton Studio: Keaton and Samuels, 125.

46. He broke his ankle in February: " 'Buster' Breaks Ankle," *Variety*, February 25, 1921.

46. was in a cast for months: Blesh, 154.

46. he signed with First National: "Buster Keaton Signs with First National," *Exhibitors Herald*, May 21, 1921.

46. The scenario department was headed by ex-vaudevillian: Foote, 169.

46. Joe Mitchell: Fred Schrader, "Coast Film Notes," *Variety*, July 1, 1921.

46. Fred Gabouri had been recently hired: Blesh, 154.

46. Elgin Lessley, a one-time still photographer: Foote, 43.

46. ex-Keystone Kop: Ibid., 98.

46. Malcolm St. Clair: "Coast Picture News," *Variety*, February 11, 1921.

46. Clyde's workday started at the civilized hour: Keaton and Samuels, 129–130.

47. landing at Special Pictures while Clyde was there: "Jean Havez's Switch," *Variety*, April 22, 1921.

47. when the company collapsed: "Coast Brevities," *Wid's Daily*, June 23, 1921.

47. until he switched to features in 1923: J. C. Jessen, "Studio And Player Brevities," *Motion Picture News*, January 20, 1923.

48. "He built a lightproof black box: Blesh, 152.

48. The secret to getting the timing right: Ibid., 168.

50. "Only someone as athletic as Buster Keaton: Patricia Eliot Tobias, "The Playhouse: An Accidental Masterpiece," video essay on *The Buster Keaton Collection* (2011; New York, Kino Lorber), Blu-ray.

50. "a phantasmagoria of masks,": Blesh, 168.

50. Members of the International Buster Keaton Society: "Damfinos," *The International Buster Keaton Society*, http://www.busterkeaton.com.

50. shortly before the release of *The Playhouse*: Keaton and Samuels, 156.

51. Arbuckle was tried three times: "Arbuckle Acquitted," *The Film Daily*, April 13, 1922.

51. he had to sell his remaining interest in Comique: "Inside Stuff," *Variety*, May 5, 1922.

51. the publicity destroyed his career: Keaton and Samuels, 156–161.

51. the idea came from Arbuckle himself: Marion Meade, *Buster Keaton: Cut to the Chase* (New York: Da Capo Press, 1997), 130.

51. Hart didn't speak to Keaton for two years afterward: Keaton and Samuels, unnumbered photo insert between 142–143.

51. "We were one big happy family: Blesh, 149.

52. Keaton had finished eleven of the twelve films: "Coast Brevities," *The Film Daily*, October 24, 1922 for completion of "The Balloonatic"; "4 New First Nationals Finished," *Exhibitors Trade Review*, August 19, 1922, for completion of "Day Dreams" and beginning production on "The Love Nest."

52. First National sent a regrettable telegram: Keaton and Samuels, 172.

52. Buster called their bluff: Edward McPherson, *Buster Keaton: Tempest In A Flat Hat* (New York: Newmarket Press, 2004), 120.

52. His new contract with Metro: "Coogan and Keaton Signed by Metro; Navarro to Star," *Exhibitors Herald*, January 27, 1923.

52. Clyde was already at Metro: "David Kirkland and Clyde Bruckman Are Now On Montana Staff," *Exhibitors Trade Review*, October 21, 1922.

52. *Rob 'Em Good*: Bruckman isn't mentioned in the trades or reviews of this short but his name's on the one-sheet, which can be seen at http://movieposters.ha.com/itm/comedy/rob-em-good-metro-1923-one-sheet-27-x-41-/a/7029-83753.s#Photo.

52. *and even Jean Havez,*:: J. C. Jessen, "Studio And Player Brevities," *Motion Picture News*, January 20, 1923.

Navigators

53. he'd had little creative control: Dardis, *Keaton*, 66–67.

53. Griffith's 1916 film had been a boondoggle for the director: Iris Barry, *D. W. Griffith: American Film Master* (New York: The Museum of Modern Art, 1940), 22–26.

54. "Cut the film apart: Blesh, 217.

55. The production seems like it was a nightmare: Blesh, 217–218.

55. "The making of a comedy is a severe nerve strain,": "Buster Keaton Works to Radio," *Vancouver Daily World*, September 8, 1923.

55. "ceaseless parties,": Blesh, 221.

56. In one or two of my later two-reelers: Keaton and Samuels, 173.

56. by all accounts had a wonderful summer: Blesh, 223–225.

56. He insisted on finishing the film: Ibid., 231–232.

56. adapted from a Rita Weiman short story: Ad for *Rouged Lips*, *Motion Picture News*, October 20, 1923.

56. The film shot in May: "Cast Is Selected for 'Rouged Lips,' " *Motion Picture News*, May 12, 1923.

56. production was finished by early June: "Some Coast-Made Pictures," *The Film Daily*, June 7, 1923.

56. "whose main ambition is to yawn without stretching.": "Rouged Lips," *Variety*, August 30, 1923.

57. "Were it forty-five minutes: Ibid.

57. That fall the Keaton features opened two months apart: Dardis, *Keaton*, 290.

57. he and Lola had moved to 1660 North Orange Drive: *Los Angeles City Directory: 1924* (Los Angeles: The Los Angeles Directory Co., 1924), 592.

57. Sid Grauman wouldn't announce construction: "New Grauman Playhouse," *Los Angeles Times*, September 12, 1924.

57. the Roosevelt Hotel: "Hollywood to Get New Hotel," *Los Angeles Times*, October 22, 1925.

57. landing its star, Glenn Hunter, a five year movie contract: "Glenn Hunter Signs Five-Year Contract with F.P.L.," *Exhibitors Trade Review*, March 24, 1923.

57. It's hard to imagine Keaton overacting, but both he: "Players We Know," *Exhibitors Trade Review*, December 15, 1923.

57. and Chaplin: " 'Merton' In Pictures?," *Film Daily*, January 1, 1923.

58. bought their new star the role he'd originated: "Cruze to Direct Hunter in 'Merton Of Movies'," *Exhibitors Trade Review*, January 12, 1924.

58. "You can't do it and tell a legitimate story: Buster Keaton, interview by Robert and Joan Franklin, in *Buster Keaton: Interviews*, ed. Kevin W. Sweeney (Jackson, MS: University Press of Mississippi, 2007), 90.

58. "the picture has about all the old hoke: "Sherlock Jr.," *Variety*, May 28, 1924.

58. "That is clever. The rest is bunk.": Ibid.

59. While travelling along the Northwest coast: Buster Keaton, interview by Arthur B. Friedman, in *Buster Keaton: Interviews*, ed. Kevin W. Sweeney (Jackson, MS: University Press of Mississippi, 2007), 23–24.

59. "You can do anything you damn please with her: Blesh, 252.

59. he was wary of destroying luxury property: Ibid., 253.

59. "There's the boat, now write me a comedy.": "Humorists All at Sea," *Los Angeles Times*, May 25, 1924.

59. Jean Havez had the idea: Blesh, 253.

59. Shooting involved ten weeks at sea: Meade, 149.

59. shared the *Buford*'s Imperial Japanese Suite: "He Admits It" (Ad for *The Navigator*), *Logansport Pharos-Tribune*, October 10, 1924.

59. Despite conflicts with director Donald Crisp: Buster Keaton, interview by Kevin Brownlow, *Buster Keaton:* Interviews, ed. Kevin W. Sweeney (University Press of Mississippi, Jackson, 2007): 203–205.

59. was his favorite after *The General*: Dardis, *Keaton*, 109.

60. It took us a while to figure out: Keaton and Samuels, 175.

60. It didn't matter what terrific gag you gave them: Ibid., 174.

60. no one but Schenck was thrilled about it: McPherson, 161–162.

61. Keaton owed Schenck favors: Meade, 153–154.

61. in the ads, mentioned he and the other gag men by name: "He Admits It" (Ad for *The Navigator*), *Logansport Pharos-Tribune*, October 10, 1924.

61. He spent the fall working on adapting the play: "The Studio Directory: West Coast," *Photoplay*, November 1924.

61. filming began in January: Meade, 154.

Built-To-Order Comedies

63. bit parts for D. W. Griffith: Brent E. Walker, *Mack Sennett's Fun Factory: A History and Filmography of his Keystone and Mack Sennett Comedies, with Biographies of Players and Personnel* (Jefferson, NC: McFarland and Company, 2010), 9–10.

63. He'd bought out Thomas Ince's studio: Mack Sennett and Cameron Shipp, *King of Comedy* (Garden City, NJ: Doubleday and Company, 1954), 85.

63. they got poached away by other studios: Keaton and Samuels, 111.

63. headed by Arthur Ripley, his coworkers were: "Sennett Outlines Plans For New Year," *Mack Sennett News Bulletin*, January 10, 1925, Mack Sen-

nett Papers, Margaret Herrick Library, Academy of Motion Picture Arts and Sciences.

64. "Bashful Jim" on the title page: Clyde Bruckman and Brian Foy, "Graves Story no. 171," Mack Sennett Papers, Margaret Herrick Library, Academy of Motion Picture Arts and Sciences.

64. Clyde and Brian Foy were credited for the film's scenario: Final Continuity Sheet, "Bashful Jim," Mack Sennett Papers, Margaret Herrick Library, Academy of Motion Picture Arts and Sciences.

64. Pick up on [Marvin] Loback driving his Ford: Clyde Bruckman and Brian Foy, "Graves Story no. 171," Mack Sennett Papers, Margaret Herrick Library, Academy of Motion Picture Arts and Sciences.

65. "This is a spot: Ibid.

65. Loback and the girl arrive: Ibid.

65. Title for picture within a picture: "Title Spots Kline [sic]-Graves Picture," Mack Sennett Papers, Margaret Herrick Library, Academy of Motion Picture Arts and Sciences.

66. "If he don't kiss her pretty soon I'll scream!": Subtitles folder, "Bashful Jim," Mack Sennett Papers, Margaret Herrick Library, Academy of Motion Picture Arts and Sciences.

66. In this case he crossed out "picture": Ibid.

67. "I got his photo in a box of prunes!": Final Continuity Sheet, "Bashful Jim," Mack Sennett Papers, Margaret Herrick Library, Academy of Motion Picture Arts and Sciences.

67. Clyde wrote at least one more short: "Langdon Circus Story no. 174," Mack Sennett Papers, Margaret Herrick Library, Academy of Motion Picture Arts and Sciences.

67. Clyde was hired away to work for Harold Lloyd: Dardis, *Harold Lloyd*, 156.

67. "As a moral lesson: Harold Lloyd and Wesley Stout, *An American Comedy* (New York: Longmans, Green and Co., 1928), 25–30.

67. Lloyd had come up from theater: Ibid., 69.

68. there he met Hal Roach: Ibid., 79.

68. Lloyd joined him: Ibid., 82.

68. left briefly for Sennett: Ibid., 87–88.

68. put on the horn-rimmed glasses that would make him famous: Ibid., 105.
68. In 1918 he'd blown off most of his own hand: "Harold Lloyd's Accident," *Variety Daily Bulletin*, August 27, 1919.
68. "masked and justified the nakedness of the aggression.": Walter Kern, *The Silent Clowns* (New York: Alfred A. Knopf, 1975), 191.
68. had grossed $680,406 domestically: Meade, 151.
68. *Girl Shy* and *Hot Water* had grossed more than $1.7 million: Dardis, *Harold Lloyd*, 155.
68. Lloyd's production company was his own: "Lloyd an Independent," *Film Daily*, June 17, 1923.
68. Clyde came on board on February 23: Dardis, *Harold Lloyd*, 156.
69. Lloyd had started shooting football footage in October: Harold Lloyd Corporation v. Witwer, 65 F.2d 1 (9th Cir. 1933).
69. It isn't going to work, boys: Dardis, *Harold Lloyd*, 157.
69. production wrapped at the end of March: Harold Lloyd Corporation v. Witwer, 65 F.2d 1 (9th Cir. 1933).
69. his contributions were crucial: Dardis, *Harold Lloyd*, 156.
69. formed his own production company: "Banks in New Company," *Film Daily*, November 26, 1924.
69. he began shooting his new film: Harvey E. Gausman, "Hollywood Happenings," *Film Daily*, March 15, 1925.
70. "a corking motor boat thriller,": "Monty Banks in a Corking Motorboat Thriller," *Exhibitors Trade Review*, July 11, 1925.
70. One of those built-to-order comedies: "Keep Smiling," *Variety*, January 20, 1926.
70. "In which Monty Banks again tries to prove that he is a comedian.": "Brief Reviews of Current Pictures," *Photoplay*, November 1925.
70. It made $2.6 million: Dardis, *Harold Lloyd*, 166.
71. then selling her house out from under her: "Foreigner Claims Eviction Unjust," *Los Angeles Times*, October 8, 1916.
71. It wasn't even his first offense: "Judge Finds Real Estate Dealer Tricks Poor Woman," *Los Angeles Times*, October 10, 1916.

71. Clark had met Bertha's family: "Holiday Visitors at the Chan W. Smith Home," *San Bernardino Daily Sun*, December 22, 1923.

71. Chauncey W. Smith died in 1924: "In the Shadow," *San Bernardino Daily Sun*, February 6, 1924.

71. "have ridden in an automobile together: "Sister Accused in Divorce Suit," *Los Angeles Times*, November 19, 1925.

71. the *Los Angeles Times* running photos: "Two Sides of Unusual Triangle," *Los Angeles Times*, November 19, 1925.

71. "Mrs. Hersford [*sic*] was my husband's favorite sister: "Wife Is Suing Sister-in-Law," *San Bernardino Daily Sun*, November 19, 1925.

72. they buried the story on the last page: "Wife Names Other Woman in Divorce," *Los Angeles Examiner*, November 19, 1925.

72. "nervous attacks": "Mystery Shrouds Death of Mrs. Chan Smith in Fall Off Porch," *San Bernardino Daily Sun*, September 11, 1927.

72. 77.5 percent of domestic gross: Dardis, *Harold Lloyd*, 167.

72. *For Heaven's Sake* was the first feature produced: "Lloyd making first for Paramount," *Motion Picture News*, October 31, 1925.

72. he hired Clyde back again in March of 1926: "Clyde Bruckman Added to Keaton 'Gag' Staff," *Motion Picture News*, March 20, 1926.

An Important Place In Motion Picture History

73. the first edition was published in 1863: William Pittenger, *Daring and Suffering: A History of The Great Railroad Adventure* (Philadelphia: J.W. Daughaday, 1863), 5.

74. It is painful for me to recall the adventures: William Pittenger, *The Great Locomotive Chase: A History of the Andrews Railroad Raid Into Georgia In 1862* (Philadelphia: The Penn Publishing Company, 1908), 13.

74. Clyde Bruckman run into this book: Buster Keaton, interview by George C. Pratt, *Buster Keaton: Interviews*, ed. Kevin W. Sweeney (Jackson, MS: University Press of Mississippi, 2007), 44–45.

75. "The audience resents it: Buster Keaton, interview by Kevin Brownlow, *Buster Keaton: Interviews*, ed. Kevin W. Sweeney (Jackson, MS: University Press of Mississippi, 2007), 206.

75. Though Keaton always claimed: Buster Keaton, interview by George

C. Pratt, *Buster Keaton: Interviews*, ed. Kevin W. Sweeney (Jackson, MS: University Press of Mississippi, 2007), 34–35.

75. Clyde's copy of the script resurfaced: "Lot 876 of 1049: Original Script for Buster Keaton Film *The General*, Hollywood Legends 2014 (no. 41214)," *Julien's Auctions*, http://www.julienslive.com/view-auctions/catalog/id/120/lot/51955.

75. Scene 310. Profile long shot of switch and loading trestle: Ibid.

76. *The General*, Buster's first UA film: Dardis, *Keaton*, 137.

76. They had originally planned to shoot in Tennessee: "4 Gag Men—1 Film," *Variety*, April 4, 1926.

76. the scenery didn't look very good: Buster Keaton, interview by Kevin Brownlow, *Buster Keaton: Interviews*, ed. Kevin W. Sweeney (Jackson, MS: University Press of Mississippi, 2007), 179.

76. Marion Meade gives a different explanation: Meade, 161.

76. toured the area in early May: "Buster Keaton Decides to Film 'The General' in Row River Section," *Cottage Grove Sentinel*, May 10, 1926.

76. the rest of the crew returned to begin shooting: "Buster and Mrs. Keaton Arrive to Start on Film," *Cottage Grove Sentinel*, May 31, 1926.

77. "Oh, I'd put one of my writers' names: Buster Keaton, interview by Kevin Brownlow, *Buster Keaton: Interviews*, ed. Kevin W. Sweeney (Jackson, MS: University Press of Mississippi, 2007), 175.

77. *Variety* reported that he would be co-directing: "Gag Man Co-Directing," *Variety*, June 1, 1926.

77. *What exactly would the co-director do?*: Buster Keaton, interview by John Gillet and James Blue, *Buster Keaton: Interviews*, ed. Kevin W. Sweeney (Jackson, MS: University Press of Mississippi, 2007), 221–222.

78. "You seldom saw his name in the story credits: Blesh, 149–150.

78. the entire town of Cottage Grove was commandeered: "Many Come to Hollywood of Oregon to See Buster Keaton Company in Action," *Cottage Grove Sentinel*, June 10, 1926.

78. extras lived in train cars: Buster Keaton, interview by George C. Pratt, *Buster Keaton: Interviews*, ed. Kevin W. Sweeney (Jackson, MS: University Press of Mississippi, 2007), 46.

78. that single stunt cost $42,000: Meade, 163–166.

78. more than half a million dollars today: "US Inflation Calculator," http://usinflationcalculator.com.

79. paying to have the local baseball field leveled: "Many Come to Hollywood of Oregon to See Buster Keaton Company in Action," *Cottage Grove Sentinel*, June 10, 1926.

79. playing third base on a local team: "Buster to Play Ball on Eugene Team," *Cottage Grove Sentinel*, June 17, 1926.

79. the *Sentinel* ran features and interviews: "900 Show Up Ready for Filming Battle Scenes," *Cottage Grove Sentinel*, June 22, 1926.

79. "important copy has failed to arrive from Hollywood: "Movie Edition Delayed," *Cottage Grove Sentinel*, August 16, 1926.

79. everyone got roaring drunk: Meade, 169.

80. he had to leave town before the film finally screened: Meade, 171–172.

80. "The action is placed entirely in the hands of the star: "The General," *Variety*, Feb. 9, 1927.

80. in its day it was a financial disaster: Meade, 173.

80. about five million dollars today: "US Inflation Calculator," http://usinflationcalculator.com.

81. "it was understood that Buster intended to favor this city.": "Buster Keaton Picture Ready to Be Shown," *Cottage Grove Sentinel*, November 8, 1926.

81. "the Arcade theater here will have the first booking: "Buster Keaton Is Not to Return Here," *Cottage Grove Sentinel*, November 15, 1926.

81. Cottage Grove was invited to send a delegation: "Buster's Picture on in Portland," *Cottage Grove Sentinel*, December 9, 1926.

81. "to make certain that there shall be no slip-up in these arrangements.": "Cottage Grove Is to Be First on Keaton Film," *Cottage Grove Sentinel*, December 16, 1926.

81. "There Is Slip Up Somewhere in Contract with Film Exchange,": "Keaton Picture Already Shown at O.A.C. City," *Cottage Grove Sentinel*, January 6, 1927.

81. they didn't manage to get a print: "The General to Show Arcade Theater Jan. 25 to 29," *Cottage Grove Sentinel*, January 13, 1927.

81. One of the important men in the Keaton organization: The Cottage

Grove Historical Society, ed., *The Day Buster Smiled: The 1926 Filming of "The General" by Buster Keaton as Chronicled in the Cottage Grove Sentinel Newspaper, Cottage Grove, Oregon*, 3rd ed. (Cottage Grove, OR: Eugene Print, Inc., 2002), 45.

License to Drive

83. **Lloyd didn't know any better:** Buster Keaton, interview by Kevin Brownlow, *Buster Keaton: Interviews*, ed. Kevin W. Sweeney (Jackson, MS: University Press of Mississippi, 2007), 175.

83. **When Lloyd left Pathé:** Dardis, *Harold Lloyd*, 167–168.

83. **"Merit Won His Start:** "Merit Won His Start in Films," *Los Angeles Times*, September 27, 1925.

83. **"Comedian Winner by Hard Work:** "Comedian Winner by Hard Work," *Los Angeles Times*, November 22, 1925.

84. **In April of 1926, Pathé signed Monty Banks:** "Mr. Banks Takes the Spotlight," *Los Angeles Times*, April 25, 1926.

84. **his first feature under the new contract:** " 'Atta Boy' Unit Only One at Hal Roach Studio," *Motion Picture News*, August 7, 1926.

84. **"It was the friendliest lot in Hollywood.":** Skretvedt, 36–39.

84. **Beanie Walker, his old boss from *The Examiner*:** "Hal Roach Reorganizes," *Los Angeles Times*, May 22, 1923.

84. **Clyde began his first job as a genuine director:** Grace Kingsley, "Star Plays Baseball Hero," *Los Angeles Times*, Nov. 5, 1926.

84. **Arthur turns out to be the daughter:** "*Horse Shoes* Is Highly Amusing Comedy," *Los Angeles Times*, April 3, 1927.

85. **he hired Clyde for his next feature:** "Bruckman to Direct Banks's Next," *The Film Daily*, December 17, 1926.

85. **he and Clyde went to work on their next film:** Grace Kingsley, "Ben Hecht in the Movies," *Los Angeles Times*, January 19, 1927.

85. **There's also an elaborate subplot:** Raymond Ganly, "A Perfect Gentleman," *Motion Picture News*, January 14, 1928.

85. **a new title, *A Perfect Gentleman*:** "Coast Studios," *Variety*, March 2, 1927.

85. **shot aboard the SS *Ruth Alexander*:** "Ship Passengers to See Comedy Filmed," *Los Angeles Times*, March 5, 1927.

85. Buster Keaton bought an enormous Italian villa in Beverly Hills: Dardis, *Keaton*, 116–118.

85. Clyde helped him move in: Blesh, 280.

85. Greenacres, his Beverly Hills estate: Dardis, *Harold Lloyd*, 219–222.

86. The house is still standing: "Assessor's ID no. 4341-020-017," *Property Assessment Information System*, Los Angeles County Office of the Assessor, http://maps.assessor.lacounty.gov.

86. visited often as a child: Donald P. Swisher, in discussion with author, November 29, 2014.

86. a baby grand piano: "Furniture at Auction," Classified Ad, *The Los Angeles Times*, April 27, 1941.

86. "The house became *the house*.": Richard Hamblin, in discussion with author, February 20, 2015.

86. "Lola attracted people: Ibid.

87. "a very funny, exceptionally human comedy: " 'Horse Shoes' Is Highly Amusing Comedy, *Los Angeles Times*, April 3, 1927.

87. "the production has its slow moments: Raymond Ganly, "Horse Shoes," *Motion Picture News*, April 15, 1927.

87. It is almost impossible now to describe: Kerr, 292.

87. Clyde was tapped to direct: "Banks Prepares for New Comedy," *Hollywood Vagabond*, May 5, 1927.

87. unaccountably decided to retitle his film *The Flying Fool*: "Banks Changes Title," *Film Daily*, June 5, 1927.

87. "Walking is good for one's health, I've heard,": "Car Too Fast So Actor Walks," *Los Angeles Times*, June 16, 1927.

87. MacArthur was eventually barred from going to the lot: "MacArthur Gets Orders to Stay Off Monty's Lot," *Los Angeles Times*, July 21, 1927.

88. "I believe the man who swore to the warrant: "Monty Banks Again in Toils Over Driving," *Los Angeles Times*, September 30, 1927.

88. "he does more harm than good.": "Slander Action Started Against Actor in Films," *Los Angeles Times*, October 8, 1927.

88. "in a desperate effort to avoid financial ruin.": "Actor Has Auto Trial Continued," *Los Angeles Times*, October 27, 1927.

88. "I am taking no chances,": "Monty Not to Chance Court's Ire," *Los Angeles Times*, November 25, 1927.

88. He ended up with a suspended sentence of thirty days in jail: "Suspended Sentence for Banks," *Los Angeles Times*, November 22, 1927.

88. "Funny Now and Then,": Raymond Ganly, "A Perfect Gentleman," *Motion Picture News*, January 14 1928.

88. he was down to $150 in assets: "Bankrupt Plea of Monty Banks Filed in East," *Los Angeles Times*, June 21, 1929.

88. Unable to work in sound film because of his accent: "Monty Banks Dies Suddenly on Italian Train," *Los Angeles Times*, January 9, 1950.

89. In May, he signed a long-term contract: Harvey E. Gausman, "Roach Signs New Director," *The Film Daily*, May 15, 1927.

89. Roach had just promoted: "Title Writer Promoted by Roach Studio," *Los Angeles Times*, March 5, 1927.

The Boys

91. the biggest stars on the lot: Ward, 67.

91. its final film starring Rex the Wonder Horse: Ibid., 56.

91. "What's typical about an L&H movie: Skretvedt, 107.

92. The solution they arrived at was removing Pallette: Ted Okuda and James L. Neibaur, *Stan Without Ollie: The Stan Laurel Solo Films 1917–1927* (Jefferson, NC: McFarland & Company, 2012), 210 – 211.

92. "one of the unfunniest comedians around,": Skretvedt, 17.

92. Laurel was initially barred from appearing in Roach films: Ibid., 42–44.

93. neither Laurel nor co-star James Finleyson: Okuda and Neibaur, 209–212.

93. Pathé was also distributing Mack Sennett's films: Skretvedt, 91.

93. the deal was arranged by Fred Quimby: "Quimby with Roach, Indirectly with M-G-M," *Variety*, January 26, 1927.

93. Hardy's injury: Skretvedt, 46.

94. Stan Laurel, despite his minor role in the film itself: Okuda and Neibaur, 209–212.

94. Roach decided to test Laurel: Skretvedt, 95.

94. he decided he could do no worse: Ibid., 24.

94. New York studios spent winters there: Walter R. Early, "The Call of Jacksonville," *Motography*, March 11, 1916.

94. Hardy found steady work as a comic villain: Skretvedt, 25–28.

94. headed west in late 1918: John McCabe, *Mr. Laurel and Mr. Hardy* (Garden City, NY: Doubleday and Company, 1961), 72–73.

95. "He was anxious to be part of a team: Skretvedt, 97.

95. "Stan Laurel and Oliver Hardy,": Ibid., 95–98.

95. he would be sidelined at the request of MGM executives: Richard W. Bann, "Max Davidson: Blow by Blow," *Laurel and Hardy: The Official Website*, http://www.laurel-and-hardy.com/archive/articles/2011-01-davidson/ davidson-1.html.

96. "the boys were just too good to be kept inactive,": Skretvedt, 99.

96. Clyde took the reins from Roach: Richard W. Bann, "Max Davidson: Blow by Blow," *Laurel and Hardy: The Official Website*, http://www.laurel-and-hardy.com/archive/articles/2011-01-davidson/davidson-1.html.

97. he misremembered it as being the first: Stan Laurel to John McCabe, March 20, 1956, *The Stan Laurel Archive Correspondence Project*, http://www.lettersfromstan.com.

97. the first film made after Roach Studios announced: Skretvedt, 104.

97. not quite a Laurel and Hardy film: Ibid., 107.

97. reediting films after timing the laughs: McCabe, 140–142.

98. "one of the funniest things I have ever looked at": Skredvedt, 107.

98. "Pandemonium was loose in the vast arena,": Alan J. Gould, "Dempsey Defeated by Single Second," *Los Angeles Times*, September 23, 1927.

98. his father was a boxing promoter: Wes D. Gehring, *Laurel and Hardy: A Bio-bibliography* (Westport, CT: Greenwood Press, 1990), 27.

99. "seized on the commotion": Bill Henry, "Handball Great Help to Leo McCarey," *Los Angeles Times*, March 14, 1937.

99. Lola Bruckman, who had traveled to Chicago: Myra Nye, "Society of Cinemaland," *Los Angeles Times*, September 25, 1927.

99. Harold Lloyd's frequent comic foil, Noah Young: Skretvedt, 107.

99. a strict rule against pie-throwing: Keaton and Samuels, 173–174.

99. "early Sennett, mid-Chaplin, and late everybody,": McCabe, 127.

99. His method would consist, simply and directly, of throwing more pies:

Philip K. Scheuer, "Comics Famous 'by Accident,' " *Los Angeles Times*, December 29, 1929.

99. owed his career to Charles Van Loan: Bill Henry, "Handball Great Help to Leo McCarey," *Los Angeles Times*, March 14, 1937.

100. "It wasn't just that we threw hundreds of pies,": Ibid.

100. McCarey's "supervisor" credit: Skretvedt, 110.

101. he credits Clyde with *The Battle of the Century*: Stan Laurel to John McCabe, March 20, 1956, *The Stan Laurel Archive Correspondence Project*, http://www.lettersfromstan.com.

101. was reportedly rarely on sets: Skretvedt, 63.

101. Stan Laurel eventually took more control: Ibid., 61–64.

102. the only version of the second reel known to have survived: Ibid., 109.

102. It wasn't until 2015 that film collector and historian Jon Mirsalis realized: Jon Mirsalis, e-mail message to author, June 15, 2015.

103. Blake Edwards: Skretvedt, 109.

103. James Agee: James Agee, "Comedy's Greatest Era," *LIFE*, September 5, 1949.

103. John Ford: Scott Eyman, *Print the Legend: The Life and Times of John Ford* (New York: Simon and Schuster, 2015), 278.

103. "the greatest comic film ever made.": Henry Miller, "The Golden Age," in *The Cosmological Eye* (New York: New Directions, 1939), 54.

103. projecting an infantile asexuality: Kyp Harness, *The Art of Laurel and Hardy: Graceful Calamity in the Films* (Jefferson, NC: McFarland and Company, 2006), 100.

105. due to a construction screw-up: Skretvedt, 112–114.

105. they were both frequent visitors: Richard Hamblin, in discussion with author, February 20, 2015.

106. he left Roach Studios to rejoin him: Keaton and Samuels, 201.

Tong Wars

107. it was meant to be a safe bet: Dardis, *Keaton*, 146–149.

107. a box-office fiasco: Ibid., 155.

107. Jean Havez had died: Foote, 163.

107. Joe Mitchell was working freelance: Ibid., 170.

107. Eddie Cline was trying, unsuccessfully: Ibid., 66–67.

107. With the sole exception of Charles Reisner: Keaton and Samuels, 203.

107. "He was a good one,": Buster Keaton, interview by Kevin Brownlow, *Buster Keaton: Interviews*, ed. Kevin W. Sweeney (Jackson, MS: University Press of Mississippi, 2007), 186.

107. "absolutely useless to me.": Ibid., 210.

108. He didn't write nothing: Ibid., 175.

108. once he was on the job he suddenly turned serious: Blesh, 284.

108. Brand went over his head: Ibid., 285.

108. Keaton openly loathed him: Dardis, *Keaton*, 146–149.

109. bored in his work, bored in his marriage: Ibid.

109. Buster Keaton Studios was shuttering for good: Blesh, 298–299.

109. "all softened up.": Ibid.

109. he was able to use MGM's money: Dardis, *Keaton*, 162.

110. he was paid $34,866: Ibid., 171.

110. nearly half a million dollars today: "US Inflation Calculator," http://usinflationcalculator.com.

110. twice what Stan Laurel and Oliver Hardy had made: Skretvedt, 119.

110. that would yield further promotional opportunities in Hearst's papers: Keaton and Samuels, 207.

110. the *crème de la crème* of the M-G-M writing staff: Ibid., 208.

111. Well, now here is rule number one with us: Buster Keaton, interview by Herbert Feinstein, *Buster Keaton: Interviews*, ed. Kevin W. Sweeney (Jackson, MS: University Press of Mississippi, 2007), 144.

111. Clyde gave them both what they wanted: Dardis, *Keaton*, 166.

111. Thalberg assigned Lawrence Weingarten: Blesh, 299.

112. they couldn't plan his budgets: Dardis, *Keaton*, 162.

112. After insisting on shooting in New York: Ibid., 165.

112. he was too famous to shoot on public streets: Keaton and Samuels, 209.

112. Keaton went over his head: Blesh, 203.

112. Not being on a team: Keaton and Samuels, 213.

113. promoted to head MGM's technical department: Ibid., 205.

113. He then sat down amidst the wreckage: Dardis, *Keaton*, 166–169.

113. he left Keaton once more for Paramount: "Protege Wins Out," *Los Angeles Times*, August 10, 1928.

113. he'd been poached once again: "Lloyd's Gag Staff," *Variety*, August 22, 1928.

113. more than two million dollars: Dardis, *Harold Lloyd*, 200.

114. I do not believe the talking motion picture: "When We Will Really Have Talking Movies," *Motion Picture Magazine*, June 1927.

114. There is so much money invested: Ibid.

114. he was considering using sound: "Lloyd May Use Sound," *Exhibitors Herald and Moving Picture World*, June 23, 1928.

114. he described sound as "doomed,": Dardis, *Harold Lloyd*, 207–208.

114. his next film might feature sound effects and music: "No Talkies For Leading Stars," *Exhibitors Daily Review*, July 19, 1928.

115. "I am thoroughly convinced that talking pictures are here to stay,": "Harold Lloyd Plans to Use Both Sound, Dialogue in His Next," *Exhibitors Herald and Moving Picture World*, September 8, 1928.

115. his plan was to create the silent version first: Dardis, *Harold Lloyd*, 207–208.

115. Ted Wilde, who'd just directed Lloyd in *Speedy*: "Lloyd's Gag Staff," *Variety*, August 22, 1928.

115. *Welcome Danger* was to start in June: "Lloyd May Use Sound," *Exhibitors Herald and Moving Picture World*, June 23, 1928.

115. Among those struck ill in late November was Ted Wilde: "Flu Epidemic on Coast Hits 500 Studio People of All Classes," *Variety*, November 28, 1928.

115. Lloyd shut down everything: "Flu Stops Lloyd," *Variety*, December 19, 1928.

115. The gag staff came back, but Wilde didn't: "Wilde's Ordered Rest," *Variety*, January 2, 1929.

116. He wouldn't be well enough to work again until summer: "Back Again, and Ready to Direct a New Personality," *Hollywood Filmograph*, June 15, 1929.

116. negotiations with unnamed "Top Playwrights.": "Harold Lloyd Negoti-

ating with Top Playwrights on Dialogue," *Exhibitors Herald and Moving Picture World*, December 1, 1928.

116. **After only five days:** Hubert I. Cohen, "The Serious Business of Being Funny: Harold Lloyd Looks Back On His Career As A Great Film Comic," *Film Comment*, Fall 1969.

116. **Under the deal just negotiated:** "Harold Lloyd Signs for Metropolitan Studios for First Dialogue Picture," *Exhibitors Herald and Moving Picture World*, December 15, 1928.

117. **"provided there is a place and a need for it:** "Mal St. Clair Lands Rich Plum for 1929—Will Direct Lloyd-Paramount Production," *Exhibitors Daily Review*, December 29, 1928.

117. **Lloyd vowed to remove nearly half:** "Lloyd's 16-Reel Preview," *Variety*, May 22, 1929.

117. **Lloyd thought this was as much a function of audiences:** Dardis, *Harold Lloyd*, 209.

117. **"My God, we worked our hearts out:** Harold Lloyd, American Film Institute Seminar, September 23, 1969, in *Conversations with the Great Moviemakers of Hollywood's Golden Age at the American Film Institute*, ed. George Stevens Jr. (New York: Alfred A. Knopf, 2006), 12.

117. **"Maybe we've kind of missed the boat,":** Hubert I. Cohen, "The Serious Business of Being Funny: Harold Lloyd Looks Back on His Career as a Great Film Comic," *Film Comment*, Fall 1969.

118. **"Nobody knew what they were doing,"** Ibid.

118. **the dubbing was horrible:** Harold Lloyd, American Film Institute Seminar, September 23, 1969, in *Conversations with the Great Moviemakers of Hollywood's Golden Age at the American Film* Institute, ed. George Stevens Jr. (New York: Alfred A. Knopf, 2006), 12–13.

118. **"Well, I've heard of strawberry and raspberry,":** Dardis, *Harold Lloyd*, 213.

119. **"certain that it will please the public:** Dardis, *Harold Lloyd*, 215.

119. **"ordered the negative sent forthwith:** "Lloyd's First Talkie Beset with Tribulation," *Los Angeles Times*, September 22, 1929.

119. **but the sound version was all Clyde:** Susan King, "It Was Lloyd's First Talkie and Last Silent," *Los Angeles Times*, August 13, 2008.

119. *Welcome Danger* grossed $23,000 in its first two days: Norbert Lusk, "Lloyd's First Talkie A Hit," *Los Angeles Times*, October 27, 1929.

120. One saw Mr. Lloyd move his lips: Martin Dickstein, "Harold Lloyd in First Talkie—Other Films at Fox and Albee—Rian James," *The Brooklyn Daily Eagle*, October 21, 1929.

120. rioted at a screening: "Chinese Students Riot Over Talkie," *Washington Post*, February 24, 1930.

120. When we made "Welcome Danger,": "Bull-etin," *Logansport Pharos-Tribune*, March 28, 1930.

120. Chiang Kai-shek's Nationalist government banned the film: "Lloyd Film Banned In All of China," *New York Times*, April 16, 1930.

121. *Welcome Danger* grossed more than anything else: Dardis, *Harold Lloyd*, 215.

Queen of Angels

123. Clyde would direct his next film: "Coast Notes," *Variety*, December 11, 1929.

123. in January they were still torn: "Lloyd Chooses Director," *Los Angeles Times*, January 28, 1930.

123. I am more enthused over this story: Dan Thomas, "Harold Gets His Wish—He's Going to Go to Sea," *Santa Cruz Evening News*, April 12, 1930.

124. Departure was scheduled for May 24: "Lloyd to Take Scenes of New Film on Island," *Los Angeles Times*, April 28, 1930.

124. an attack of appendicitis: "Harold Lloyd Stricken," *New York Times*, May 20, 1930.

124. managed to avoid one until the next year: "Harold Lloyd's Condition Good," *Los Angeles Times*, April 13, 1931.

124. Filming began with the *Malolo*'s next voyage: Clyde Bruckman, SS *Malolo* Passenger Manifest, June 7, 1930; Stamped Page 273, Line 11, *Passenger Lists of Vessels Arriving at Honolulu, Hawaii, compiled 2/13/1900–12/30/1953* (National Archives Microfilm Publication A4156, roll 184); *Records of the Immigration and Naturalization Service 1784–2004*, Record Group 85, database online, Ancestry.com.

124. a proof-of-concept for making sound films at sea: "Steamer to Become Studio," *Los Angeles Times*, May 11, 1930.

124. Lloyd attended a Luau: "Comedian Back from Honolulu," *Los Angeles Times*, June 22, 1930.

124. a gale which nearly washed the sound equipment overboard: Speed Kendall, "Lloyd's Newest Work Replete with Thrills," *Los Angeles Times*, October 5, 1930.

124. on June 21 cast and crew returned: "Comedian Back from Honolulu," *Los Angeles Times*, June 22, 1930.

125. *Feet First* was released that October: Dardis, *Harold Lloyd*, 224–227.

126. "state of horror all the way through.": George C. Pratt, "Mind Over Matter: Harold Lloyd Remembers," *Image*, September 1976.

126. "In *Safety Last* we had what we call an idea: Ibid.

127. "literally rolled in the aisles": Whitney Williams, "Hilarity Runs Rampant in 'Feet First,'" *Los Angeles Times*, November 2, 1930.

127. grossed just over half as much: Dardis, *Harold Lloyd*, 230.

127. another college film next: "Forthcoming Pictorial Features," *New York Times*, September 7, 1930.

128. a parody of Westerns: "Lloyd Abandoning College Picture," *Los Angeles Times*, November 29, 1930.

128. The old Harold Lloyd is no more: Jessie F. Edgerly, "Turn Back the Movie Universe," *Screenland*, May 1931.

128. decided to see if Wheeler and Woolsey could sell tickets on their own: Edward Watz, *Wheeler and Woolsey: The Vaudeville Comic Duo and Their Films, 1929–1937* (Jefferson, NC: McFarland Classics, 2001), 124.

129. from $750 to $1,250 a week: "Harold Lloyd Corporation Increase Card," February 16, 1931, Clyde Bruckman Pay Records, Harold Lloyd Papers, Margaret Herrick Library, Academy of Motion Picture Arts and Sciences.

129. *Variety* reported that RKO had hired Clyde: "Hollywood Bulletins," *Variety*, February 18, 1931.

129. *Los Angeles Times* had him working with Robert Woolsey: Grace Kingsley, "Helen Johnson Wins Contract," *Los Angeles Times*, February 16, 1931.

129. which he shot in two weeks: Watz, 125.

129. rushing through the first four days: "Hollywood," *Variety*, April 29, 1931.

129. the film's one innovation: Ralph Wilk, "A Little from 'Lots,' " *Film Daily*, April 10, 1931.

130. Woolsey was responsible this time around: Watz, 311.

130. "It stinks, but they gotta pay us for doing *something*.": Ibid., 124.

131. One of cinema's minor indiscretions: Andre Sennwald, "The Medicine Man: *Everything's Rosie*," *New York Times*, May 22, 1931.

131. Exculpation should be granted to Clyde Bruckman: "Everything's Rosie," *Variety*, May 27, 1931.

131. hung onto each other's bad reviews: Watz, 127.

132. Harold Jr., born prematurely in January: "Physicians Battle To Save Lloyds' 4-Pound Baby," *Chicago Daily Tribune*, January 26, 1931.

132. another bout of appendicitis: "Harold Lloyd Fighting Appendicitis Operation," *Chicago Daily Tribune*, March 18, 1931.

132. his long-overdue appendectomy: "Comedian's Condition Favorable," *Los Angeles Times*, April 10, 1931.

132. he'd make a movie about the foreign legion: "Lloyd Discovers Legion," *Variety*, July 14, 1931.

132. a Hollywood satire: "Lloyd Would Rib," *Variety*, September 1, 1931.

132. she suspected he was having an affair: Richard Hamblin, in discussion with author, February 20, 2015.

132. "emergency operation.": "Mrs. Bruckman's Last Rites Set for Tomorrow," *Los Angeles Times*, October 9, 1931.

132. adhesions, intestinal obstruction, and gangrene: "Death Certificate: Lola Bruckman," Los Angeles County Department of Registrar-Recorder/County Clerk, Norwalk, California.

132. Her funeral was held on Saturday, October 10: "Mrs. Bruckman's Last Rites Set for Tomorrow," *Los Angeles Times*, October 9, 1931.

133. Da Vinci's *Last Supper*: " 'Last Supper' Unveiled," *Los Angeles Times*, April 29, 1931.

The Wash-Out

135. knew to go looking for him at the Bruckmans': Richard Hamblin, in discussion with author, February 20, 2015.

135. even briefly lived with them: George Hamblin, p. 9B [handwritten], Line 53, Enumeration District 0820, Beverly Hills, Los Angeles County, California, California Census of Population, *Fifteenth Census of the United States, 1930* (National Archives Microfilm Publication T626, Roll 124), database online at Ancestry.com.

135. They thought in some way he was responsible: Richard Hamblin, in discussion with author, February 20, 2015.

136. they never spoke to him again: Ibid.

136. Filming began on February 27, 1932: Grace Kingsley, "Lloyd Cameras to Grind Today," *Los Angeles Times*, February 27. 1932.

136. hiring playwright Vincent Lawrence: "Inside Stuff—Pictures," *Variety*, August 30, 1932.

136. Lloyd has been using a great variety of camera equipment: Edwin Schallert, "Lloyd Title Duly Picked," *Los Angeles Times*, March 23, 1932.

137. Universal managed to build a camera crane: "U's Camera Crane Replaces 'Parallels,' " *Variety*, December 5, 1928.

137. Lloyd was fascinated with its possibilities: John Scott, "Lloyd Wrapped Up in Love Plot," *Los Angeles Times*, April 10, 1932.

137. Even in pictures where I directed: Hubert I. Cohen, "The Serious Business of Being Funny: Harold Lloyd Looks Back on His Career as a Great Film Comic," *Film Comment*, fall 1969.

137. there are photographs of him on set: Dardis, *Harold Lloyd*, 234.

138. Clyde was quietly married in a civil ceremony: Clyde A. Bruckman and Gladys Marie Meals, Marriage License and Certificate no. 768-O.M. (March 26, 1932), copy from Ventura County Clerk and Recorder.

138. Joseph lost several fingers: Donald P. Swisher, in discussion with author, November 29, 2014.

138. became a clerk at a local jewelry store: *Orange County Directory, 1924: South Orange County*, (Long Beach, California: Western Directory Co., 1923), 538.

138. she married a doctor named Robert Meals: "Miss Gladys Prevost Weds Young Medico in Hollywood," *Santa Ana Register*, November 26, 1926.

138. "to test my mental discipline,": "Why He Cut Own Appendix," *Los Angeles Times*, October 13, 1928.

138. got his face in the papers: See, e.g., *The Daily Northwestern*, Oshkosh, Wisconsin, October 18, 1928.

139. 6777 Hollywood Boulevard: *Los Angeles City Directory, 1932* (Los Angeles: Los Angeles Directory Co., 1932), 1440.

139. Dr. Meals had delivered Clyde's nephew: Jeff Hamblin, e-mail message to author, February 11, 2015.

139. a divorce from Dr. Meals in Carson City: "Three Divorces Granted by Court in Carson," *Nevada State Journal*, Reno, Nevada, March 5, 1932.

139. spending the summer learning to fly: Terrel DeLapp, "Skyways," *Los Angeles Times*, September 4, 1932.

139. remarrying a year later: "Intention to Marry," *Los Angeles Times*, April 27. 1933.

139. Despite a story in *Variety* in mid-April: "Inside Stuff—Pictures," *Variety*, April 5, 1932.

139. the film wrapped by early May: "Flashes from Studios," *New York Times*, May 1, 1932.

139. first in San Francisco: "Lloyd to Test Film," *Motion Picture Daily*, May 17, 1932.

139. and then in Los Angeles: "Chatter," *Variety*, June 7, 1932.

140. Harold Lloyd cut him loose: "Harold Lloyd Corporation Closing Card," June 11, 1932, Clyde Bruckman Pay Records, Harold Lloyd Papers, Margaret Herrick Library, Academy of Motion Picture Arts and Sciences.

140. Lloyd had taken *himself* off the payroll on May 31: Dardis, *Harold Lloyd*, 243.

141. "avoided the mistakes of his early talkie days,": Martin Dickstein, "The Screen," *Brooklyn Daily Eagle*, September 15, 1932.

141. "Lengthy Comedy Scene Keeps Audience Roaring.": "Lengthy Comedy Scene Keeps Audience Roaring," *Los Angeles Times*, October 26, 1932.

141. Too long between Lloyd pictures: "What the Picture Did For Me," *Motion Picture Herald*, December 24, 1932.

142. I still gave the directing credit to this other boy: Hubert I. Cohen, "The Serious Business of Being Funny: Harold Lloyd Looks Back on His Career as a Great Film Comic," *Film Comment*, fall 1969.

142. at $1,000 per week: Clyde Bruckman, Contract with Mack Sennett, Signed November 8, 1932, Mack Sennett Papers, Margaret Herrick Library, Academy of Motion Picture Arts and Sciences.

The Human Fish

143. they'd replaced Clyde with Mark Sandrich: "Sandrich for Masquers," *Film Daily*, October 28, 1932.

143. "Famed white hunter Trader Cohen leads the Chuzzlebottom: "Thru Thin and Thicket; or, Who's Zoo In Africa," *Internet Movie Database*, http://www.imdb.com/title/tt0024667.

144. won gold medals in all three of her events: "Helene Madison," *Olympic.org: Official Website of the Olympic Movement*, http://www.olympic.org/helene-madison.

144. announcing she would retire: Muriel Babcock, "Queen Helene Through Racing: It Costs Too Much to Be Champion," *Los Angeles Times*, August 9, 1932.

144. Sennett. . . signed her that fall: "Sennett Signs Swimmer," *Film Daily*, November 15, 1932.

144. a rather ominous production photo: E.g., "Ex-Sun Sports Editor to Direct Olympic Champion," *San Bernardino Daily Sun*, December 2, 1932.

144. shot from Tuesday, November 15 to Saturday, November 19: Production Files, *The Human Fish*, Mack Sennett Papers, Margaret Herrick Library, Academy of Motion Picture Arts and Sciences.

144. "What the famous Olympic swimming champ lacks: "What The Picture Did For Me," *Motion Picture Herald*, August 5, 1933.

144. "the most improbable star in the first century of movies.": Roger Ebert, "Great Movies: The Bank Dick," *RogerEbert.com*, http://www.rogerebert.com/reviews/great-movie-the-bank-dick-1940.

145. Born in Philadelphia in 1880: James Curtis, *W. C. Fields: A Biography* (New York: Alfred A. Knopf, 2003), 9.

145. "the pay-if-you-can-catch-us plan.": Ibid., 27–28.

145. he'd risen through the minstrel shows and burlesques: Ibid., 40–41.

145. joining the *Ziegfeld Follies* in 1915: Ibid., 99–100.

145. *Pool Sharks*, his first short film: Ibid., 103.

145. he became a Broadway star: Ibid., 149.

145. *Sally of the Sawdust*: Ibid., 175–176.

145. arranged a lucrative contract that year: Ibid., 249.

145. Fields had rarely touched a drink: Ibid., 50–51.

145. he'd picked up the habit: Ibid., 116.

146. I'm an advocate of moderation: Ibid., 300–301.

146. After breakfast he downed a solid glass of bourbon: Ibid., 301.

146. five days of shooting: *The Fatal Glass of Beer* Shooting Schedule, Mack Sennett Papers, Margaret Herrick Library, Academy of Motion Picture Arts and Sciences.

147. "a reckless lack of finesse": William K. Everson, *The Art of W. C. Fields* (New York: Bonanza Books, 1967), 85.

147. You are probably one hundred percent right: W. C. Fields to Mack Sennett, December 7, 1932, in *W. C. Fields by Himself: His Intended Autobiography*, ed. Ronald J. Fields (Englewood Cliffs, NJ: Prentice-Hall, Inc., 1973), 269.

148. Sennett insisted on cutting away: Ibid.

148. this was more of an editing dispute: *The Fatal Glass of Beer* Working Draft Script dated November 17, 1932, Mack Sennett Papers, Margaret Herrick Library, Academy of Motion Picture Arts and Sciences.

148. "Top-Notch Comedy,": "Short Subject Reviews," *Film Daily*, June 3, 1933.

148. "No real laffs and hardly a snicker.": "Talking Shorts," *Variety*, June 20, 1933.

148. "This is the worst comedy we have played: "What the Picture Did for Me," *Motion Picture Herald*, July 8, 1933.

148. "Inexplicable. Rank. Uncalled for.": Ibid.

Too Many Highballs

151. **I worked on the last story ten full days:** W. C. Fields to Mack Sennett, December 18, 1932, in *W. C. Fields by Himself: His Intended Autobiography*, ed. Ronald J. Fields, (Englewood Cliffs, NJ: Prentice-Hall, Inc., 1973), 269.

152. **the ensuing scandal torpedoed his career:** Anthony Balducci, *Lloyd Hamilton: Poor Boy Comedian of Silent Cinema* (Jefferson, NC: McFarland and Company, 2009), 138–141.

152. **temporarily sobering up:** Ibid., 147–149.

152. **"very quiet and extremely sad man.":** Ibid., 168.

152. **Among the comic set pieces:** Ralph Wilk, "A Little From 'Lots,' " *Film Daily*, December 23, 1932.

152. **"quite a favorite here,":** "What the Picture Did for Me," *Motion Picture Herald*, August 5, 1933.

152. **"disturbing appearance . . . spoiled the fun.":** Balducci, 170.

152. **a drinking-related, hemorrhaging ulcer:** "Death Calls Hamilton, Pioneer Film Comedian," *Los Angeles Times*, January 19, 1935.

153. **They go on the picnic:** Felix Adler and Clyde Bruckman, "Notes on Vacation Story," January 17, 1933, Mack Sennett Papers, Margaret Herrick Library, Academy of Motion Picture Arts and Sciences.

153. **"notes and gags for picnic,":** Felix Adler and Clyde Bruckman, "Notes and Gags for Picnic," undated, Mack Sennett Papers, Margaret Herrick Library, Academy of Motion Picture Arts and Sciences.

153. **the rough draft of** *Daddy Knows Best***:** Felix Adler, Clyde Bruckman, and John A. Waldron, "Daddy Knows Best," Rough Draft, February 8, 1933, Mack Sennett Papers, Margaret Herrick Library, Academy of Motion Picture Arts and Sciences.

154. **In the shooting script:** Felix Adler, Clyde Bruckman, and John A. Waldron, "Daddy Knows Best," Shooting Script, February 13, 1933, Mack Sennett Papers, Margaret Herrick Library, Academy of Motion Picture Arts and Sciences.

154. **Sennett was in serious financial trouble:** Walker, 218.

155. **Sennett was looking into stunts:** Ibid. 220–221.

155. hired to direct the first of a new series: Arthur Forde, "As Seen and Heard," *Hollywood Filmograph*, July 8, 1933.

155. Lloyd hired him back again: "Lloyd Keeps Megger," *Variety*, July 11, 1933.

155. He returned in March 1933: Dardis, *Harold Lloyd*, 241–242.

155. he bought the film rights to a novel: Ibid. 246–247.

155. he'd rehired Clyde to direct once again: "Lloyd Keeps Megger," *Variety*, July 11, 1933.

155. his payroll card has him in the scenario department: "Harold Lloyd Corporation Starting Card," July 10, 1933, Clyde Bruckman Pay Records, Harold Lloyd Papers, Margaret Herrick Library, Academy of Motion Picture Arts and Sciences.

155. Lloyd let him go on September 2: "Harold Lloyd Corporation Closing Card," September 2, 1933, Clyde Bruckman Pay Records, Harold Lloyd Papers, Margaret Herrick Library, Academy of Motion Picture Arts and Sciences.

155. this time he lasted three months: "Harold Lloyd Corporation Closing Card," December 23, 1933, Clyde Bruckman Pay Records, Harold Lloyd Papers, Margaret Herrick Library, Academy of Motion Picture Arts and Sciences.

156. lining up a production organization: Harold Lloyd to Sidney Kent, January 22, 1934, Harold Lloyd Papers, Margaret Herrick Library, Academy of Motion Picture Arts and Sciences.

156. *Variety* reported he'd been signed to MGM: "MG Tags Scrib Duo," *Daily Variety*, April 27, 1934.

156. Clyde and Sherman wrote the outline and first draft: Joe Sherman and Clyde Bruckman, "Death on the Diamond Temporary Complete Screenplay," May 5, 1934, Turner/MGM Scripts, Margaret Herrick Library, Academy of Motion Picture Arts and Sciences.

156. hired him to direct the Three Stooges: Ralph Wick, "A Little from Hollywood 'Lots,' " *Film Daily*, November 20, 1934.

156. Larry, Curly, and Moe had split with their old mentor: Michael Fleming, *From Amalgamated Morons to American Icons: The Three Stooges: An Illustrated History* (New York: Broadway Books, 1999), 38–40.

157. Lloyd had knowingly lifted it from *Horse Shoes*: Clyde Bruckman, "Offer

of Proof on Behalf of Defendants," filed September 13, 1945, Case 4361, Box 751, Civil Case Files 1938–1950, Records of the District Court of the United States for the Southern District of California, Central Division, Record Group 21, National Archives at Riverside, Riverside, CA.

158. "There were three stooges: Clyde Bruckman, "Depositions of Edward Muhl, Leonard Lee, Maurice Leo, Jean W. Yarbrough, and Clyde Bruckman," Deposition taken June 5, 1945, filed September 11, 1945, Case 4361, Box 751, Civil Case Files 1938–1950, Records of the District Court of the United States for the Southern District of California, Central Division, Record Group 21, National Archives at Riverside, Riverside, CA.

158. hire him to direct three more Stooges films: "Studio Placements," *Weekly Variety*, Nov. 13, 1934.

158. "A steal. 4 bedrms., 3 baths, libr., game rm., 2 servants rms.": Classified Ad for 717 N. Elm, *Los Angeles Times*, January 22, 1935.

159. A few weeks later, he listed it again: Classified Ad for 717 N. Elm, *Los Angeles Times*, February 17, 1935.

159. Clyde went to Fox: "Director Details!," *Daily Variety*, February 5, 1934.

159. "dissatisfied with the treatment of the story,": "Brown No Like Story, Nixes 'Tiger' Chore," *Weekly Variety*, February 12, 1935.

160. This picture has every appearance of being ad libbed: "Spring Tonic," *Weekly Variety*, June 12, 1935.

161. *The Plot Thickens*: "Bruckman Directing Next Fields at Par," *Daily Variety*, March 15, 1935.

161. *The Flying Trapeze*: "Field's 'Flying Trapeze,' " *Weekly Variety*, March 20, 1935.

161. Filming began on April 27: George Hippard, "Assistant Director's Report," April 27, 1935, *Man on the Flying Trapeze: Assistant director's reports 1935*, Paramount Pictures Production Records, Margaret Herrick Library, Academy of Motion Picture Arts and Sciences.

161. Fields and Hardy wrote nights and mornings: Curtis, 331.

161. "Reason for Delay": George Hippard, "Assistant Director's Report," April 29, 1935, *Man on the Flying Trapeze: Assistant director's reports 1935*, Paramount Pictures Production Records, Margaret Herrick Library, Academy of Motion Picture Arts and Sciences.

161. "LATE START DUE TO MR. BRUCKMAN'S ABSENCE: George Hippard, "Assistant Director's Report," May 13, 1935, *Man on the Flying Trapeze: Assistant director's reports 1935*, Paramount Pictures Production Records, Margaret Herrick Library, Academy of Motion Picture Arts and Sciences.

162. "flu attack": "Emergency," *Daily Variety*, May 14, 1935.

162. Ronald Fields's account of the film: Simon Louvish, *Man on the Flying Trapeze: The Life and Times of W. C. Fields*, (New York: W. W. Norton and Company, 1997), 392–393.

162. "MR. FIELDS ILL, NOT ON SET UNTIL 11:05: George Hippard, "Assistant Director's Report," May 24, 1935, *Man on the Flying Trapeze: Assistant director's reports 1935*, Paramount Pictures Production Records, Margaret Herrick Library, Academy of Motion Picture Arts and Sciences.

162. "MR. FIELDS NOT ON SET UNTIL 10:45: George Hippard, "Assistant Director's Report," May 31, 1935, *Man on the Flying Trapeze: Assistant director's reports 1935*, Paramount Pictures Production Records, Margaret Herrick Library, Academy of Motion Picture Arts and Sciences.

162. wrapping on June 4: George Hippard, "Assistant Director's Report," June 4, 1935, *Man on the Flying Trapeze: Assistant director's reports 1935*, Paramount Pictures Production Records, Margaret Herrick Library, Academy of Motion Picture Arts and Sciences.

162. two days of reshoots later in June: Harry Scott, "Assistant Director's Report," June 21, 1935, *Man on the Flying Trapeze: Assistant director's reports 1935*, Paramount Pictures Production Records, Margaret Herrick Library, Academy of Motion Picture Arts and Sciences.

162. It didn't help matters that the finished film wasn't well received: Curtis, 333.

163. a not-so-secret attempt to dry out: Louvish, 399.

163. "four weeks idler,": "Chatter," *Daily Variety*, Jul. 31, 1935.

163. "back at grind after month on an island.": "Chatter," *Weekly Variety*, Aug. 7, 1935.

Slapstick

165. They took him back, but not as a director: "Columbia Adds Writers," *Film Daily*, September 28, 1935.

165. their first Best Picture nomination: "The Official Academy Awards Database," *Academy of Motion Picture Arts and Sciences*, http://awardsdatabase.oscars.org.

165. In 1933 the studio had begun production: Okuda and Watz, 3–4.

165. we, the short subjects people: Edward Bernds, Introduction to *The Columbia Comedy Shorts: Two-Reel Hollywood Film Comedies 1933–1958*, by Ted Okuda and Edward Watz (Jefferson, North Carolina: McFarland Classics, 1986) 1–2.

166. White had started out as a child actor: Jules White, interview by David Bruskin, *Behind the Three Stooges: The White Brothers: Conversations with David N. Bruskin*, (Los Angeles, Directors Guild of America, 1993), 37.

166. The original plan, as pitched by Zion Myers and Mark Sandrich: Ibid., 59–62.

166. Mack Sennett's bankruptcy: Walker, 220–221.

166. selling used Buicks: Bruskin, 51.

167. on Sundays, Felix and I used to write a script: Bruskin, 78–79.

167. On October 1, 1935, he handed in his first script: Clyde Bruckman, *Three Little Beers* final screenplay dated October 1, 1935, Jules White Papers, Margaret Herrick Library, Academy of Motion Picture Arts and Sciences.

167. White picked up Clyde's option: Ralph Wick, "A Little from Hollywood 'Lots,'" *Film Daily*, October 21, 1935.

170. a detailed family tree for this bit: Anthony Balducci, *The Funny Parts: A History of Film Comedy Routines and Gags* (Jefferson, NC: McFarland and Company, 2012), 84–85.

170. had failed utterly at the box office: Dardis, *Harold Lloyd*, 252.

170. a critical success but a box-office flop: Ibid., 256–257.

170. "whittled down.": "Lloyd Set on Next Yarn," *Daily Variety*, September 2, 1936.

170. have the film in front of cameras by November 1: "Harold Lloyd Rushing Next Script for Par," *Daily Variety*, September 23, 1936.

170. he rehired Clyde, Felix Adler, and Eddie Moran: Philip K. Scheuer, "Harold Lloyd to Star in New Story Written by Himself," *Los Angeles Times*, September 1, 1936.

171. they set to work at the Bel-Air Bay Club: "Lloyd's Brigade Whittling His Pic Gags," *Daily Variety*, September 17, 1936.

171. he only lasted two weeks: "Harold Lloyd Corporation Closing Card," September 19, 1936, Clyde Bruckman Pay Records, Harold Lloyd Papers, Margaret Herrick Library, Academy of Motion Picture Arts and Sciences.

171. writing another Stooges short: Clyde Bruckman, *Grips, Grunts and Groans*, final draft screenplay dated October 23, 1936, Jules White Papers, Margaret Herrick Library, Academy of Motion Picture Arts and Sciences.

171. returned to work with Lloyd on October 26: "Harold Lloyd Corporation Starting Card," October 26, 1936, Clyde Bruckman Pay Records, Harold Lloyd Papers, Margaret Herrick Library, Academy of Motion Picture Arts and Sciences.

171. His distribution deal with Paramount: "Lloyd's Two a Year for Par," *Daily Variety*, November 11, 1936.

171. news broke that Simpson was divorcing her second husband: "King Edward's Favorite Files Suit for Divorce," *Los Angeles Times*, October 15, 1936.

171. "at any cost,": "King to Wed Mrs. Simpson 'at Any Cost,' *Post* Learns," *Washington Post*, October 17, 1936.

171. no one in Hollywood would touch the story: "World's Greatest Story Shunned by Producers," *Los Angeles Times*, December 13, 1936.

172. "out of deference to the people of the British Empire.": Ralph Wilk, "A 'Little' from Hollywood 'Lots,' " *Film Daily*, December 17. 1936.

172. writing *3 Dumb Clucks* in January: Clyde Bruckman, *Three Dumb Clucks*, final screenplay dated January 25, 1937, Jules White Papers, Margaret Herrick Library, Academy of Motion Picture Arts and Sciences.

172. **who'd replaced him at the** *Examiner*: Mark Kelly, "Angels Defeat Seattle in Opening Game by 8 to 1 Count," *Los Angeles Examiner*, April 6, 1921.

172. **were signed by Paramount to write**: Ralph Wick, "A 'Little' from Hollywood 'Lots,' " *Film Daily*, February 24, 1937.

172. **Jack Benny was attached to star**: Ralph Wick, "A 'Little' from Hollywood 'Lots,' " *Film Daily*, January 21, 1937.

172. **On his return, he asked Paramount**: "McCarey Leaving Par," *Weekly Variety*, September 1, 1937.

172. **Clyde picked up a Stooges assignment**: Clyde Bruckman and Elwood Ullman, *Cash and Carry*, fifth draft continuity dated April 28, 1937, Jules White Papers, Margaret Herrick Library, Academy of Motion Picture Arts and Sciences.

173. **John L. Murphy signed off and wrote "OK,"**: "Harold Lloyd Corporation Starting Card," June 29, 1936, Clyde Bruckman Pay Records, Harold Lloyd Papers, Margaret Herrick Library, Academy of Motion Picture Arts and Sciences.

173. **the production started in late November**: "New Film Productions Started During Week," *Los Angeles Times*, November 28, 1937.

173. **the company made its way to Kernville, California**: John Summer, Harold Lloyd Productions Press Release dated November 29, 1937, "*Professor, Beware*—Press Releases 1937, undated," Harold Lloyd Papers, Margaret Herrick Library, Academy of Motion Picture Arts and Sciences.

173. **Clyde was assigned second unit work**: "Daily Production Report," December 2, 1937, "*Professor, Beware*—Production Reports 1937–1938," Harold Lloyd Papers, Margaret Herrick Library, Academy of Motion Picture Arts and Sciences.

173. **the film company introducing the latest dances**: John Summer, Harold Lloyd Productions Press Release dated December 2, 1937, "*Professor, Beware*—Press Releases 1937, undated," Harold Lloyd Papers, Margaret Herrick Library, Academy of Motion Picture Arts and Sciences.

173. **Harold Lloyd talking about his favorite comedies**: John Summer, Harold Lloyd Productions Press Release, undated, "*Professor, Beware*—Press Releases 1937, undated," Harold Lloyd Papers, Margaret Herrick Library, Academy of Motion Picture Arts and Sciences.

173. **so work began at 5:30 every morning:** John Summer, Harold Lloyd Productions Press Release dated December 2, 1937, "*Professor, Beware*—Press Releases 1937, undated," Harold Lloyd Papers, Margaret Herrick Library, Academy of Motion Picture Arts and Sciences.

173. **on December 9, the rains came:** "Daily Production Report," December 9, 1937, "*Professor, Beware*—Production Reports 1937–1938," Harold Lloyd Papers, Margaret Herrick Library, Academy of Motion Picture Arts and Sciences.

173. **the production would still be on schedule:** John Summer, Harold Lloyd Productions Press Release, undated, "*Professor, Beware*—Press Releases 1937, undated," Harold Lloyd Papers, Margaret Herrick Library, Academy of Motion Picture Arts and Sciences.

173. **performed in the garage-studio:** John Summer, Harold Lloyd Productions Press Release, undated, "*Professor, Beware*—Press Releases 1937, undated," Harold Lloyd Papers, Margaret Herrick Library, Academy of Motion Picture Arts and Sciences.

173. **enlisted the help of an army air force pilot:** John Summer, Harold Lloyd Productions Press Release, undated, "*Professor, Beware*—Press Releases 1937, undated," Harold Lloyd Papers, Margaret Herrick Library, Academy of Motion Picture Arts and Sciences.

174. **Eddie Adams had to be rushed by ambulance:** John Summer, Harold Lloyd Productions Press Release, undated, "*Professor, Beware*—Press Releases 1937, undated," Harold Lloyd Papers, Margaret Herrick Library, Academy of Motion Picture Arts and Sciences.

174. **Or the story about a wildcat:** John Summer, Harold Lloyd Productions Press Release, undated, "*Professor, Beware*—Press Releases 1937, undated," Harold Lloyd Papers, Margaret Herrick Library, Academy of Motion Picture Arts and Sciences.

174. **Harold Lloyd's trailer reportedly caught fire:** John Summer, Harold Lloyd Productions Press Release, undated, "*Professor, Beware*—Press Releases 1937, undated," Harold Lloyd Papers, Margaret Herrick Library, Academy of Motion Picture Arts and Sciences.

174. **the production returned to shoot interiors:** "Daily Production Report," December 16, 1937, "*Professor, Beware*—Production Reports 1937–1938,"

Harold Lloyd Papers, Margaret Herrick Library, Academy of Motion Picture Arts and Sciences.

174. **Clyde was done on January 8:** "Harold Lloyd Corporation Closing Card," January 8, 1938, Clyde Bruckman Pay Records, Harold Lloyd Papers, Margaret Herrick Library, Academy of Motion Picture Arts and Sciences.

174. **to get Lloyd tickets to the Rose Bowl:** John Summer, Harold Lloyd Productions Press Release, undated, "*Professor, Beware—Press Releases 1937,* undated," Harold Lloyd Papers, Margaret Herrick Library, Academy of Motion Picture Arts and Sciences.

174. **their regular "Kernville" column:** E.g., "Kernville," *Bakersfield Californian*, December 8, 1937.

174. **The *Washington Post* published the story:** "Harold Lloyd Uses Army Weather Tip," *Washington Post*, February 10, 1938.

174. **unaccountably ran an undated two sentences:** "Extended Location," *Ames Daily Tribune*, April 30, 1938.

175. **a personal loss of $100,000:** Dardis, *Harold Lloyd*, 267.

175. **immediately hiring Delmer Daves:** "To Do New Lloyd Story," *Motion Picture Daily*, Mar. 17, 1938.

Bonfire

177. **It was difficult for Keaton to convince anyone at MGM:** Dardis, *Keaton*, 190.

177. **"I knew before the camera turned on:** Blesh, 313.

178. **her husband got into a brawl in his MGM bungalow:** Dardis, *Keaton*, 194–195.

178. **"to show who wears the trousers around our house.":** Dardis, *Keaton*, 206.

178. **as a husband, Buster was an excellent comedian:** "Keaton's Wife Wins Divorce," *Los Angeles Times*, August 9, 1932.

178. **"the land yacht,":** Doris Janeway, "Keaton Buys 'Land Yacht' as Big Joke," *Movie Classic*, November 1932.

178. **"Most of them wish Buster had never heard of a land yacht!":** Carol

Maynard, "The Stars Are At It Again—Giving Bigger And Better Parties," *Movie Classic*, January 1933.

179. "a new kind of divorce: Nancy Pryor, "Stars Invent a New Kind of Divorce," *Movie Classic*, November 1932.

179. a blackout bender in Ensenada: McPherson, 231.

179. MGM finally fired him: Dardis, *Keaton*, 224–225.

179. The sheriff threw him out of town: Blesh, 334–335.

179. He eventually found his way to Educational Pictures: Dardis, *Keaton*, 234.

179. His second marriage failed in 1936: Ibid., 242.

179. Educational Pictures failed in 1937: Ibid., 245.

179. They hired him as a gag man: Ibid., 246–248.

179. he'd just finished writing *Three Sappy People* for the Stooges: Clyde Bruckman, *Three Sappy People*, final draft screenplay dated January 13, 1939, Jules White Papers, Margaret Herrick Library, Academy of Motion Picture Arts and Sciences.

179. One day Bruckman came to me: Okuda and Watz, 139.

180. I'd pick up the stars who had refused to work for me: Bruskin, 85.

180. "felt Buster would be more comfortable": Okuda and Watz, 139.

180. "White was being moved up from dogs to people: Meade, 205.

180. alternated telling me how to walk, how to talk, how to stand: Blesh, 324.

181. announced in March of 1939: "Keaton's Comeback," *Daily Variety*, March 8, 1939.

181. Keaton would be paid $1,000 per short: Okuda and Watz, 49.

181. *Pest from the West*: Clyde Bruckman, *Pest From The West*, final draft continuity dated March 10, 1939, Jules White Papers, Margaret Herrick Library, Academy of Motion Picture Arts and Sciences.

181. a reworking of *The Invader*: Meade, 234.

181. He received screen credit for *She's Oil Mine*: Felix Adler, *She's Oil Mine*, final draft continuity dated October 6, 1941, Jules White Papers, Margaret Herrick Library, Academy of Motion Picture Arts and Sciences.

181. an assignment creating a new character: "Screen News," *Brooklyn Daily Eagle*, September 6, 1939.

181. which he wrote with L. A. Sarecky: Clyde Bruckman and L. A. Sarecky,

Glove Slingers, incomplete final draft continuity dated August 11, 1939, Jules White Papers, Margaret Herrick Library, Academy of Motion Picture Arts and Sciences.

181. turned into an eleven-film series: Okuda and Watz, 145–147.

182. he had begun work on *The Great Dictator*: "Chaplin's 'Great Dictator' Will Start in Early July," *Film Daily*, June 28, 1939.

182. budgeted at more than two million, all of it Chaplin's: "Chaplin's $2,200,000 'Dictator' to Be Shown at Upped 'Gone' Scale," *Weekly Variety*, August 14, 1940.

182. By late October, they'd written a script: Clyde Bruckman and Felix Adler, *You Nazty Spy!* final draft continuity dated October 31, 1939, Jules White Papers, Margaret Herrick Library, Academy of Motion Picture Arts and Sciences.

182. Clyde must have disagreed: Balducci, *The Funny Parts*, 83–84.

183. *I'll Never Heil Again*, which Clyde and Felix wrote: Clyde Bruckman and Felix Adler, *I'll Never Heil Again*, final draft continuity dated March 11, 1941, Jules White Papers, Margaret Herrick Library, Academy of Motion Picture Arts and Sciences.

183. In 1944, he'd join a "Writers for Roosevelt" group: "Writers for Roosevelt Ad," *Daily Variety*, Sep. 5, 1944.

184. written in October of 1943: Clyde Bruckman, *The Yoke's on Me*, final continuity dated October 27, 1943, Jules White Papers, Margaret Herrick Library, Academy of Motion Picture Arts and Sciences.

184. thrown in jail for being German: "Seeing San Bernardino in Five Minutes," *San Bernardino Daily Sun*, June 8, 1918.

184. He'd briefly tried to sell it in 1935: Classified Ad for 177 N. Elm, *Los Angeles Times*, January 22, 1935.

184. a few days in November of 1936: Classified Ad for 177 N. Elm, *Los Angeles Times*, November 12, 1936.

185. from August through October of 1937: Classified Ad for 177 N. Elm, *Los Angeles Times*, August 8, 1937.

185. In the fall of 1940: Classified Ad for 177 N. Elm, *Los Angeles Times*, September 4, 1940.

185. "A VERY REAL BUY: Classified Ad for 177 N. Elm, *Los Angeles Times*, January 12, 1941.

185. "THE HOUSE OF IDEAS: Classified Ad for 177 N. Elm, *Los Angeles Times*, January 19, 1941.

185. "WANT reasonable offer: Classified Ad for 177 N. Elm, *Los Angeles Times*, April 5, 1941.

185. "HOUSE SOLD. MUST VACATE.": "Furniture At Auction," Classified Ad, *The Los Angeles Times*, Apr. 27, 1941.

185. they'd barely been managing to pay the interest: Donald P. Swisher, in discussion with author, November 29, 2014.

Song and Dance Man

187. The practice of showing a second, cheap, short feature: Ward, 89.

188. a 1937 *Motion Picture Herald* editorial: J. H. Thompson, "Calls Double Feature Octopus Strangling Quality and Receipts," *Motion Picture Herald*, February 13, 1937.

188. That left Columbia, which had entered the field late: Ward, 91–94.

188. "I want one good picture a year: Gene Blottner, *Columbia Pictures Movie Series, 1926–1955: The Harry Cohn Years* (Jefferson, NC: McFarland and Company, 2012), 7.

189. Columbia eventually made twenty-eight *Blondie* films: Ibid, 15.

189. a different facility a few miles away: Okuda and Watz, 9.

189. "the faithful standbys go on: Philip K. Scheuer, "Town Called Hollywood," *Los Angeles Times*, April 12, 1942.

189. Most "legitimate" players are leery: Ibid.

191. *Behind the Rising Sun*: Ad for *Behind the Rising Sun* and *Honeymoon Lodge*, *Los Angeles Times*, September 12, 1943.

191. "pleasantly accomplishes goal: "Film Preview: Honeymoon Lodge," *Daily Variety*, July 23, 1943.

191. Clyde's $275 a week from Universal: "Universal Studios Production Company, Inc. Production Estimate: *South of Dixie*," January 14, 1944, Universal Studios Collection, Cinema Library Archive of Performing Arts, University of Southern California.

191. $3,667 a week in 2015 dollars: "US Inflation Calculator," http://usinflationcalculator.com.

191. Andrews Sisters vehicles *Swingtime Johnnie*: "Universal Studios Production Company, Inc. Production Estimate: *Swingtime Johnnie*," September 24, 1943, Universal Studios Collection, Cinema Library Archive of Performing Arts, University of Southern California.

191. *Her Lucky Night*: "Universal Studios Production Company, Inc. Story & Continuity Estimate: *Stars Over Manhattan* [*Her Lucky Night*]," July 1, 1944, Universal Studios Collection, Cinema Library Archive of Performing Arts, University of Southern California.

192. he worked on *In Society* for Bud Abbott and Lou Costello: "Short Shorts," *Daily Variety*, June 22, 1944.

192. he was assigned to *She Gets Her Man*: "Short Shorts," *Daily Variety*, October 19, 1944.

192. Universal has a winner here: "Film Preview: She Gets Her Man," *Daily Variety*, January 5, 1945.

Special Damages

193. the *Los Angeles Times* had dedicated an entire article to it: "Lengthy Comedy Scene Keeps Audience Roaring," *Los Angeles Times*, October 26, 1932.

193. Lloyd thought the movie was terrible: Harold Lloyd Deposition, taken August 20, 1945, Case 4361, Box 751, Civil Case Files 1938–1950, Records of the District Court of the United States for the Southern District of California, Central Division, Record Group 21, National Archives at Riverside, Riverside, CA.

193. After going through the necessary formalities: Harold A. Fendler, "Complaint for Damages and Other Relief from Copyright Infringement," Filed April 4, 1945, Case 4361, Box 751, Civil Case Files 1938–1950, Records of the District Court of the United States for the Southern District of California, Central Division, Record Group 21, National Archives at Riverside, Riverside, CA.

194. Lloyd filed three lawsuits: "Lloyd Sues U In $1,700,000 Piracy Action," *Daily Variety*, April 5, 1945.

194. Lloyd wanted $200,000 in general damages: Harold A. Fendler, "Complaint for Damages and Other Relief from Copyright Infringement," Filed April 4, 1945, Case 4361, Box 750, Civil Case Files 1938–1950, Records of the District Court of the United States for the Southern District of California, Central Division, Record Group 21, National Archives at Riverside, Riverside, CA.

194. For the gags in *Welcome Danger* taken from *She Gets Her Man*: Ibid.

194. And for ripping off *The Freshman*: Ibid.

194. Harold Lloyd had been sued by short story writer H. C. Witwer: "Harold Lloyd Sued by Author," *Los Angeles Times*, January 5, 1926.

195. That initial case was dismissed: Dardis, *Harold Lloyd*, 159.

195. they'd even had a story in the same issue: "*The Popular Magazine* [v.46 #2 October 7, 1917]", *The FictionMags Index* http://www.philsp.com/homeville/fmi/t2598.htm#A55599.

195. he bought back his copyright and sued Lloyd for $2,300,000: "H. C. Witwer Sues Lloyd Over Story," *Los Angeles Times*, April 12, 1929.

195. Lloyd lost the original case outright in 1930: Witwer v. Harold Lloyd Corporation, 46 F.2d 792 (S.D. Cal. 1930).

195. ordered to hand over every dime of *The Freshman*'s profits: Harold Lloyd Corporation v. Witwer, 65 F.2d 1 (9th Cir. 1933).

195. all negatives and prints of *The Freshman*: Ibid.

195. the petition for writ of certiorari: Harry G. Henn, "'Magazine Rights'—A Division of Indivisible Copyright," in *Copyright And Related Topics: A Choice of Articles*, ed. The Los Angeles Copyright Society and The UCLA School of Law (Los Angeles: University of California Press, 1964), 200.

196. At one point, the two judges had to issue parallel orders: Benjamin Harrison, "Order Removing Brief Filed by Plaintiff in 4363-H and Filing in Correct File 4361-BH," Filed November 13, 1945, Case 4361, Box 751, Civil Case Files 1938–1950, Records of the District Court of the United States for the Southern District of California, Central Division, Record Group 21, National Archives at Riverside, Riverside, CA.

196. a demand that Lloyd's attorneys explain, in detail: Joseph L. Lewinson, "Motions to Dismiss, to Make Certain, or for Bill of Particulars, and

to Strike," Filed April 26, 1945, Case 4361, Box 750, Civil Case Files 1938–1950, Records of the District Court of the United States for the Southern District of California, Central Division, Record Group 21, National Archives at Riverside, Riverside, CA.

196. **It is obvious that it is "impracticable":** Harold A. Fendler, "Plaintiff's Objections to Defendants' Motion for a More Definite Statement and/ or Bill of Particulars," filed May 10, 1945, Case 4361, Box 750, Civil Case Files 1938–1950, Records of the District Court of the United States for the Southern District of California, Central Division, Record Group 21, National Archives at Riverside, Riverside, CA.

196. **asking Universal to produce a list of every single showtime:** Harold A. Fendler, "Interrogatories to Be Answered by or on Behalf of Defendant Universal Pictures Company," filed July 2, 1945, Case 4361, Box 750, Civil Case Files 1938–1950, Records of the District Court of the United States for the Southern District of California, Central Division, Record Group 21, National Archives at Riverside, Riverside, CA.

196. **there was a chance they'd be charged with a crime:** Joseph L. Lewinson, "Affidavit of Joseph L. Lewinson in Opposition to Motion to Require Defendants to Answer Questions Propounded upon Deposition," Filed May 14, 1945, Case 4361, Box 750, Civil Case Files 1938–1950, Records of the District Court of the United States for the Southern District of California, Central Division, Record Group 21, National Archives at Riverside, Riverside, CA.

197. **and then declined to answer anything else:** Harold A. Fendler, "Plaintiff's Points and Authorities in Support of Motion to Require Defendants to Answer Questions Propounded upon Deposition, and in Opposition to Motion to Vacate Order for Taking Depositions and to Quash Subpoenas," Filed May 10, 1945, Case 4361, Box 750, Civil Case Files 1938–1950, Records of the District Court of the United States for the Southern District of California, Central Division, Record Group 21, National Archives at Riverside, Riverside, CA.

197. **Their attorneys filed motions to quash the subpoenas:** Loeb and Loeb, "Notice of Motion to Vacate Order and to Quash Subpoenas," Filed April 28, 1945, Case 4361, Box 750, Civil Case Files 1938–1950, Records of

the District Court of the United States for the Southern District of California, Central Division, Record Group 21, National Archives at Riverside, Riverside, CA.

197. it was customary when studios were sued for copyright infringement: Harold A. Fendler, "Affidavit in Support of Motion to Require Defendants to Answer Questions Propounded upon Deposition," filed May 10, 1945, Case 4361, Box 750, Civil Case Files 1938–1950, Records of the District Court of the United States for the Southern District of California, Central Division, Record Group 21, National Archives at Riverside, Riverside, CA.

197. Universal, of course, claimed to have never heard of anyone: Edward Muhl, "Affidavit in Opposition to Motion to Require Defendants to Answer Questions Propounded upon Deposition," Filed May 14, 1945, Case 4361, Box 750, Civil Case Files 1938–1950, Records of the District Court of the United States for the Southern District of California, Central Division, Record Group 21, National Archives at Riverside, Riverside, CA.

198. his general manager, Creed Neeper: "Pictorial Section," *Exhibitors Herald-World*, January 5, 1929.

198. "practically identical,": Creed Neeper to William Fraser, February 15, 1934, Harold Lloyd Papers, Margaret Herrick Library, Academy of Motion Picture Arts and Sciences.

198. I do feel that there is a chance: Ibid.

198. "He is a very sociable fellow: Creed Neeper to William Fraser, February 17, 1934, Harold Lloyd Papers, Margaret Herrick Library, Academy of Motion Picture Arts and Sciences.

198. Lloyd hired him to produce a second report: Ibid.

199. This letter would not be a good thing: Creed Neeper to William Fraser, February 15, 1934, Harold Lloyd Papers, Margaret Herrick Library, Academy of Motion Picture Arts and Sciences.

199. they devolved into a fistfight: H. A. Dewing, "Reporter's Transcript of Proceedings: Case 4361-BH, Los Angeles, California, May 14, 1945," filed May 28, 1945, Case 4361, Box 750, Civil Case Files 1938–1950, Records of the District Court of the United States for the Southern District of Cal-

ifornia, Central Division, Record Group 21, National Archives at River-side, Riverside, CA.

199. It looks like horseplay: Ibid.

199. Fendler asked that the charges be dismissed: Harold A. Fendler, "Dis-missal Without Prejudice," filed May 28, 1945, Case 4362, Box 751, Civil Case Files 1938–1950, Records of the District Court of the United States for the Southern District of California, Central Division, Record Group 21, National Archives at Riverside, Riverside, CA.

200. the print he'd been provided did not have any on-screen notice of copy-right: Guy Knupp, "Affidavit of Guy Knupp," filed May 7, 1946, Case 4363, Box 752, Civil Case Files 1938–1950, Records of the District Court of the United States for the Southern District of California, Central Division, Record Group 21, National Archives at Riverside, Riverside, CA.

200. it had been among the films destroyed in a huge nitrate fire: Harold A. Fendler, "Motion to Vacate Order for Inspection of Negative Film Destroyed by Fire," filed August 30, 1945, Case 4363, Box 752, Civil Case Files 1938–1950, Records of the District Court of the United States for the Southern District of California, Central Division, Record Group 21, National Archives at Riverside, Riverside, CA.

200. a surviving 16mm print surfaced at the Museum of Modern Art: Guy Knupp, "Affidavit of Guy Knupp," filed May 7, 1946, Case 4363, Box 752, Civil Case Files 1938–1950, Records of the District Court of the United States for the Southern District of California, Central Division, Record Group 21, National Archives at Riverside, Riverside, CA.

200. They dug up everyone they could find: E.g., Herman F. Selvin, "Affi-davit of Herman F. Selvin," filed May 7, 1946, Case 4363, Box 752, Civil Case Files 1938–1950, Records of the District Court of the United States for the Southern District of California, Central Division, Record Group 21, National Archives at Riverside, Riverside, CA.

201. Judge Hollzer had a heart attack on January 3, 1946: "Harry A. Hollzer, Veteran Jurist, Taken by Death," Los Angeles Times, January 15, 1946.

201. "I will be frank with you: H. A. Dewing, "Reporter's Transcript of Pro-ceedings: Case 4361-BH, Los Angeles, California, May 14, 1945," filed

May 28, 1945, Case 4361, Box 750, Civil Case Files 1938–1950, Records of the District Court of the United States for the Southern District of California, Central Division, Record Group 21, National Archives at Riverside, Riverside, CA.

201. **The opening day's arguments, like so many conversations in Los Angeles:** "Reporter's Transcript of Proceedings: Case 4361-BH, Los Angeles, California, September 10–13 1945, filed Oct. 10, 1945, Case 4361, Box 751, Civil Case Files 1938–1950, Records of the District Court of the United States for the Southern District of California, Central Division, Record Group 21, National Archives at Riverside, Riverside, CA.

201. **"it is clear to the court:** Ibid.

203. **I am free to receive any memorandum:** "Reporter's Transcript of Proceedings: Case 4361-BH, Los Angeles, California, December 17 1945, filed December 31, 1945, Case 4361, Box 751, Civil Case Files 1938–1950, Records of the District Court of the United States for the Southern District of California, Central Division, Record Group 21, National Archives at Riverside, Riverside, CA.

203. **The plaintiff corporation, I take it, is inactive at the present time?:** Harold Lloyd, "Deposition of Harold Lloyd," deposition taken August 20, 1945, filed September 10, 1945, Case 4361, Box 751, Civil Case Files 1938–1950, Records of the District Court of the United States for the Southern District of California, Central Division, Record Group 21, National Archives at Riverside, Riverside, CA.

203. **Has the Harold Lloyd Corporation produced a picture:** Ibid.

204. **"Mr. Lloyd, you are 51 years old, I believe?":** "Reporter's Transcript of Proceedings: Case 4361-BH, Los Angeles, California, September 10–13 1945, filed October 10, 1945, Case 4361, Box 751, Civil Case Files 1938–1950, Records of the District Court of the United States for the Southern District of California, Central Division, Record Group 21, National Archives at Riverside, Riverside, CA.

204. **he wasn't even aware of *Loco Boy Makes Good*:** Ibid.

204. **I was not too enthusiastic over it:** Maurice Leo, "Depositions of Edward Muhl, Leonard Lee, Maurice Leo, Jean W. Yarbrough, and Clyde Bruckman," Deposition taken June 5, 1945, filed September 11, 1945, Case 4361,

Box 751, Civil Case Files 1938–1950, Records of the District Court of the United States for the Southern District of California, Central Division, Record Group 21, National Archives at Riverside, Riverside, CA.

204. "old and hokey.": Jean W. Yarbrough, Ibid.

204. I felt so honestly because in the 25 years: Clyde Bruckman, Ibid.

205. Lloyd was well aware of this: Clyde Bruckman, "Offer of Proof on Behalf of Defendants," filed September 13, 1945, Case 4361, Box 751, Civil Case Files 1938–1950, Records of the District Court of the United States for the Southern District of California, Central Division, Record Group 21, National Archives at Riverside, Riverside, CA.

205. if other people felt Harold Lloyd was reusing their gags: "Reporter's Transcript of Proceedings: Case 4361-BH, Los Angeles, California, September 10–13 1945, filed October 10, 1945, Case 4361, Box 751, Civil Case Files 1938–1950, Records of the District Court of the United States for the Southern District of California, Central Division, Record Group 21, National Archives at Riverside, Riverside, CA.

205. "one of the worst pictures I have ever seen: Ibid.

206. "I could rather believe that after seeing the picture.": Ibid.

206. "Gentlemen, I have viewed the Columbia short: "Reporter's Transcript of Proceedings: Case 4361-BH, Los Angeles, California, Decebmer 17 1945, filed Decebmer 31, 1945, Case 4361, Box 751, Civil Case Files 1938–1950, Records of the District Court of the United States for the Southern District of California, Central Division, Record Group 21, National Archives at Riverside, Riverside, CA.

206. "I would say you were good all the way through.": "Reporter's Transcript of Proceedings: Case 4361-BH, Los Angeles, California, September 10–13 1945, filed October 10, 1945, Case 4361, Box 751, Civil Case Files 1938–1950, Records of the District Court of the United States for the Southern District of California, Central Division, Record Group 21, National Archives at Riverside, Riverside, CA.

206. "the figures that come out of Hollywood: Ibid.

206. awarded him $40,000 in damages: Judge Ben Harrison, Findings of Fact and Conclusions of Law, filed January 8, 1946, Case 4361, Box 751, Civil Case Files 1938–1950, Records of the District Court of the United

States for the Southern District of California, Central Division, Record Group 21, National Archives at Riverside, Riverside, CA.

206. **filing two suits against Columbia:** "Harold Lloyd Sues Columbia for 500G," *Daily Variety*, March 7, 1946.

207. **Here, we find 57 consecutive scenes:** Universal Pictures Co. v. Harold Lloyd Corporation, 162 F.2d 354 (9th Cir. 1947).

207. **the other cases were rapidly settled:** "Stipulation for Dismissal With Prejudice" filed November 14, 1947, Case 4363, Box 752, Civil Case Files 1938–1950, Records of the District Court of the United States for the Southern District of California, Central Division, Record Group 21, National Archives at Riverside, Riverside, CA. Similar filings, also dated November 19, 1947 can be found for cases 5184 and 5185 (the Columbia cases) in boxes 846 and 847.

207. **he handed in his last screenplay for Universal:** "Production Notes from the Studios, *Showmen's Trade Review*, August 11, 1945.

207. **Abbott and Costello bought it from the studio:** "Abbott and Costello Sign for E-L Film," *Daily Variety*, July 1, 1947.

207. **"It is one of these bitter end situations.":** H. A. Dewing, "Reporter's Transcript of Proceedings: Case 4361-BH, Los Angeles, California, May 14, 1945," filed May 28, 1945, Case 4361, Box 750, Civil Case Files 1938–1950, Records of the District Court of the United States for the Southern District of California, Central Division, Record Group 21, National Archives at Riverside, Riverside, CA.

207. **Mr. Bruckman, up until the time:** Harold Lloyd, "Deposition of Harold Lloyd," Deposition taken October 30, 1945, filed May 6, 1946, Case 4363, Box 752, Civil Case Files 1938–1950, Records of the District Court of the United States for the Southern District of California, Central Division, Record Group 21, National Archives at Riverside, Riverside, CA.

Waxworks

209. **working title *Wilbur Goes Wild*:** Clyde Bruckman, *Andy Plays Hookey Final Draft Continuity*, November 16, 1945, Jules White Papers, Margaret Herrick Library, Academy of Motion Picture Arts and Sciences.

209. It's nothing more than a two-reel, condensed version: Okuda and Watz, 32–33.

210. six in all: All dates from final drafts or final draft continuities in the Jules White Papers, Margaret Herrick Library, Academy of Motion Picture Arts and Sciences.

210. because White stockpiled them to film later: Bruskin, 76.

210. Clyde simply transcribed the routine: Okuda and Watz, 36.

210. "the worst Stooge comedies to date,": Ibid., 67.

210. *Three Little Pirates* was the last full performance he gave: Fleming, 79–81.

210. White had more writers on staff: "Five Writers Hurry Stories for Stooges," *Daily Variety*, April 9, 1947.

210. "Felix [Adler] or Jack [White, Jules's brother] or Clyde, in that order.": Bruskin, 79.

211. "Bruckman's scripts were very sloppy: Okuda and Watz, 32.

211. Clyde wrote five scripts: All dates from final drafts or final draft continuities in the Jules White Papers, Margaret Herrick Library, Academy of Motion Picture Arts and Sciences.

211. he sold it in January: Classified Ad for 1826 Prosser, *Los Angeles Times*, January 11, 1948.

211. an apartment near UCLA: Donald P. Swisher, in discussion with author, November 29, 2014.

211. 934 6th Street in Santa Monica: Dep. Chief C. Brown, Santa Monica Police Department, "Death (Suicide): Bruckman, Clyde Adolph," Report #55-117, January 4, 1955.

211. someone who always needed to be occupied: Donald P. Swisher, in discussion with author, November 29, 2014.

212. It didn't even last a year: John Dunning, *On the Air: The Encyclopedia of Old-Time Radio* (New York: Oxford University Press, 1998), 172.

212. recut it to include a talking horse: Dardis, *Lloyd*, 283.

212. "All those sight gags!": Dardis, *Keaton*, 259.

212. The marriage turned out to be good for him: Keaton and Samuels, 258–260.

213. a joint venture between CBS and the *Los Angeles Times*: "Television KTTV Makes Bow Today," *Los Angeles Times*, January 1, 1949.

213. Buster came by the offices the next day: Dardis, *Keaton*, 260.

213. The night Pearson visited Buster's house: Ibid.

214. Donald Swisher recalls a family gathering: Donald P. Swisher, in discussion with author, November 29, 2014.

214. Columbia Short department veteran Henry Taylor: Okuda and Watz, 181.

214. "It looks like television has a new 'must-see' program,": "Television Review: Buster Keaton Show," *Daily Variety*, December 23, 1949.

214. the transcontinental microwave relay: "85,000,000 Can See Television of Peace Treaty Sessions," *Los Angeles Times*, September 4, 1951.

215. He was unable to meet his deadlines: Dardis, *Keaton*, 260–261.

215. Costar Shirley Tegge remembered him showing up tipsy: Meade, 240–241.

215. In April, the live show went off the air: "KTTV Telefilming Bus Keaton Show for Syndication," *Daily Variety*, June 26, 1950.

215. The revamped show aired beginning in the spring of 1951: Walter Ames, "Buster Keaton Show Returns to Screens May 9; Navy to Get 'Pharmacist's Mate' Film," *Los Angeles Times*, April 28, 1951.

215. and in other markets: "New Business," *Broadcasting Telecasting*, July 23, 1951.

215. rereleased under the title *Life with Buster Keaton*: "Availabilities," *Broadcasting Telecasting*, June 16, 1952.

215. "only partially successful": "Life with Buster Keaton," *Weekly Variety*, December 10, 1952.

215. The day Buster filmed his final episode: Keaton and Samuels, 272.

216. *Variety* reported that Clyde was directing: "Chatter," *Daily Variety*, November 17, 1952.

216. It had premiered on December 5, 1952: Jim Mulholland, *The Abbott and Costello Book* (New York: Popular Library, 1975), 183.

216. Abbott & Costello have proved too often: "Abbott and Costello Show," *Daily Variety*, December 10, 1953.

217. The first season had virtually nothing in the way of plot: Mulholland, 188.

217. After six shows produced by Alex Gottlieb: Ibid., 183.

217. The second season began airing on New York's WNBT: "TV Key," *Brooklyn Daily Eagle*, October 10, 1953.

217. a fifty-two-episode package by MCA-TV: "Checklist for a Busy Film Buyer" (Ad for MCA-TV), *Sponsor*, December 28, 1953.

217. one episode is a recreation of *One Week*: Mulholland, 191–192.

217. "the comedy of least resistance,": "Telepix Followup: Abbott and Costello," *Daily Variety*, March 5, 1954.

217. "Clyde Bruckman and [co-writer] Jack Townley: Ibid.

217. WNBT aired the last episode: "TV Key," *Brooklyn Daily Eagle*, March 13, 1954.

218. all the way back in August of 1922: "4 New First Nationals Finished," *Exhibitors Trade Review*, August 19, 1922.

The Gentlemen of the Santa Monica Police Department

219. "Gradually and then suddenly.": Ernest Hemingway, *The Sun Also Rises* (1926; Repr. New York: Charles Scribner's Sons, 1954), 136.

219. Clyde's mother, Bertha, died in Santa Ana: State of California, *California Death Index, 1940–1997* (Sacramento: State of California Department of Health Services, Center for Health Statistics), database online, Ancestry.com.

219. she'd had a nurse well before her death: Donald P. Swisher, in discussion with author, November 29, 2014.

219. resurfaced in 2014 and were sold at auction: "Lot 234 of 641: An Archive of Clyde Bruckman Material, Julien's 90210 Exclusive Spring Online Entertainment Auction (#3314)," *Julien's Auctions*, http://www.julienslive.com/view-auctions/catalog/id/118/lot/49087/.

219. who'd appeared in Columbia shorts: Okuda and Watz, 78.

219. "Miss San Fernando Valley 1951,": Joanne Anderson, "State Contest Next Step For 'Miss San Fernando Valley,'" *The Van Nuys News*, May 26, 1952.

220. "the fearless Inspector Braddock of 'Racket Squad,' ": Erskine Johnson, "Hollywood Today!" *Eureka California Times-Standard*, June 26, 1953.

220. Ronald Colman might be the right person to play him: "Suspected

Murderer Tries to Sell Life Story for Film," *Lubbock Evening Journal*, July 11, 1957.

220. **was convicted:** Gene Blake, "Scott Sentenced to Life in Prison," *Los Angeles Times*, December 27, 1957.

220. **he confessed to the crime in 1986:** David Johnston, "30 Years Later, a Case of Murder Is Admitted—but Questions Linger," *Los Angeles Times*, February 23, 1986.

220. **He paid a visit to Stan Laurel:** Stan Laurel to John McCabe, March 20, 1956, *The Stan Laurel Archive Correspondence Project*, http://www.lettersfromstan.com.

220. **"under way or out for consideration":** Clyde A. Bruckman, "Contemporary Writers and Their Work: A Series of Autobiographical Letters: 122: Clyde A. Bruckman," *The Editor*, January 25, 1918, 53–54.

220. **The reason I called you the other day:** Clyde Bruckman to George Stevens, November 14, 1954, George Stevens Papers, Margaret Herrick Library, Academy of Motion Picture Arts and Sciences.

222. **Have your letter before me this morning:** George Stevens to Clyde Bruckman, November 16, 1954, George Stevens Papers, Margaret Herrick Library, Academy of Motion Picture Arts and Sciences.

222. **I wish to express my deep appreciation:** Clyde Bruckman to George Stevens, November 25, 1954, George Stevens Papers, Margaret Herrick Library, Academy of Motion Picture Arts and Sciences.

224. **"I had no idea he was that desperate.":** Bruskin, 77.

224. **a brand new building at 2001 Wilshire Boulevard:** "Announcing the Grand Opening of Bess Eiler's Beautiful Location," Ad for Bess Eiler's, *Los Angeles Times*, September 10, 1954.

224. **Gentlemen of Santa Monica Police Department:** Dep. Chief C. Brown, Santa Monica Police Department, "Death (Suicide): Bruckman, Clyde Adolph," Report no. 55-117, January 4, 1955.

225. **Mel Sevland is a teacher at Santa Monica High School:** Ibid.

226. **The police respected Clyde's wishes:** Ibid.

226. **Buster even got his gun back:** Meade, 409.

226. **Clyde's suicide made the AP wires and was picked up nationally:** E.g.,

"Film Writer Borrows Gun to Kill Himself," *Provo Daily Herald*, January 6, 1955.

226. "Film Writer": "Bruckman, Film Writer, Ends His Life," *Los Angeles Times*, January 5, 1955.

226. "Film Veteran,": "Film Veteran Shoots Self," *Los Angeles Examiner*, January 5, 1955.

226. Bruckman most recently worked as a writer at Columbia: "Obituaries: Clyde Bruckman," *Daily Variety*, January 6, 1955.

226. Two days after Clyde's death: Okuda and Watz, 98.

226. The film lifts the plot, the gags, and, in fact, most of the footage: Okuda and Watz, 16–17.

Magic Lamps

227. "Life,": Blesh, 253.

228. "the real end": Ibid., 256.

228. "The story really ended when you two dove in and sank,": Ibid.

228. his heart gave out in 1925: Foote, 163.

228. W. C. Fields's drinking caught up with him: "Death Takes W. C. Fields, Famed Film Comedian," *Los Angeles Times*, December 26, 1946.

228. Joe Mitchell got Alzheimer's and died of pneumonia: Foote, 163.

228. Monty Banks, who'd had so much trouble with driving: "Monty Banks Dies Suddenly on Italian Train," *Los Angeles Times*, January 9, 1950.

228. Oliver Hardy had a stroke in 1957: "Oliver Hardy of Famous Movies Comedy Team Dies," *Los Angeles Times*, August 8, 1957.

228. Eddie Cline drank himself to death in 1961: Foote, 73.

228. Felix Adler died of cancer: "Movie Comic Writer Felix Adler Dies at 72," *Los Angeles Times*, March 26, 1963.

228. And in 1965, it was Stan Laurel's turn: Art Berman, "Film Comic Stan Laurel Dies at 74," *Los Angeles Times*, February 24, 1965.

229. He took virtually every job he was offered: Dardis, *Keaton*, 267–269.

229. when he was diagnosed with terminal lung cancer: Meade, 304.

229. "the living room became a hazardous labyrinth: Dardis, *Harold Lloyd*, 302.

229. He died in March of 1971: Ibid., 303.

230. **By 1975, even the Stooges were gone:** "Moe Howard, Last of 3 Stooges, Dies at 78," *Los Angeles Times*, May 7, 1975.

230. **She blamed Buster:** Meade, 261.

230. **working at Virginia's Gift Shop:** Donald P. Swisher, in discussion with author, November 29, 2014.

230. **She died on June 9, 1983:** State of California, *California Death Index, 1940–1997* (Sacramento: State of California Department of Health Services, Center for Health Statistics), database online, Ancestry.com.

230. **After White's death in 1985:** "Jules J. White, 'The Fourth Stooge,' Dies at 84," *Los Angeles Times*, May 4, 1985.

231. **"I often wish,":** Blesh, 152.

Works Cited

Archives and Special Collections

Arda Haenszel California Room. Norman F. Feldhelm Central Library. San Bernardino, California.

George Stevens Papers. Margaret Herrick Library, Academy of Motion Picture Arts and Sciences. Beverly Hills, California.

Harold Lloyd Papers. Margaret Herrick Library, Academy of Motion Picture Arts and Sciences. Beverly Hills, California.

Jules White Papers. Margaret Herrick Library, Academy of Motion Picture Arts and Sciences. Beverly Hills, California.

Los Angeles County Department of Registrar-Recorder/County Clerk. Norwalk, California.

Mack Sennett Papers. Margaret Herrick Library, Academy of Motion Picture Arts and Sciences. Beverly Hills, California.

Paramount Pictures Production Records, Margaret Herrick Library. Academy of Motion Picture Arts and Sciences. Beverly Hills, California.

Records of the District Court of the United States for the Southern District of California, Central Division. National Archives at Riverside. Riverside, California.

San Bernardino County Historical Archives. San Bernardino, California.

Santa Monica Police Department Records Section. Santa Monica Police Department. Santa Monica, California.

Turner/MGM Scripts. Margaret Herrick Library, Academy of Motion Picture Arts and Sciences. Beverly Hills, California.

Universal Studios Collection. Cinema Library Archive of Performing Arts, University of Southern California. Los Angeles, California.

W. C. Fields Papers. Margaret Herrick Library, Academy of Motion Picture Arts and Sciences. Beverly Hills, California.

Books

Balducci, Anthony. *The Funny Parts: A History of Film Comedy Routines and Gags*. Jefferson, NC: McFarland and Company, 2012.

Balducci, Anthony. *Lloyd Hamilton: Poor Boy Comedian of Silent Cinema*. Jefferson, NC: McFarland and Company, 2009.

Barry, Iris. *D. W. Griffith: American Film Master*. New York: The Museum of Modern Art, 1940.

Blesh, Rudi. *Keaton*. New York: The MacMillan Company, 1966.

Blottner, Gene. *Columbia Pictures Movie Series, 1926–1955: The Harry Cohn Years*. Jefferson, NC: McFarland and Company, 2012.

Bruskin, David. *Behind The Three Stooges: The White Brothers: Conversations with David N. Bruskin*. Los Angeles: Directors Guild of America, 1993.

The Cottage Grove Historical Society, ed. *The Day Buster Smiled: The 1926 Filming of "The General" by Buster Keaton as Chronicled in the Cottage Grove Sentinel Newspaper, Cottage Grove, Oregon*. 3rd Ed. Cottage Grove, Oregon: Eugene Print, Inc., 2002.

Curtis, James. *W. C. Fields: A Biography*. New York: Alfred A. Knopf, 2003.

Dardis, Tom. *Buster Keaton: The Man Who Wouldn't Lie Down*. New York: Charles Scribner's Sons, 1979.

Dardis, Tom. *Harold Lloyd: The Man on the Clock*. New York: Viking, 1983.

Dick, Bernard F. *Engulfed: The Death of Paramount Pictures and the Birth of Corporate Hollywood*. Lexington, KY: University Press of Kentucky, 2001.

Dunning, John. *On The Air: The Encyclopedia of Old-Time Radio*. New York: Oxford University Press, 1998.

Everson, William K. *The Art of W. C. Fields*. New York: Bonanza Books, 1967.

Fields, Ronald J., ed. *W. C. Fields by Himself: His Intended Autobiography*. Englewood Cliffs, NJ: Prentice-Hall, Inc., 1973.

Fischer, Claude S. *America Calling: A Social History of the Telephone to 1940*. Los Angeles: University of California Press, 1992.

Fleming, Michael. *From Amalgamated Morons to American Icons: The Three Stooges: An Illustrated History*. New York: Broadway Books, 1999.

Foote, Lisle. *Buster Keaton's Crew: The Team Behind His Silent Films*. Jefferson, NC: McFarland and Company, 2014.

Gehring, Wes D. *Laurel and Hardy: A Bio-bibliography*. Westport, CT: Greenwood Press, 1990.

Harness, Kyp. *The Art of Laurel and Hardy: Graceful Calamity in the Films*. Jefferson, NC: McFarland and Company, 2006.

Hemingway, Ernest. *The Sun Also Rises*. 1926; Repr. New York: Charles Scribner's Sons, 1954.

Henn, Harry G. " 'Magazine Rights'—A Division of Indivisible Copyright." In *Copyright and Related Topics: A Choice of Articles*, ed. The Los Angeles Copyright Society and The UCLA School of Law. Los Angeles: University of California Press, 1964.

Ingersoll, Luther A. *Ingersoll's Century Annals of San Bernardino County, 1769 to 1904: Prefaced with a Brief History of the State of California: Supplemented with an Encyclopedia of Local Biography and Embellished with Views of Historic Subjects and Portraits of Many of Its Representative People*. Los Angeles: L. A. Ingersoll, 1904.

1912 Kansas City Directory. Kansas City, MO: Gate City Directory Co., 1912.

Keaton, Buster, and Charles Samuels. *My Wonderful World of Slapstick*. New York: Doubleday and Co., 1960.

Kern, Walter. *The Silent Clowns*. New York: Alfred A. Knopf, 1975.

Kowalksi, Dean A. " 'Clyde Bruckman's Final Repose': Reprised 2009." In *The Philosophy of the X-Files*, ed. Dean A. Kowalski, 189–208. Lexington, KY: University Press of Kentucky, 2009.

Lloyd, Harold and Wesley Stout. *An American Comedy*. New York: Longmans, Green and Co., 1928.

Los Angeles City Directory 1914. Los Angeles: Los Angeles Directory Company, 1914.

Los Angeles City Directory 1915. Los Angeles: Los Angeles Directory Co., 1915.

Los Angeles City Directory 1917. Los Angeles: Los Angeles Directory Co., 1917.

Los Angeles City Directory 1924. Los Angeles: The Los Angeles Directory Co., 1924.

Los Angeles City Directory, 1932. Los Angeles: Los Angeles Directory Co., 1932.

Louvish, Simon. *Man on the Flying Trapeze: The Life and Times of W. C. Fields.* New York: W. W. Norton and Company, 1997.

McCabe, John. *Mr. Laurel and Mr. Hardy.* Garden City, NY: Doubleday and Company, 1961

McPherson, Edward. *Buster Keaton: Tempest in a Flat Hat.* New York: Newmarket Press, 2004.

Meade, Marion. *Buster Keaton: Cut to the Chase.* New York: Da Capo Press, 1997.

Miller, Henry. *The Cosmological Eye.* New York: New Directions, 1939.

Mulholland, Jim. *The Abbott and Costello Book.* New York: Popular Library, 1975.

Okuda, Ted, and James L. Neibaur. *Stan Without Ollie: The Stan Laurel Solo Films 1917–1927.* Jefferson, NC: McFarland and Company, 2012.

Okuda, Ted, and Edward Watz. *The Columbia Comedy Shorts: Two-Reel Hollywood Film Comedies, 1933–1958.* Jefferson, NC: McFarland and Company, 1986.

Orange County Directory, 1924: South Orange County. Long Beach, California: Western Directory Co., 1923.

Pittenger, William. *Daring and Suffering: A History of the Great Railroad Adventure.* Philadelphia: J. W. Daughaday, 1863.

Pittenger, William. *The Great Locomotive Chase: A History of the Andrews Railroad Raid into Georgia in 1862.* Philadelphia: The Penn Publishing Company, 1908.

Richardson, James. *For the Life of Me: Memoirs of a City Editor.* New York: G. P. Putnam's Sons, 1954.

Roots, James. *The 100 Greatest Silent Comedians.* London: Rowman and Littlefield, 2014.

Eyman, Scott. *Print the Legend: The Life and Times of John Ford.* New York: Simon and Schuster, 2015.

Sennett, Mack and Cameron Shipp. *King of Comedy* Garden City, NJ: Doubleday and Company, 1954.

Skretvedt, Randy. *Laurel and Hardy: The Magic Behind the Movies*. Beverly Hills, CA: Moonstone Press, 1987.

Stevens, Jr., George, ed. *Conversations with the Great Moviemakers of Hollywood's Golden Age at the American Film Institute*. New York: Alfred A. Knopf, 2006.

Strecker, Trey. Introduction to *The Collected Baseball Stories*, by Charles Emmett Van Loan, 1–4. Edited by Trey Strecker. Jefferson, NC: McFarland and Company, 2004.

Sweeney, Kevin W., ed. *Buster Keaton: Interviews*. Jackson, MS: University Press of Mississippi, 2007.

Universal Exposition Saint Louis, 1904: Preliminary Programme of Physical Culture: Olympic Games and World's Championship Contests. St. Louis, MO: St. Louis Universal Exposition, 1904.

Walker, Brent E. *Mack Sennett's Fun Factory: A History and Filmography of his Keystone and Mack Sennett Comedies, with Biographies of Players and Personnel*. Jefferson, NC: McFarland and Company, 2010.

Ward, Richard Lewis. *A History of the Hal Roach Studios*. Carbondale, IL: Southern Illinois University, 2006.

Watz, Edward. *Wheeler and Woolsey: The Vaudeville Comic Duo and Their Films, 1929–1937*. Jefferson, NC: McFarland Classics, 2001.

Periodicals and Newspapers

Ames Daily Tribune. Ames, Iowa. *Newspapers.com*. http://newspapers.com.

Bakersfield Californian. Bakersfield, California. *Newspapers.com*. http://newspapers.com.

Boston Post. Boston, Massachusetts. *Newspapers.com*. http://newspapers.com.

Broadcasting Telecasting. Washington, DC. *Media History Digital Library*, http://mediahistoryproject.org.

The Brooklyn Daily Eagle. Brooklyn, New York. *Newspapers.com*. http://newspapers.com.

Buffalo Evening News. Buffalo, New York. *Old Fulton New York Post Cards,* http://fultonhistory.com.

The Cinema News and Property Gazette. London, England. *Media History Digital Library,* http://mediahistoryproject.org.

Chicago Daily Tribune. (also *Chicago Tribune*). Chicago, Illinois. *Chicago Tribune Archives,* http://archives.chicagotribune.com.

The Cincinnati Enquirer. Cincinnati, Ohio. *Newspapers.com.* http://newspapers.com.

The Cottage Grove Sentinel. Cottage Grove, Oregon. Published by The Cottage Grove Historical Society in *The Day Buster Smiled: The 1926 Filming of "The General" by Buster Keaton as Chronicled in the Cottage Grove Sentinel Newspaper, Cottage Grove, Oregon.* 3rd ed. Cottage Grove, Oregon: Eugene Print, Inc., 2002.

The Daily Courier (and *Weekly Courier*). San Bernardino, California. *Newspapers.com.* http://newspapers.com.

The Editor. Ridgewood, New Jersey. *Google Books,* http://books.google.com.

Emerging Infectious Diseases. Atlanta, Georgia. *Centers for Disease Control and Prevention,* http://wwwnc.cdc.gov/eid.

Eureka California Times-Standard. Eureka, California. *Newspapers.com.* http://newspapers.com.

The Evening Herald. Klamath Falls, Oregon. *Newspapers.com.* http://newspapers.com.

Exhibitors Herald. Chicago, Illinois. *Media History Digital Library,* http://mediahistoryproject.org.

Exhibitors Trade Review. New York, New York. *Media History Digital Library,* http://mediahistoryproject.org.

The Film Daily (Also known as *Wid's Daily*). New York, New York. *Media History Digital Library,* http://mediahistoryproject.org.

Film Comment. New York, New York. *Magzter,* http://magzter.com.

Hollywood Filmograph. Los Angeles, California. *Media History Digital Library,* http://mediahistoryproject.org.

Hollywood Vagabond. Los Angeles, California. *Media History Digital Library,* http://mediahistoryproject.org.

Image. Rochester, New York. *George Eastman House,*
http://image.eastmanhouse.org.

The Implet. New York, New York. *Media History Digital Library,*
http://mediahistoryproject.org.

LIFE Magazine. New York, New York. *Google Books,*
http://books.google.com.

Logansport Pharos-Tribune. Logansport, Indiana. *Newspapers.com,*
http://newspapers.com.

The Los Angeles Examiner, Los Angeles, California. Microfilm, Los Angeles
Public Library.

The Los Angeles Herald. Los Angeles, California. *Newspapers.com,*
http://newspapers.com.

The Los Angeles Times. Los Angeles, California. ProQuest,
http://proquest.com.

Lubbock Evening Journal. Lubbock, Texas. *Newspapers.com,*
http://newspapers.com.

Motion Picture Magazine. New York, New York. *Media History Digital Library,*
http://mediahistoryproject.org.

The Moving Picture News, New York, New York. *Media History Digital
Library,* http://mediahistoryproject.org.

Motion Picture News, New York, New York, *Media History Digital Library,*
http://mediahistoryproject.org.

Motography, Chicago, Illinois, *Media History Digital Library,*
http://mediahistoryproject.org.

The Moving Picture World. New York, New York. *Media History Digital
Library,* http://mediahistoryproject.org.

Movie Classic. New York, New York. *Media History Digital Library,*
http://mediahistoryproject.org.

Nevada State Journal. Reno, Nevada. *Newspapers.com.*
http://newspapers.com.

The New York Clipper. New York, New York. *Media History Digital Library,*
http://mediahistoryproject.org.

The New York Times. New York, New York. *ProQuest,* http://proquest.com.

The Daily Northwestern. Oshkosh, Wisconsin. *Newspapers.com*.
http://newspapers.com.

The Oakland Tribune. Oakland, California. *Newspapers.com*.
http://newspapers.com.

The Photodramatist. Los Angeles, California. *Media History Digital Library*,
http://mediahistoryproject.org.

Photoplay. Chicago, Illinois. *Media History Digital Library*,
http://mediahistoryproject.org.

Picture-Play Magazine. New York, New York. *Media History Digital Library*,
http://mediahistoryproject.org.

Provo Daily Herald. Provo, Utah. *Newspapers.com*. http://newspapers.com.

The San Bernardino Daily Sun (also known as *Weekly Sun* and *Sun-Telegram*).
San Bernardino, California. *Newspapers.com*. http://newspapers.com.

San Bernardino News and the Free Press. San Bernardino, California. *Newspapers.com*. http://newspapers.com.

The San Francisco Chronicle. San Francisco, California. *Newspapers.com*.
http://newspapers.com.

Santa Ana Register. Santa Ana, California. *Newspapers.com*.
http://newspapers.com.

Santa Cruz Evening News. Santa Cruz, California. *Newspapers.com*.
http://newspapers.com.

The Saturday Evening Post. Philadelphia, Pennsylvania. Microfilm, Los
Angeles Public Library.

Screenland. New York, New York. *Media History Digital Library*,
http://mediahistoryproject.org.

Showmen's Trade Review. New York, New York. *Media History Digital Library*,
http://mediahistoryproject.org.

Sponsor. New York, New York. *Media History Digital Library*,
http://mediahistoryproject.org.

The Typographical Journal. Indianapolis, Indiana. *Google Books*,
http://books.google.com.

The Tyro. San Bernardino, California. Arda Haenszel California Room,
Norman F. Feldhelm Central Library, San Bernardino, California.

The Van Nuys News. Van Nuys, California. *Newspapers.com*.
    http://newspapers.com.

Daily Variety. Los Angeles, California. Variety Archives,
    http://varietyultimate.com.

Variety (Also known as *Weekly Variety, Variety Daily Bulletin*). New York,
    New York. Variety Archives, http://varietyultimate.com.

Vancouver Daily World. Vancouver, British Columbia. *Newspapers.com*.
    http://newspapers.com.

The Washington Herald, Washington, DC. *Newspapers.com*.
    http://newspapers.com.

The Washington Post, Washington, DC. *ProQuest*, http://proquest.com.

Washington Times. Washington, DC. *Newspapers.com*.
    http://newspapers.com.

Weekly World News, Boca Raton, Florida. *Google Books*,
    http://books.google.com.

Index

CPSIA information can be obtained
at www.ICGtesting.com
Printed in the USA
LVOW01*0024260516
489976LV00007B/9/P